Wickets, Catches and the Odd Run

TREVOR·BAILEY
Wickets, Catches and the Odd Run

Every Good Wish

[signature]

Willow Books
Collins
8 Grafton Street, London W1
1986

To my long-suffering wife, Greta . . .
and with apologies to the composers
and publishers of the quoted
songs which have been especially
relevant to my life

Willow Books
William Collins Sons & Co. Ltd, Glasgow
London · Glasgow · Sydney · Auckland
Toronto · Johannesburg

First published 1986
© Trevor Bailey 1986

British Library Cataloguing in Publication Data
Bailey, Trevor, *1923–*
Trevor Bailey's autobiography.
1. Bailey, Trevor, *1923–*   2. Cricket players
——Great Britain——Biography
I. Title
796.35'8'0924   GV915.B/

ISBN 0 00 218127 4
Set by Wyvern Typesetting Ltd, Bristol
Printed and bound in Great Britain by
Mackays of Chatham

CONTENTS

	Introduction	7
1	HOME TOWN	11
2	A LIFE ON THE OCEAN WAVE	26
3	THEY SAID WE SHOULDN'T LOOK BACK	36
4	WE'RE A COUPLE OF SWELLS	47
5	I'VE BEEN EVERYWHERE, MAN	74
6	WON'T YOU COME HOME, BILL BAILEY	144
7	I'VE GROWN ACCUSTOMED TO HER FACE	163
8	FANAGALO	178
9	BROWN SKIN GAL	185
10	FOOTBALL CRAZY	197
11	QUE SERA, SERA	208
12	SEND IN THE CLOWNS	220
	Index	233

INTRODUCTION

Like everybody, I have experienced some pain, some sorrow, some disappointment and a few regrets, but unquestionably I have had a very happy life. I would love to have been able to play a reasonable piano, not well, but well enough to have been able to hammer out a recognizable tune. It would have been satisfying to have been able to speak, read and think in another language, preferably French because of its beauty. But what I failed to realize early enough, except in the sporting field, was that nothing which is really worth having can be acquired without hard work. However, despite this weakness I can claim that I have been remarkably successful in my pursuit of happiness.

Many things have contributed to my having enjoyed myself so much. First and foremost, I have remained remarkably healthy, which is just as well as I am a bad patient with little patience when I am ill.

Second, I was blessed with a sense of humour which has grown over the years and has enabled me to laugh at the world, at other people and at myself. For me, life without laughter and humour would be unthinkable.

Third, I have avoided catching 'obsessionitis'. It is dangerous to be cornered by a sufferer from this particular disease, because he is unwilling to talk on any other subject. So often a bore, he is usually a bigot as well.

Fourth, friendship has been one of the most vital ingredients in my life and I have been fortunate in having acquired a number of real friends, people who will stand by you during the bad as well as the good times, as distinct from pleasant acquaintances. Where I have been unfortunate is the high number who have died, while I have chugged contentedly along.

At school I had seven close mates. Four were killed in the war: Don was blown up in his flak-ship off Walcharen; Horace failed to return from a training flight with the RAF, thus depriving cricket of a fast bowler of considerable potential; Gordon went down in a destroyer; and Alan crashed his plane in the States. I also lost my boon companion in the Royal Marines, shot through the head by a sniper. I suppose these events may have made me somewhat intolerant when people start talking about human rights as if these were ordained by God, rather than fought for and died for by man. The high death rate among my personal friends continued after the war. My choice in them was, like my taste in wine and food, essentially catholic, half of them being sports lovers and the other half having little or no interest in sport.

Fifth, I was given the instinctive eye and physical co-ordination required to play any moving ball game above average. This gift, combined with stamina, a good physique and a love for games, supplied me with an interest which began at the age of three and has continued throughout my life. Sport has provided me with a stage, a continual challenge and that special excitement which comes from winning, particularly as a member of a team.

Sixth, I was lucky in where and when I was born. I was not born with a silver spoon in my mouth, just one of metal alloy, but my parents did give me a great deal of their time, and plenty of encouragement. They provided me with a happy home and an education, both scholastic and sporting, which was above average. Cricket is not a natural game so it helps enormously to be well coached, and the earlier the better. It was not pure coincidence that half of the 1984–85 England party in India were taught the game at private schools; yet the number of private schools compared with state schools is microscopic.

Seventh, I have never been especially ambitious, am comparatively easy to satisfy, and have always tried not to expect too much. I never possessed a craving to make a vast fortune. My aim has been simply to acquire sufficient money to satisfy my own tastes, and I know the difference between a necessity and a luxury. I like driving a 'Roller' but have never had any desire to own one. To me a car has always been a vehicle to transport me from A to B. It should never break down, must start immediately and should not be an alcoholic in terms of petrol consumption.

Southend-on-Sea still is a large, mundane, sprawling, commuter/day-tripper town with little aesthetic appeal. However, both my wife and I were born there and, apart from the war years, have dwelt there all our lives. It is where we shall leave our ashes. Our four married homes, as well as those in which we lived as children, are within a radius of a quarter of a mile, which may not be adventurous but has made moving simple.

Southend does possess some good features to compensate for a train service where for the past forty years they have apologized to travellers when a train arrived on time; for the candy floss; for charabancs awash with brown ale; and for a football team which has recently captured the headlines, not for the football but for dubious off-the-field activities by directors. The weather is above average, it is within easy reach of London and it is at its best during the winter. The great attraction for me is the people. It has always baffled me why a married couple who have spent their entire working life in, shall we say, Bootle should retire to Bournemouth, where they have neither friends, nor relatives. The odds on the wife finding herself a widow, surrounded by mere acquaintants, must be high. Although I was far too lazy and lacked the passion and the ability needed to climb that material mountain, there have been few occasions when I have not been contented with my lot. I have never had any desire to swap places with anybody and have never been consciously jealous of anybody's success; indeed it invariably gives me pleasure whenever a friend does well.

Finally, I have been blessed with a marriage which, largely as a result of my wife's toleration, has been a success, lasted and produced three children who have grown up relatively sane and civilized. We have remained close, as one hopes a family will, but have avoided that overpossessiveness which can suffocate any relationship.

Marriage is inevitably a gamble as there is no way that two people in their early twenties can have any idea what they will like, or be like, in twenty, thirty, or forty years' time. The chances of a marriage breaking down are more probable for an international cricketer than for a person in a steady nine-to-five occupation. Although in my era divorce was neither as common nor as easy as it is today, I reckon that at least half of my cricketing contemporaries have been divorced and remarried. Our matrimonial casualty list was not as horrendous as that of the theatrical world, where a wedding invitation can almost become a season ticket, but it was still high. The reasons were obvious: frequent and long separations, though these might be claimed to reduce the amount of boredom liable to occur in the conventional marriage, and the glamour (often false) which is accorded to an international sportsman. I have always maintained that a woman must be mad to marry a cricketer, but I am thankful that there are some mad women in the world.

There are three basic types of cricket wives: those who hate the game, those who love it, and those who tolerate it. The chances of the first category achieving a marriage which lasts are remote. For me to have married somebody from the second category would have been a disaster, as the last thing I wanted to discuss on returning home was cricket. I could not possibly have remained with a woman who was worried about a pitch breaking up on the third day, or my weakness against off-spin bowling, or did not approve of the captain's or, far worse, my tactics. Nevertheless, several players have been happy with a wife who was a cricket fanatic. Not surprisingly, these are feared and dreaded by every tour manager.

My wife, Greta, has enjoyed cricket in small doses. Far more important, she instantly read the game as it had affected me as soon as I opened the door. I did not have to say a word. She could always tell whether it had been one of those good days, or one of those when runs and wickets had been in unpleasantly short supply. We hardly ever discussed cricket, except in the most general terms, which was ideal. I have always enjoyed talking about cricket and have done so much that I have never wanted or needed to bring the subject home. This has enabled me to divide my existence into two departments, marked sport and normal life.

HOME TOWN

My father was a minor civil servant in the Admiralty, who commuted by train to London and earned £500 per annum. We lived in a fairly typical four-bedroom semi-detached house in a Leigh-on-Sea street, originally costing about £400 and now probably fetching between £55,000 and £60,000. We did not own a car, but, until the outbreak of war, we always employed a maid, who lived in, normally stayed a couple of years, and was paid 12 shillings a week. In retrospect, the maid seems superfluous: though useful as a baby-sitter, my parents did not often go out in the evening, the house was comparatively small, and my mother, who did all the cooking, was a capable fulltime housewife. On the other hand, she herself had been brought up in a Victorian household where servants were considered normal essentials – rather like the dishwasher and fridge are today.

The other members of the household were my parents, my brother, a dog (originally a delightful mongrel, then followed by a succession of not quite so nice toy Pomeranians) and the inevitable cat. My mother had me somewhat late in life, but I never discovered whether I was an accident or intended. Basil, my only brother, was in fact 11 years older than me, so I was in effect an only child, with a young uncle living in the same house. He was prepared to play with me for hours and we never experienced any of those arguments and fights that erupt between brothers and sisters of similar ages.

Mine was a contented childhood as I was seldom bored: I had inherited a vivid imagination which enabled me to disappear into my own make-believe world; my mother was happy to devote hours of her time to me; and I had been given a natural aptitude and a passion for ball games, which was encouraged.

Shopping with my mother before I was old enough to go to school became an adventure because I used to turn the trips into hunting expeditions. By the time I was nine, my toy soldier battles would last at least a couple of hours. And I can still remember the pain, and the embarrassment, of running into a wooden fence on my first road bike with my eyes closed, because I had just been shot through the back by an Indian arrow.

The benefits of having a parent who has patience, time and an affinity with children are considerable. It was from my mother that I acquired a love for the written word, especially fiction. She started by telling me stories, of which she had a fund, and then she introduced me to Christopher Robin and his friends at Pooh Corner. Next came the classic Victorian school stories, including *Tom Brown's Schooldays*. Unbelievably, I even enjoyed *Eric, or Little by Little* at that stage. From there it was into that wonderful world of historical adventure, *Treasure Island, Kidnapped, Mr Midshipman Easy* and *The Scarlet Pimpernel*. Finally, she read Scott and Dickens to me, usually for an hour at a time, in front of the fire when it was becoming dark. As a result, by the time I could read fluently I had become an addict of the romantic historical novel. By the age of 12 I had gone through, and enjoyed, most of the Waverley novels, nearly all of Dumas, the whole of Sherlock Holmes and most of H. G. Wells and Charles Dickens.

I collected and avidly read secondhand books, and I believe I was fortunate not to have been brought up in the television age. With its effortless and instant entertainment provided by simply turning a knob, I would never have read as much if I had been born forty years later.

I am not sure when I first played cricket, but I was very keen on the game by the age of three. According to my mother, my favourite toy in my pram days was a woolly ball which I liked to throw at ornaments. My earliest recollections of cricket are in my back garden and on the beach, where I acquired the rudiments from my father and brother.

We had a tent on the beach at Westcliff and I spent a large part of each summer there. When the tide was out there was plenty of space on the mud. Midweek, the game usually consisted of Tony, the boy in the next tent, and myself plus any recruits we could find. This encouraged my wish to become an allrounder as one was either batting or bowling most of the time. At the weekends we were joined by the adults, including my father and brother, and it was during one of these impromptu games that I learned about one of the Laws of Cricket.

Like most small boys I found I was unable to bowl overarm, so I simply threw the ball. Nobody complained and I continued to use this method, which had certain definite advantages – like pace and accuracy – until I was seven. One Sunday we acquired for our pick-up game a number of grown-ups, who were not too happy when I managed to dismiss them with quickly propelled, well directed yorkers to the base of the spade 'stumps'. I was told I must either bowl underarm or throw more slowly, which was really an impossible choice for someone who had already decided to become a fast bowler. There was only one solution. I had to learn to bowl. The following day my brother showed me the basic requirements and by the end of the morning I could bowl properly. This was followed by hours of practising bowling at a target in my garden. As a result, I was able to take wickets on the beach the following weekend, though it was a long, long time before I was as effective a bowler as I had been a thrower.

I loved those days on the beach at Westcliff – the picnic lunches and teas, which always seem so much nicer when eaten in the open, sailing boats, ice-cream, catching crabs, swimming and, above all else, hours and hours of playing cricket on the mud. Even when the tide was in and the beach packed, I was able to practise throwing and catching. The outcome was that I viewed holidays at other places in England with both suspicion and dislike, until the year we went to Walton-on-the-Naze. Here there was not only a much better beach for cricket – which, to be honest, was not difficult – but also a collection of kindred spirits that came to the same beach and the same huts year after year. In addition to the ordinary pick-up games, there were organized matches with teams, even a scorebook, and we took sides to play against rather posher opposition at Frinton.

I had discovered my perfect holiday and continued to go to Walton and the same boarding house year after year except for one visit to France, which I bitterly resented even though, like most of my generation, I had never been abroad.

Our garden was not really big enough for cricket, but fortunately my father was not a keen gardener (a trait which I have inherited) and he allowed us to use it as a cricket ground in the summer and a football ground in the winter. As a result, the flower-beds were small, the flowers few, the lawn heavily scarred and broken windows frequent – a state of affairs which was viewed with remarkable tolerance.

Two forms of cricket took place in the garden, the traditional game and my special version. Most of the former was played with my brother, occasionally with my father, and sometimes with other friends of my own age in the vicinity. My mates and I normally used the car runway of an empty house further down the road, rather than our garden, because the garage doors provided a safe wicketkeeper, the pitch was longer, the bounce from concrete truer, and there was less likelihood of losing the ball.

One valuable lesson garden cricket taught me was the importance of keeping the ball on the ground as you were automatically out if you hit it over the fence, and I have never liked losing my wicket. Even worse, hitting a ball into another garden was liable to terminate the game because one of our neighbours did not share my passion for cricket. The man in the house on the leg side would refuse permission to retrieve the ball, then return it later carefully cut in half. As I grew older, my brother and I used a composition ball which not only increased the number of broken windows, but also did considerable damage to the fences. Fortunately it was more difficult to cut in half.

My own version of cricket was a solitary game which required a vivid imagination. At the back there was a concrete strip where the coal-shed and outside toilet extended from the house. I would pitch three stumps at the end of this and bowl an old tennis ball at the house, between the kitchen window and the drain-pipe, and attempt to hit the return after it had bounced with a stick about 18 inches long and as thick as a child's stump. In addition, pieces of garden equipment and the dustbin were employed as fieldsmen. Initially, it was just a case of bowling a ball and hitting the return, but this gradually grew into matches, complete with individual and team scores, recorded in a scorebook.

The first matches were between those fictional schools Greyfriars and St Jims, when I would open the bowling with Harry Wharton and have Tom Merry coming on as first change. Later, when I began following first-class cricket in the press, Essex naturally featured heavily – and just as naturally met with more success than they did in reality. Even the great Australian side of 1934 was repeatedly trounced by Morris Nichols and company.

During the holidays my imaginary matches usually commenced at six o'clock and would often last all day with intervals for breakfast, lunch and tea. My parents wisely slept in the front of the house and I assume the nextdoor neighbours adopted the same precaution, because the incessant banging of a tennis ball against a wall at that hour in the morning must have been disturbing.

Normally, these games took place in the summer. During the winter my garden was transformed into various football grounds on which, with the aid of a tennis ball and a vivid imagination, I played my solitary football matches. However, in 1934 I was given *The Fight for the Ashes 1932–33* by Jack Hobbs, an account of the Bodyline tour, as a Christmas present. On Boxing Day I made my initial trip to Australia under the captaincy of D. R. Jardine for the first of many 'Tests' to be staged at 36 Fillebrook Avenue. Subsequently, I was to make three tours to Australia as a player with varying degrees of success, but without ever approaching the runs I scored and the wickets I took in that Bodyline tour – Don Bradman was my rabbit and I experienced very little difficulty against the spin of Bill O'Reilly and Clarrie Grimmett.

There can be no doubt that those matches and the countless hours they absorbed were beneficial, but if I had not possessed the imagination required to transform them into what was, to me, a real game, I would never have spent quite so much time hitting a tennis ball with a piece of wood. I enjoyed my own dream cricket world enormously and can remember how I would sometimes prefer to remain there rather than go out with friends, unless they were off to play cricket or football. My imaginary matches also taught me the pleasure of being an allrounder, as I was always batsman and bowler.

On leaving my kindergarten at the age of seven, I had the good fortune to become a pupil at Alleyn Court Preparatory School, founded in 1904 by the Wilcox family. It is difficult to imagine a better place for a young boy whose consuming interests were cricket and football. Denys Wilcox, who was to captain both Cambridge University and Essex, had just become joint-headmaster as his father had recently died. He brought with him all the passion for sport, especially cricket and football, that one associates with an undergraduate of the 1930s. Later, Denys became an outstanding allround headmaster, but when I was at his school games were almost an obsession with him. In addition to possessing the chief requirements of every coach, burning enthusiasm and patience, he was technically excellent.

I was eight when he gave me my first net and it turned out to be an experience that I will never forget. My batting at that time relied on a very good eye, plenty of right hand, the ability to hit the bad ball, a healthy 'mow', a reasonable cut and instinctive forward movement, but no defence. Denys proceeded to bowl at me a series of good length underarm deliveries which I tried to hit as hard as I could. To my anger and dismay I found that not only was I usually failing to make any contact, but my stumps were also being hit with monotonous regularity. The final indignity was, of course, that he was bowling underarm. In ten minutes I had learned two vital lessons: first, I was not nearly as good as I had imagined; second, there was much I needed to learn about batting if I was to score runs with the necessary regularity.

Under the guidance of Denys I acquired the fundamentals of batting, so that by the time I was 13 I was able to play all the strokes, other than the hook, and also possessed a solid defence. In addition, he taught me to enjoy every aspect of the game – nets and practice, though strictly controlled, were fun. I developed a tactical appreciation, knew how to set a field and call correctly and was learning to spot the weaknesses of an opponent. The last was the result of Denys asking us in the nets the reason why the batsman was edging the ball when off driving, or was so often lbw when playing back. The grounding I received from Denys helped enormously when I started to coach: teach a boy how to keep out the good ball, but never forget to give him plenty of practice at hitting the bad.

I spent six very happy years at Alleyn Court. The school had 120 boys, about 30 of whom were boarders. The scholastic objective was to make sure the boys were able to pass Common Entrance which was required by the majority of the public schools. In addition there was a small but highly successful scholarship class, for which I never strived. The classes were small and the teaching was above average though I always felt that it would have been better if we had spent more time, until the age of ten, on reading, writing and arithmetic, and less on Latin and French. I might then have acquired a legible hand.

There were organized games for every boy on Wednesdays and

Saturdays, as well as a large number of matches against other schools. Those who wanted were able to play football or cricket on the other days after school, providing the weather allowed. I seldom returned home much before six o'clock, although I did cycle back for lunch as I wisely preferred my mother's cooking.

In addition to work and games, great stress was put on manners and behaviour. I once let out a subdued 'damn', having missed a tackle in football, and was immediately dismissed from the field. Swearing was regarded as a very serious offence.

We learned respect for authority and other people, particularly older people. We were proud of our country and our King. Henry Newbolt and his sentiments seemed perfectly acceptable to an 11-year-old in the 1930s. Life was uncomplicated and straightforward and we were too young for the cynicism which some of us would acquire at our public schools, and nearly all of us by the end of the war that lay ahead.

What was I like when I was at Alleyn Court? Definitely spoilt, though not materially; decidedly petulant; a bad loser, because winning was so important to me; rather selfish; useless with my hands, except when hitting a ball, as I could not draw or make anything; an insatiable reader with a fairly catholic taste; baffled by the simplest arithmetical problem; very gregarious; tended to do reasonably well at only those subjects which interested me; never bored, as there simply was not the time; adored all moving ball games.

At Alleyn Court there was no shortage of both football and cricket matches, with under-10, under-11, and under-12 teams as well as the First XI. Matches provided that extra bite and competition I wanted. At nine I gained my cricket colours as a minute fast bowler, and at ten I was playing inside forward for the First XI football team. The school had an outstanding cricket record because we were so well coached, but we were not nearly as impressive at football, where our toughest matches were invariably against the under-14 side of the local high school. In addition to having so many more boys of 12 and 13 to choose from, a high percentage of them had already reached a good standard of football at primary-school level. In contrast, they had experienced little, or no, organized cricket.

An outstanding prep-school cricketer is able to dominate a game to a greater extent than at any other time in his career, which, as I possessed an insatiable appetite for both runs and wickets, I found much to my taste. However, this domination by an individual is less appreciated by opponents, or indeed the members of his own side. This point was first really drawn to my attention by the late Harry Crabtree. In his capacity as County Physical Education Officer, he had been to see a cricket game at a secondary school. The two batsmen were thoroughly enjoying themselves but the rest of the batting side were showing little interest, which rather baffled Harry until he found out this was the second afternoon the pair had been together. In the early stages, cricket must involve everybody. Although England want to see a Boycott or a Gooch engaged in enormous partnerships, 10- and 11-year-olds lose interest in a game when they do not have the chance to bat.

Obviously such thoughts did not occur to me as a 13-year-old. I was much too busy and happy enjoying what was easily the finest allround season of my life. Alleyn Court won all 11 matches and my batting and bowling figures were: 11 innings, 3 not outs, 1109 runs, average 138.62; and 137 overs, 46 maidens, 366 runs, 52 wickets, average 7.03. As I normally bowled unchanged throughout the innings, my lowest score was 50 and I fielded in the highly lucrative position of silly mid-off, I had good reason to believe that cricket was a splendid game. I realized that this state of paradise would never occur again and, as I had already played in senior cricket, I understood the problems ahead. Although at prep-school level the batsman who could keep out the good ball and score off the bad had to make runs, because there were plenty of loose deliveries, it would not always be quite so simple.

My first experience of adult cricket was at the age of 11. It was August bank holiday and, as usual, I was playing cricket on the mud, when I was asked if I would like to make up the number for Westcliff B who found themselves one short. A quick wash, a dash home to change into whites, and I arrived at Priory Park late, but with sufficient time for me to bat. The opposing captain was plainly incensed at having to bowl at anyone quite so small and decided for the first over to bowl underarm, a tactic which both insulted and pleased me. Runs are runs, whatever the bowling, and they all look exactly the same in the scorebook. I was more than capable of taking toll of badly directed adult underarm bowling. It provided me with the confidence which runs at the start of an innings produce, and the opposition reverted to their normal attack after that one over. Although at 11 I found B XI bowling a little too fast, my fielding and catching was up to the standard. It was the first of many matches I was to play for Westcliff, the last being more than 45 years later.

By the time I was 11, Denys had decided that I had the ability to develop into a first-class cricketer. He believed it would be wiser if I concentrated on my batting – a batsman who could turn his arm over, as distinct from an allrounder. This is what he wrote in the school magazine after my last term:

> His batting and fielding reached as high a standard as anyone could expect of a Preparatory Schoolboy. There are immense possibilities about his bowling too, but perhaps it will be wise for him to concentrate on his batting in the future. Allrounders are invaluable, but one often sees a young cricketer who is a good batsman and a good bowler, but never reaches the highest class at either.
>
> In county cricket today there are very few players who are first-class with the bat and the ball. There is so much cricket played now that it requires a man of exceptional stamina to do both. It is noticeable that when an allrounder is in exceptional form with the ball, his batting often suffers, and vice versa.

Denys maintained that as the standard of cricket improved my ability to make runs would suffer if I bowled too much, especially if I continued in my pursuit of becoming a fast bowler. He was of course right. Furthermore, if there was a shortage of allrounders in county cricket, they were even rarer in Test cricket until a remarkable glut appeared in the 1980s. I have no doubt that if I had concentrated mainly on my batting I would have scored many more runs; likewise, I would have taken more wickets if I had concentrated on my bowling. However, had I followed Denys's advice I am sure I would never have enjoyed cricket as much.

Being an allrounder suited my temperament, because I was always in the game and an integral part of the side. If I failed with the bat, then there was always the opportunity to remedy matters with the ball. It also meant that the demands were not quite so high. I remember Len Hutton lamenting that anything less than a hundred by him in a county match was inclined to be regarded by the press as a failure, while I was more than content with a fifty. Similarly, Fred Trueman would want five wickets in an innings, whereas I considered three was just about my par for the course.

Had I concentrated solely on batting, my whole career would have been very different. If I had not been a fast bowler I would not have been awarded my colours for Alleyn Court at nine, Dulwich at 14, or made the same impression when chosen in a four-counties match at Lord's during the war. In addition, I was first selected for England against New Zealand as an opening bowler, my batting being regarded as a useful bonus.

At 13 I was, of course, not seriously concerned about the distant future, though I occasionally used to think to myself that cricket would not be nearly so much fun if I did not bowl.

The transformation from the gentle, rather narrow, fairly spoilt life as a day boy at prep school, where I had become one of its most important members, to that of a fag at a pre-war public school was considerable. For a delicate, sensitive, artistic youth who did not like games and lacked a sense of humour, Dulwich College could be unpalatable, but I took to it immediately. There were about forty boys in my house, Ivyholme, a tight-knit community, which was admirably controlled by the housemaster, largely administered by the senior boys, and was self sufficient and satisfying. The curriculum was so packed with work, games and companionship that there was not much time for anything else. Although I neither appreciated nor liked the cold bath we had every day, was not over impressed with some of the more absurd rules, and found Sundays with the long church service and ban on sport rather monotonous, I fitted comfortably and easily into the system. However, although I enjoyed boarding school I always treasured that first morning of the holidays when I awoke in my own bedroom with the knowledge that I could relax and do more or less what I wished at my own pace.

I had not wanted to go to Dulwich because it was a rugger, not a soccer, school and I loved football. I did learn to like and enjoy the oval-ball game, though never with as much passion as I had for the round-ball one. The first thing I discovered about rugby was that if one side-footed the ball, as if taking a corner in football, it was virtually impossible to miss a conversion in front of the posts, whereas it was easy to slice using the toe. This was even truer with the rugby ball of that period. The outside cover was not so well protected as it is today, so those old ones used for junior rugby tended to be rather more round than oval.

My junior housemaster was G. W. Parker, who made two appearances for England at full-back in the 1937–38 season. Their recognized place-kicker, he used the then accepted style. It was probably not entirely wise for me to point out to him the advantages of soccer-style conversions, but then I never was a diplomat. But I did have a point, as I never failed to convert in front of the posts throughout five seasons of rugby and also recorded a high percentage from the left-hand side of the pitch. I reverted to the toe method for distance and from the right-hand touchline.

The gap between prep and public school cricket was considerable, and was probably wider before the war, when it was by no means unusual to have 18- and 19-year-olds in a First XI. The difference was rather like that which exists between village and county cricket. In my first summer at Dulwich I could see no likelihood of my playing for, or even being considered for, the First XI, especially as they had what was generally reckoned to be the most powerful side in the history of the school. I played for the Colts, where I scored runs and took wickets but not with the profusion or frequency of my previous summer at Alleyn Court. Although at the start of the term I thought there might be an outside chance of making it into the First XI, by the end of May I had given up hope as I had never even had nets with them.

Fate, in the elegant shape of Jack Robertson, who was trying to establish himself in the Middlesex side, then took a hand. He came down with MCC and scored a classic century, in the process exposing the one basic weakness of the Dulwich First XI. It had only three mainline bowlers. The outcome was that I was chosen for the next match against Bedford School, because I happened to be the fastest bowler available. The master in charge of cricket, 'Father' Marriott, had doubts about including me because I was only 14. My only worry was whether I was good enough – if the player has the ability, throw him in the deep end, has always been my belief.

Being selected for the first time for Dulwich was probably the most exciting moment of my entire cricket career. I can recall asking to be excused, and leaving the classroom, simply to go and look at my name at the bottom of the First XI team list, which had been put up on the notice board. I could not really believe it. A dream had come true. I was actually going to play in the same side as the head of Ivyholme, David Knight (father of Roger Knight, the former Surrey captain).

We beat Bedford. I batted at number ten, bowled as fast as I could and picked up a couple of important wickets, which guaranteed me a place in the next game against St Paul's. Even more important, our captain Alan Shirreff – an outstanding schoolboy cricketer and an above average captain – had realized that a fourth bowler gave his attack extra bite and variety.

The rest of the season was very similar to the first match. I continued picking up a few useful wickets, batted occasionally low in the order and was an asset in the field. We won all our school matches and P. G. Wodehouse, an Old Alleynian, decided to celebrate our performance by taking the entire team out to dinner and then on to the London Palladium. This was, in those days, something very special, as I had never been to a major London restaurant, let alone seen a show at the Palladium. My housemaster thought I was too young, but my parents persuaded him otherwise and I took part in my first ever celebration cricket dinner.

The cricket facilities at Dulwich College before the war could scarcely have been bettered. The master in charge, 'Father' Marriott, was that cricketing rarity, a bowler pure and simple. He could neither bat nor field for the very good reason that he was not a natural ball player and was unable to coordinate. I shall always remember when he unwisely decided to take a highish catch off his own bowling and called 'mine'. It was not a case of him simply dropping it: he never made, nor looked like making, any contact whatsoever. He was, however, a very fine legbreak bowler, who took 11 for 96 in his only Test in 1933.

The fact that he was understandably not the most efficient coach of batting and fielding did not matter, because on the staff we also had S. C. Griffith (Cambridge University, Surrey, Sussex, and later England), G. W. Parker (Cambridge University and Gloucestershire) and several other masters who were up to Minor County standard. We also had two professionals, the senior of which was George Brown, formerly with Surrey. He was an excellent umpire, while at medium pace he could be relied upon to drop the ball exactly where he wanted. In addition, the pitches in the middle were fast and true, and, perhaps even more important, the nets were just as good if not better.

'Father' Marriott made two very important contributions. First, he had an infectious enthusiasm and was desperately keen for us to do well because it really meant so much to him. Second, he made absolutely certain that we knew how to play legbreak bowling, which so often destroys school teams. It is entirely due to the hours I spent batting against 'Father' that I fancied legbreak bowlers all my life.

In the nets he would bowl his leg-breaks and his googly slowly. He would give them plenty of air, the type of bowling we might expect to encounter in school and club matches. It was marvellous practice, especially when he deceived you in the flight after you had gone down the pitch and you realized that, providing you did not commit suicide with a hearty mow, all was not lost and you could live to face another ball. When he bowled like that you had to learn how to use your feet.

In the middle and in matches he bowled as he had done for England, Kent and Cambridge University, flat and quickly. Then it was absolutely fatal to play back, because he would have you lbw with his top-spinner. The dead-bat forward defensive was an essential stroke if you intended to stay and make runs against him.

After the triumphs of 1938, the team did not do so well in the following year, though it marked the arrival of A. W. H. Mallett in the side. I had the personal satisfaction of scoring 403 runs and heading the batting with an average of 50.38, which meant that I had improved considerably as a batsman, while my bowling remained about the same. Apart from a one-term evacuation to Tonbridge, the outbreak of war did not have that much effect on school life and I topped both the batting and bowling averages in 1940.

The Government were urging people to leave the Southend area and I suggested to my parents that Dulwich was a good place to come to. This had the considerable advantage of allowing me to become a day boy. Boarding school, with rationing and often having to sleep in shelters, had lost much of its original appeal. Also, as a day boy I would obviously have more freedom, while my interest in the other sex was steadily increasing.

The first raid on London occurred the night my parents arrived in London. Shortly afterwards the Blitz began and the rather cosy life style at school inevitably changed. Much of the fun of being a boarder vanished. Food was a problem, the houses were no longer able to dine separately and a shelter did not compare with sleeping in a cubicle, so I was very pleased to have become a day boy.

Before every rugby match the whole school would walk up and down the pitch during 'break' combing the ground for shrapnel. My friends and I used to cycle to have a look at the damage whenever a bomb landed within a radius of about eight miles, and we came to accept death and destruction philosophically. Once a week we spent the night fire watching at the school, a master and ten senior boys, which we all enjoyed. In between the duty shifts, we played endless games of table tennis and talked and talked and talked about the future, the past, the war, the school, music, sport and sex.

We did not have to go to school if the siren sounded and, as the all-clear often took a couple of hours, I would frequently turn round and head back home and, indeed, the air raids did allow one to go missing without any questions being asked. By this time I had become a prefect and was captain of cricket and squash. With no sign of the war ever ending, and with two years to go before I went into the forces, I had decided to enjoy myself as much as possible while I could.

Some of the cricket fixtures with the club sides, like the Free Foresters and I Zingari, had to be abandoned because they were unable to raise a side. This did not worry me, in fact I was delighted, because it allowed us to increase the number of matches we played against other schools and those were the ones that really mattered and we enjoyed most.

In 1941 I was lucky to have one of the most formidable attacks a school could possess, with three bowlers capable of taking wickets in first-class cricket: Tony Mallett, who went on to play for Oxford and Kent and was also a spectacular batsman; Horace Kiddle, who would have played for Surrey if he had not been killed flying during the war; and myself. The outcome was a succession of massacres of other school teams, who were not infrequently shot out for under 50.

One of my favourite big wins was over MCC because their side contained a former Oxford Blue who gave the impression that he was very special. He announced that he would be an hour or so late as a result of a business appointment. When he turned up, MCC were all back in the pavilion for 22. He did not score very many when we allowed them to have a second innings, and I fancy he regretted not wearing a thigh pad.

It was in 1941 that I decided to forget about being a quickie and concentrate on my batting, plus a little leg-break bowling. I had some back trouble and the combination of Mallett and Kiddle was proving too much for most teams, while I was having my best ever season for Dulwich with the bat, finishing with an average of 121.57. Everyone, especially 'Father', whose seldom-fulfilled dream was to have a wrist-spinner in the First XI, thought that this was a sensible step as they felt that, with my slight build (under ten stone), combining batting and pace bowling in first-class cricket would not be feasible.

I changed my mind during the match with Bedford School. For once, Mallett and Kiddle failed to make the expected breakthrough, while I had captured only one wicket for 70 with my leg-spin. This was not really surprising as I was never able to turn my leg-breaks because my fingers were much too small. My only assets as a spinner were a very graceful, almost effete, action and a good quick ball which I slipped in very frequently. In desperation I decided to bowl fast again – my back had fully recovered by this time – and finished with six wickets for 80.

That was the last time I ever seriously considered giving up pace bowling and taking the advice of the experts. From then on I remained an allrounder and, in my last year at Dulwich, although I did not make as many runs as in 1941, I had my best allround summer scoring 635 runs and capturing 66 wickets at 6.17, which was necessary as Kiddle was then in the RAF.

A LIFE ON THE OCEAN WAVE

I have long forgotten the number of times I have marched to the Royal Marine signature tune. However, crossing to Holland on tank landing craft and sailing small landing craft in the Barmouth Estuary was the sum total of my life on the ocean wave.

Of all the periods of my life, the most unreal was unquestionably the years spent in the Royal Marines. They contain so many moments of farce that I sometimes wonder whether they ever occurred and, because they did, how on earth we won a war. From the outset, I was never cut out to be a soldier, let alone a Royal Marine. I had an inquisitive mind, automatically queried anything I did not believe was right, was essentially an individualist, possessed at the time an essentially liberal outlook, hated cruelty, and had a sense of humour which made me laugh at things which my elders and betters frequently considered important and not laughing matters.

I first realized my unsuitability for a military career when, as a boy of 14, I was forced to join the OTC at Dulwich. It was not that I had any pacifist tendencies – though I seem to remember one term when I was rather impressed by Beverley Nicholls's book *The Fool Hath Said* – but I simply found puttees uncomfortable and difficult to keep straight, my uniform never seemed to fit, my webbing always acquired more of the Brasso than the brass, I found drill extremely boring, and I carefully avoided camp because it was not my scene. The summer holidays were designed for cricket, the seaside, tennis, enjoyment, cycle rides, and girlfriends, not for army manoeuvres and sleeping in a tent.

Some of my contemporaries also disliked the corps, others tolerated it and many enjoyed it enormously, especially Field Day staged on Epsom Downs, after we had all marched – why was I so often out of step – to West Dulwich station. I found even Field Day, apart from firing blanks, rather heavy going, but noticed that our military band appeared to have a rather good time. They played *Sussex, Sussex, Sussex by the Sea* – I do not think they had another tune in their repertoire – to and from the railway station. Then, while we were fighting our mock battle on the downs, they had a short practice session before spending most of the day on the swings and roundabouts.

Alan, a friend in the same boarding house, was a drummer in the band. Apparently it was easy to join but I had two particular problems. First, I was unable to blow a bugle and, even if I eventually mastered it, I would undoubtedly murder *Sussex, Sussex, Sussex by the Sea*. Second, I was obviously unwilling to spend the time required to learn the drums. It seemed unsolvable until he brought the news that the band needed somebody to play the cymbals, rather spoiling things by saying 'any fool can handle those'. He was absolutely right. Even I could manage the cymbals, apart from that occasion when I gave one extra clang after the band had completed its other number, *God Save the King*. It might be said I had found my rightful spot in the OTC, which I held until I decided to switch to the ATC.

The Air Force was the most glamorous of the forces, and to me it seemed the cleanest, even if the chances of survival as a pilot were less. One shot down another plane, or dropped a bomb, but one did not have to stick a bayonet into the enemy, a somewhat uncivilized objective, and the thought of going down in a ship depressed me as I was never entirely convinced that drowning was a fast way to go.

My initial enthusiasm for the ATC began to wane immediately I was introduced to navigation. I never saw eye to eye with it, and therefore experienced considerable problems moving from A to B – and still do.

In our last year at school everybody talked a great deal about which service they intended to volunteer for. It was a favourite topic of conversation when fire watching. One of my closest friends was Don Smith, who, apart from being head of the school, was a natural soldier and a shining light in the corps. He already had an elder brother, later to be killed, in the Fleet Air Arm and we were seeking something different. Then Don came up with a quite irresistible idea for a romantic 18-year-old: we would join the Royal Marines, but learn to fly with the Fleet Air Arm, thus becoming a real rarity, a flying marine.

This provided us with the ideal piece of one-upmanship when

asked which service we were joining. We simply tossed away a casual, 'Oh, I am going to be a flying marine.' Game, set and match anywhere, including on the local dance floor.

Don and I joined the Royal Marines together, received our call-up papers on the same day, travelled down by train to Exton for our initial training, and had a spell at the Marine camp near Dalditch. This was a distinctly primitive camp and we would sometimes go to a hotel in Exmouth for a meal and bath. Finally we were both selected for OCTU. We had learned after the six-week initial training period that there was no way we could ever become flying marines, as the Marines had no intention of training us and then allowing us to become pilots. If we wanted to fly, we would have to transfer immediately to the Fleet Air Arm.

As I mentioned earlier, Don was a born soldier. Not only did he look the part, he was also extremely efficient. Inevitably he sailed through OCTU and was commissioned. Although Don did his best to assist me, I found OCTU extremely hard. We said goodbye, wished each other luck, and I never saw him again. He was blown up off Walcheren commanding a flak ship.

Joining the Royal Marines did me a great deal of good, and broadened my outlook. Until I went into the forces my horizons had been limited, largely confined by a loving, somewhat doting family, a prep school, a public school, friends who might have different views but came from similar backgrounds, and sportsmen. When I arrived for my initial training, the next nissen hut was full of Scots of my own age from Glasgow. Although I had difficulty in understanding everything they said, apart from an over-frequent four letter word, they fascinated me. We would all line up on pay day to receive a few shillings, which was intended to last until the following week. By the end of that Friday evening half the Scots would have lost everything playing pitch and toss. It did not make any sense to me, because I have never been prepared to gamble with anything I could not afford. Nevertheless, we got on well because of a mutual passion for football, and I began to absorb views I had never encountered before.

The Marine OCTU at Thurlestone provided an interesting experience. By the end of it I was better prepared to run a marathon than to lead a platoon into battle. I was not surprised when I was not commissioned at the end of the course. Indeed, I was surprised that the powers that be had considered me officer material in the first place, apart from the obvious fact I would never have made a sergeant and would do less harm as a second lieutenant.

Although I had not acquired that little pip at the end of the course, I was not listed as an F for Failure – I was assigned the status of an NY. We Not Yets were put in a kind of marine limbo. If we impressed our commanding officer we would be considered again, but would not have to go through another OCTU. I drifted back to Devon, became a corporal, played plenty of cricket and football and rather enjoyed the existence. It was here I had one of those experiences which stay with you throughout your life.

As Corporal Bailey I found myself instructing a squad of Marines in semaphore for use in landing craft. I was having great trouble with one marine who was behaving like an imbecile, though I knew that he was not. Eventually my lance corporal called out that Marine Blank did not know his alphabet. I shouted back: 'I know that you bloody fool, that's what I'm trying to teach him.'

His reply shattered me: 'No, corp, he doesn't know the real alphabet, you know, his ABC.' I felt sick at the pain I had unintentionally inflicted.

One day I was summoned by my commanding officer, who told me that I had been appointed a second lieutenant, to take some leave and purchase a uniform. Although it seemed odd, as my military knowledge had not increased during what had been a restful period, I was both pleased and proud.

My first appointment as an officer did not prove very satisfactory. In fact, it came close to a real disaster.

A group of commissioned Not Yets were sent to Dille to undergo what, I supposed, was intended to be a post-OCTU course under a marine officer, a regular who would have been an asset to the Gestapo. We did not meld. He reminded me of Charles Laughton in *Mutiny on the Bounty*, minus ability. Later, after several years as a commissioned officer, I was still amused by the condescension with which some regular officers regarded the HO, or Hostilities Only, brigade. Understandably, my personal view that nobody in his right mind would want to be a regular did not make me universally popular with a breed not exactly famed for their sense of humour, or indeed brainpower. Rather too many were still struggling mentally in the lower fifth.

Having received a bad report for the course, and been warned as to my future behaviour, I was sent for my first job as a second lieutenant to a camp with an unpronounceable and unspellable name in North Wales, near Towyn. I reported to the adjutant, who informed me that I was the new training officer in charge of landing craft. This appointment summed up my marine career: not only did I know absolutely nothing about landing craft, but I had not even seen one, except on the screen.

It was to be the start of a happy, uneventful year or so in various North Wales camps. During this period all the marine crews who were in charge of landing craft on D-Day arrived for their initial training. My duties were not too exacting and left me plenty of time to play football and cricket. In addition I read a great deal, almost taught myself shorthand, seriously considered Roman Catholicism, and played cricket for the Marines plus several big matches for the Royal Navy. Sport was encouraged, the food, with many farms in the vicinity, was above average, and the only danger I faced was from bombs when I went home to London on leave.

What was an essentially comfortable routine was once disturbed by the arrival of a new commanding officer, who decided to shake up the regular staff by making us spend one night a week marching the coxswains we were training through the Welsh mountains, and then carry on the next day as normal. His idea was to teach men how to do without sleep, but it never seemed to work quite that way. As a result of losing my entire company on more than one occasion, I confirmed that my map and compass reading left something to be desired. Much later, an enthusiastic and slightly mad Marine Commando lieutenant-colonel arrived and I helped him to construct and try out an assault course for his troops. It was fun and he invited me to join his commando, an offer I declined with thanks. I would have jumped at the opportunity straight from school, but by then I was older, wiser and more cynical. I was already thinking about after the war and had long since decided it was more sensible, and safer, not to volunteer for that sort of job.

I was eventually moved from the comfort of Wales after a stay which I thought would be brief but lasted for more than a year. Expecting something to do with landing craft, I found instead that I had been returned to an infantry battalion for possible use in the Far East. More troops were then required in Europe, which led to a sudden reshuffle when it was realized that the Marines used a different infantry formation from the army. I never did find out why it took quite so long for this to dawn on the authorities.

After some time I found myself attached to a battalion and was asked if I had any particular platoon preference. Having attended an infantry course at Barnard Castle and acquired some knowledge of the life, I volunteered for the Pioneer platoon, which contained all the tradesmen in the company. Although the name was unglamorous, it had a big practical advantage. I would be in charge of motor vehicles and believed travelling on four wheels was preferable to my two feet. Because it was a specialist platoon, it also meant that I had to go on several specialist courses. We learned to use explosives and defuse booby traps, which was more interesting and less restrictive than general day to day life in a battalion. I was taught to drive a jeep – badly – in an afternoon, with the result that I nearly killed a high percentage of my platoon on our way back from a dance in Leamington Spa the same evening.

My battalion eventually embarked for Europe at exactly the right time for anyone, like myself, who was thinking in terms of post-war sport rather than military glory – just before Germany surrendered. We started to make our way across a battered Holland when one of the Bren carriers broke down. I was ordered to remain and join up with the rest of the brigade in Germany after it had been repaired. The outcome was that, as the war was ending, I found myself being driven across Holland, Belgium and Germany in a Bren carrier. I was never completely sure whether I had been entrusted with this particular mission because I was the most expendable of the officers, or because, with my qualifications as a navigator, we would never arrive.

It turned out to be an unforgettable journey. We drove past Belsen shortly after the British Army had arrived there. Many of the former prisoners were standing like emaciated cattle by the roadside wearing what looked like striped pyjamas. I had never seen such expressions on human faces before, and thankfully never have since.

We caught up with the brigade just before Kiel was taken. The main interest of a high percentage of British forces seemed to be the acquisition of as much loot as possible. Binoculars from the destroyers seemed fair game, but I sometimes wondered about the stripping of everything of any value from the private apartments where the brigade was billeted. At least it made me thankful that Germany had not won the war.

After the initial excitement, being stationed in Germany became a boring and monotonous exercise. In the prison we controlled there were a number of Nazis, and I witnessed several classic examples of how catching the disease of cruelty can be. One of my brother officers, with whom I had become very friendly, was a charming, liberal Jew, but placed in charge of those Nazis he acquired another personality. I began to understand how sadism can lie dormant in kindly civilized people, just waiting for the spark to set it alight.

The next episode of my Marine career, which I always think of as my court-martial period, was the most bizarre and certainly the most unexpected. It began by chance. I was sitting in the adjutant's office, because I happened to be the duty officer, reading a book and minding my own business when a wretched marine was brought in front of my commanding officer by the sergeant major for committing the heinous offence of falling asleep on guard duty. He was told that he would be court-martialled and was asked whether there was any particular officer he would like to defend him. To my horror and amazement he said, 'Could I have Lieutenant Bailey?' I had never attended a court-martial, let alone acted as a defending officer!

Fortunately, nobody at the ensuing court-martial had any practical knowledge of law and it was a straightforward case. My client admitted his guilt and I pleaded extenuating circumstances with a sincerity which was certainly not justified. Whether that had any effect on the court I never discovered, but I think it unlikely. The most likely explanation was that the officiating officer had received good news from home. Whatever the reason, the sentence passed on my client was less severe than he expected and he was so impressed by my performance that he told his mates. The outcome was that I gained an entirely undeserved reputation as a defending officer and was in considerable demand.

I was helped by three things. First, nobody at any of the courts-martial was a lawyer. Second, I had a reasonably devious mind and the ability to present an improbable tale with some conviction. Third, I enjoyed the job, because it made such a pleasant change to the normal routine, and applied myself to it as best I could.

In addition to acting as a defending officer, I found myself sitting in on the court-martial of a marine sergeant who had been accused, with an officer who happened to be a friend of mine, of fraternization with a fraulein. I had heard the whole unintentionally funny story only an hour after the alleged crime. They had just been unlucky to have been caught. Nobody seemed worried that I knew considerably more about the case than either the defence or the prosecution. Naturally both were found not guilty.

'Old Bailey's' last case was too farcical for farce. The facts were these. Three marines had taken a craft out into the harbour and gone aboard a boat which was occupied by German civilians. The trio were fully armed, partially tight and stole several things, including a clock.

It has to be stressed again that nobody in the court had the slightest knowledge of law and for some extraordinary reason the three marines were charged with piracy. The defence was based on my claim that the prosecution had not proved intent to steal; that the clock had only been borrowed as an aid to making sure they were able to parade at the correct time. To put it mildly, it was an unlikely tale, particularly as the three accused were experts at absenting themselves from parades, let alone arriving on time. The eventual outcome was that the three were acquitted. My own view of justice has never quite been the same again.

Back at headquarters, somebody with a smattering of law and probably fascinated by the dramatic original charge, realized that some of the Royal Marines' courts-martial were being badly mishandled with hilarious results and consequently an officer, who had had a legal training in civilian life, was immediately dispatched to superintend the staging of future courts-martial. I never had the opportunity of acting as defending officer at a correctly run one, because my battalion was ordered home in the summer of 1945 with a view to our providing additional troops for the Far East. I found myself back in Wales; even better was the news that Japan had surrendered. I never fancied touring the Far East as a Marine and the atom bomb had my complete approval.

During disembarkation leave I played plenty of cricket for the British Empire XI and the Royal Navy. I began playing for the British Empire XI during my school holidays of 1941 and 1942 and continued to appear for them, when my Royal Marine duties permitted, until 1945, when the club was wound up, with a record of 238 matches played, 150 won, 52 drawn and 36 lost. In that period the club raised a great deal of money for the Red Cross and provided cricket lovers with a chance to see good players in action when entertainment (and laughter) was in short supply.

It provided me with my first taste of a new cricket world which included sessions in the bar after the match, girls who liked cricketers, which added that certain something to the game, and autograph hunters. It also introduced me to a number of established players, many of whom would play with me for Essex when first-class cricket was resumed. This enabled me to compare my own performances with bat and ball with those of professionals. I was reasonably satisfied, probably too satisfied, with such comparisons as I generally managed to take some wickets and score runs, providing I was given the opportunity to bat. So saying, most of the time we were much stronger than the opposition, much of which was mundane. I cannot remember any of the games, just the fun.

The British Empire XI was led with considerable style by Ray Smith, who could have made a better than average county skipper as long as there had been somebody at hand to remind him to take himself off occasionally. Other Essex players whom I encountered in that side were Harry Crabtree, 'Sonny' Avery and Frank Appleyard, a medium-paced seamer and jovial farmer who never wore socks and whose pace was never quite fast enough for first-class cricket. However, our key bowler and the person who made the biggest impression on me was the West Indian, Bertie Clarke. Bertie, who had played for the West Indies three times in 1939, was the first black West Indian whom I got to know really well. I was impressed and fascinated by his enthusiasm, ability and unfailing cheerfulness as a player and as a person. After the war he played a certain amount for Northants, and much later we persuaded him in 1959 and 1960 to turn out in a few matches for Essex, when his medical duties allowed. He was past his peak, but his top-spinner still bounced and he always made the game sparkle.

Other players whom I remember especially well from those happy days with the British Empire XI were Harry Halliday, who never did as well for Yorkshire as I expected, A. C. L. Bennett and L. B. Thompson, who I always felt could have been an outstanding fast-medium bowler.

After my cricket-playing leave, I returned to my camp in Wales and went to see my commanding officer with a long list of invitations to take part in matches up and down the country, including several for the Royal Marines and the Royal Navy. Fortunately, he was an understanding person, not a regular, who loved cricket. He must have realized that with the war finished there was nothing much to do in Wales. I thought he would grant me some leave, but he proved to be even more helpful.

Having gone very carefully through the list of matches which stretched over a period of six weeks, finishing at the end of September, he turned to me and said: 'What you really want Bailey is to disappear until October, but you will appreciate that I cannot authorise a leave allowance.' Hardly able to believe my good fortune, I said that my allowance did not matter. I was then given the best order of my career in the Marines: 'Disappear'.

I reported back to a somewhat unusual unit stationed near Shrewsbury and found myself billeted with one other officer in what had been an old vicarage. The intention was that we should supervise the six marines who were farming, but as in addition to the two of us there were 30 NCOs, none of whom was expected to farm, it was a case of 'too many chiefs and not enough indians'. It was also such a complete and utter waste of time that I decided that the moment had come for me to leave the Marines as quickly as possible.

There was a snag – the thousands who had joined before me. I then had a brainwave. Certain categories in the forces were being released well ahead of their allocated schedule. My objective was to qualify, but the problem was how, as I had gone straight from school into the Royal Marines. One group securing an early release were schoolmasters. In addition to the shortage, many of the masters who had come out of retirement to fill in during the war had had enough. Every school was crying out for new staff and none more than preparatory schools, which had never been able to afford high wages and had always relied to some extent on young unqualified teachers, many of whom were waiting to go up to university. As I had no qualifications other than matric and A-levels in English and History, it had to be a prep school.

Alleyn Court, where I had been at school, had just returned to Westcliff after being evacuated down to Devon. This increased their staffing problems. I told Denys Wilcox, the headmaster, that I would be delighted to join Alleyn Court as a teacher and he was only too pleased to apply for my release, which, much to my surprise and delight, came through just before Christmas 1945.

It was a marvellous Christmas present, saving me from wasting several years of my life. It was also a very memorable Christmas, because during my demobilization leave I met Greta, later to become my wife, at a Christmas dance in Westcliff. Within a couple of weeks I had become a civilian and began teaching in January. Was there really a war?

35

THEY SAID WE SHOULDN'T LOOK BACK

I enjoyed teaching so much that when I went up to Cambridge in the autumn of 1946, I had already decided to become a schoolmaster. The short period I spent at Alleyn Court between leaving the Royal Marines and going to university was one of the happiest in my life. Teaching at a prep school is especially rewarding, because the boys are so enthusiastic, malleable and responsive. This was especially true immediately after the war, when standards of behaviour were much higher than today, sensible discipline was considered essential and television had not started to dominate domestic life.

My particular subjects were English and History, but I did have to fill in with others, including Maths and Latin – without, I hope, doing too much damage. In addition, twice a week I took the kindergarten for what was ostensibly History, but really consisted of stories about King Alfred and the cakes, Richard Coeur de Lion, and Lord Nelson. These two periods were fun and I was fascinated by how the children would come forth with such vital pieces of domestic information as the purchase of an alarm clock by Mother, or how delighted Daddy was that Grandma had gone home at last.

On one occasion we all became involved in a serious discussion about the inhabitants of Fairy Land. I was holding forth on the comparative magical skills of fairies, gnomes and goblins when a small, bespectacled, rather intense boy held up his hand. I told him that he could be excused, but he remained until I eventually asked what he wanted. The son of the local vicar, he came out with the devastating: 'My Daddy says there's no such thing as fairies and gnomes. There's only God and the angels.'

For anyone like myself who still believed in Santa Claus, this was close to heresy and there was consternation in the classroom. Knowing that children quickly forget, I solved the problem by ordering the milk to be handed round immediately, and telling them that when they raised their cap to a lady they were imitating knights in armour lifting their visors. For several days afterwards I noticed the class were raising their caps with rather more of a flourish.

In addition to teaching boys the delights of the split infinitive and the matrimonial complexities of Henry VIII, I coached them at football and cricket. I found this to be immensely rewarding, not only because of their enthusiasm but also because they improved so quickly.

At the start of the summer term you may well find yourself without a wicketkeeper. The best solution is to pick a well co-ordinated fielder who tackles hard on the football field, a boy with courage who is not afraid to take a knock. Within a month it is possible to turn him into a reasonable performer behind the stumps. The satisfaction when he makes a stumping in a match and the opposing master compliments you on your keeper's ability, is considerably greater than if you had done it yourself, though in a sense you had.

There was only one snag about teaching a prep school: the salary was low. Initially this was no problem as I was living at home and single, but by the time I had acquired my degree I was about to marry and therefore had to think in terms of different types of schools. My original idea was a public school, which I would have enjoyed greatly, but with my unexceptional degree in English and History, I could not see myself finishing higher than a house master – and that would have taken a long time to achieve as at most schools it was largely a case of filling deadmen's shoes.

Then I had an interview with the headmaster of Romford Royal Liberty School, who not only wanted me as a member of his staff but also reckoned that I would only have myself to blame if I had not acquired a headship at a state school by the time I was 30 – there was a real shortage at that time! It certainly provided an interesting alternative, especially as my wife was running a retail dress business for her father and therefore we had to live in the Westcliff area, and there were only a limited number of public schools in Essex.

From the financial and career angles there was much in favour of teaching in state schools. Against these was the fact that the cricket facilities were better at a public school, an important consideration as I intended to go on playing for Essex in the school holidays; and I also knew I would prefer the more relaxed atmosphere.

I am still not sure what I would have done because the choice became unnecessary. Essex offered me a post as assistant secretary, which allowed me to play first-class cricket for the whole of the summer and increased my chances of making an overseas tour with the MCC. It also allowed me to go on teaching during the two winter terms, as my duties with Essex at that time were not too demanding. The outcome was that I returned to Alleyn Court for two wonderful winters. But during this period I was chosen to play for England and became increasingly involved in cricket administration, which inevitably brought to an end my teaching career.

At school I became involved with the fundamentals of cricket, what and how it should be taught. Denys Wilcox, who was still headmaster of Alleyn Court and had played some first-class cricket with me for Essex after the war during the holidays, was an excellent mentor who had himself been greatly influenced by Bob Wyatt. As well as being a very accomplished technician, Bob's theories and views were based on practical experience and a lifetime discussing every aspect of the game with the best cricketers. The outcome of the interest which Denys and I had in cricket coaching resulted in our staging at Alleyn Court in 1949 the first-ever residential course for cricket coaches to be held in England. Shortly afterwards, the MCC began to take practical steps to find more coaches, which were certainly needed.

At that first course Harry Crabtree, then Physical Education Officer for Essex, came to demonstrate his brainchild, 'group coaching'. The objective was to enable teachers with a limited knowledge to put across to a large class the basics of cricket, particularly at schools where the facilities were limited and sometimes non-existent. Harry's concept was excellent. He correctly preached that cricket was not a natural game because it was sideways-on and some coaching was therefore essential if a cricketer, especially a batsman, was to attain his potential. Group coaching, under Harry himself, was extremely rewarding as he was an enthusiast, an expert coach and a fine teacher. Inevitably, its execution by some teachers with little or no technical knowledge was less successful: they turned it into cricket by numbers, which was never Harry's intention.

Denys Wilcox's son, John, was at the time of this coaching course for coaches a small 11-year-old who, not surprisingly, had been well instructed in the art of batting by his father. We used him as a model to show the coaches what could be achieved by a talented boy, even at that early age. It proved the highlight of the course, because everybody was surprised by the skill and the range of strokes in the demonstration – in fact, most of them were amazed. Later, Denys and I were to write *Cricketers in the Making*, which was designed especially for coaches. We used only boys as models in the action photographs, with John playing the batting strokes, because we wished to show that children under 13 were capable of being really proficient at all the basic arts of the game. John himself went on to Malvern and Cambridge University and played for Essex without ever scoring as many runs as his ability as a small boy had suggested.

I am not sure what I expected from Cambridge, but in some respects it was something of a disappointment, rather in the way that no school could ever quite measure up to Greyfriars, nor the real West possess the glamour and the code of the cinema version. On the other hand, I enjoyed immensely the two years I spent there, my major regret being that I feel I should have gained even more from the experience than I did, which was my fault not the University's.

The reader may have noticed that in the previous paragraph I mentioned my two years up at Cambridge. This was not due to my being sent down. However, I was allowed to deduct one year for war service and acquire a degree in two, instead of three years. This meant that I did not have enough time to browse and dream, which I would have had if I had been up for three or four years. As it was, I could not afford more than two years because Greta and I had decided to marry in 1948. Apart from feeling there was something rather incongruous about married undergraduates, my grant was scarcely enough for me and certainly would not have supported two.

Unquestionably, I would have found Cambridge more romantic and exciting if I had gone straight from school. Climbing into college would have been an adventure, whereas after several years in the Marines it was an unnecessary bore. My objectives were to gain a respectable degree, Blues for cricket and football, and then to become a schoolmaster when I came down. This schedule did not give me too much time for social activities at the University, especially as I went home most weekends.

It seemed to me that I would be better equipped to teach if I took a degree in English as well as History, particularly as my specialized subject was American history. However, there was one snag. I found it impossible to read, let alone digest, all the suggested literature for Part One English in one year, and this would still have been the case if I had had no other commitments. During the winter I normally played two football matches per week and spent two afternoons training, which forced me to give up squash after my first term because I simply did not have time. I rather regretted this as Tony Mallett, whom I reckoned to beat at Dulwich, gained a Blue for Oxford University and higher honours afterwards, while I never played squash seriously again.

If football took up quite a portion of my life at Cambridge, cricket was even more demanding. For most of the summer term I was playing first-class cricket against the counties six days per week and six hours a day, which did not leave too much time for study and other entertainment.

My extra-curricular activities consisted of one evening of bridge and one at the cinema and most weekends at home. A friend who worked in Cambridge drove home every Saturday and returned on Monday morning. Without him I would have had neither the time nor the money for the journey.

The bridge was essentially social and my partners had to contend with my own system, 'Bailey Bridge', a mixture of Culbertson and Blackwood which was intended to get the message across but often failed. To make things rather more difficult, I was seldom able to remember which cards below the tens had been played, a weakness which increased my excitement when attempting even a simple squeeze because I never knew whether my last card was in fact the master.

My most frequent cinema companion was Doug Insole. We both had a love for films which continued through the whole of our cricket careers. It was at Cambridge that our friendship began. I first saw him kicking a football and put him down as a professional footballer practising, because he did hit the ball uncommonly hard with his right foot. I was surprised to learn that he was an undergraduate. Within a few weeks I found myself on the right wing for the University team with Doug at inside right, a partnership which lasted until I went down.

My next mistake about Doug occurred in the summer, when he

was trying for a place in the cricket eleven and was having a net. I bowled at him and, because he was unquestionably one of the worst and ugliest net players I ever encountered, immediately wrote him off. In the nets everything seemed wrong about him and he departed to play some Crusader cricket. I was convinced that I had seen the last of him in senior University cricket, but could not have been more wrong. Despite his unusual technique, Doug forced our captain, Guy Willatt, to give him a chance in the University eleven through the simple expedient of scoring runs, something which he continued to do in profusion until he retired from the game.

The big difference between University sport of my era and today was age. The majority of players in the Cambridge rugby, soccer and cricket teams were in their twenties, so they were more experienced as well as physically and mentally more mature. This was particularly noticeable in the rugby XV, which was one of the strongest and fittest in the country. The University Match would immediately provide a number of internationals. There were only about two members in the cricket and football elevens who had come straight from school. The result was that we sometimes beat and regularly made large totals and individual scores against the counties.

In my first session at Fenner's, 1947, we drew with Sussex, Essex, Yorkshire, Worcestershire and Gloucestershire. We beat the Royal Navy and Free Foresters and lost to Middlesex. On tour we drew with Surrey, Hampshire and Somerset, lost to Lancashire and beat Warwickshire.

Our tour produced two magic moments for me, the first against Somerset at Bath where I found I was able to make the ball swing far more than usual. I had had a successful opening spell, but my day was made when our twelfth man came on with a marvellous story of the sagacity of two aged Somerset experts sitting in the pavilion.

Our slow left-arm bowler was a delightful Indian, P. B. Datta, who bowled accurately but hardly spun the ball. He and I were about the same height and build with dark complexions and dark wavy hair. The conversation of the two Somerset members, overheard by our twelfth man, was as follows:

'These Indians are marvellously supple, old man.'

'What do you mean?'

'Well, only an Indian would be able to open the attack fast right arm and then come on first change as a slow left-arm spinner.'

My second magic moment came later in the tour at Edgbaston. We won the toss and, because I have always instinctively recognized a pitch which favours seam, I suggested very forcibly that we put Warwickshire into bat. Though our batsmen did not agree, I won the day and took the new ball. Their opener, who scored a hundred in their second innings, wanted the sightscreen moved. I held up my arm for him to make the necessary adjustment and at the same time shouted to a gaggle of spectators in that area to move it. Their reply was not exactly complimentary, nor were the remarks of my batsmen colleagues at the end of six overs when not a ball had deviated. However, all was well, as the ball started to move and Warwickshire were all out before lunch, my partner, Hugh Griffiths, and myself sharing the wickets and bowling unchanged.

My first year at Cambridge assisted my cricket in two different ways. The wickets at Fenner's were so good that I was able to score sufficient runs to provide the confidence required when batting for Essex, while after the hard work of bowling there, taking wickets in county games was much easier.

What was the standard of the two University teams in which I played? Our batting, assisted by the runs one could hardly fail to acquire at Fenner's, was more than adequate; our fielding was superior to and more agile than that of the majority of county sides; but our bowling, apart from the seam bowling, was well below county standard. Five of the side would have gained a permanent place in most county elevens, two would have struggled and the rest were competent club players.

In many respects what appealed most about University sport was the Blues system, which meant that all the games, although important in their own way, were really warm-ups for the big one against Oxford – a Blue is dependent upon playing in the Varsity match. This was the match which really counted, when everyone pulled out all the stops. I have always welcomed a major occasion and a large crowd and in the 1940s 15,000 would attend the first day of the Varsity match at Lord's, while the football match at Dulwich Hamlet would draw a capacity crowd of about 10,000.

From the personal angle, I had four satisfactory Varsity matches. We won both football matches, possibly against form, but at cricket we lost one and had much the worse of the other, largely because Oxford possessed a better attack and, on the first occasion, in Martin Donnelly, had a batsman at least two classes higher than anybody on either side. He cruelly exposed the limitations of our bowling line-up which consisted of two seamers, a non-turning leftarmer and a reasonable club wrist-spinner.

In my second University match, we batted indifferently in our first innings, although, somewhat ironically in the view of future events, I was not involved in the slow scoring which produced only 134 runs for the loss of four wickets by tea. My own fifty came in about 90 minutes, but what sank us did not occur until the Monday morning, when our third seamer, 'Tonker' Urquhart, a supremely confident bowler who believed that he was capable of producing the unplayable ball more or less at will, even if his figures hardly supported this belief, went for a trundle in the nets before start of play, pulled a muscle and was unable to field, let alone bowl. As he was run out for nought it might be said that he experienced one of the less successful University matches, but it also again left us two new-ball bowlers with, on this occasion, two limited wrist-spinners. Predictably we were unable to sustain an early breakthrough and eventually went down by an innings.

Although I enjoyed neither my cricket or my football as much in my second year, this had nothing to do with that disastrous result. It was due to several different factors. First, some novelty had inevitably departed. Second, it was very necessary for me to obtain a degree. English Part One was proving more daunting than History Part One and I had arranged to marry on the day after the University match. (As I have never been able to remember numbers or dates, this proved very handy in later years because I had only to look in the relevant *Wisden* to check our wedding anniversary.) Third, I was injured at both football and cricket.

Playing for Southend United Reserves before the commencement of the winter term I was kicked in the ankle. Though painful, I was not especially concerned. However, when I began with the University team I found I was unable to kick the ball properly with my right foot, which had certain disadvantages for a right winger. The diagnosis of torn fibres and a manipulative operation under an anaesthetic for what, much later, turned out to have been a hairline fracture did nothing to improve the situation. I was even tried on the left wing which, as my left foot might be termed a swinger and was certainly incapable of providing accurate crosses, did not prove a profitable move. At one time it seemed as if I would miss the University match, then, with only about a week to go, the ankle improved sufficiently for me to be picked on the basis of the previous year's match rather than on form.

After an extremely good allround cricket season in 1947, the following summer proved disappointing. Indeed, 1948 was one of my worst summers, which was by no means entirely due to injuries although these did not help.

Despite losing our captain, Guy Willatt, it was generally felt that Cambridge should do very well as two exceptionally talented freshmen, Hubert Doggart and John Dewes, had come up; while Brian Elgood was an above average University batsman. In the first match Hubert scored a record 215 not out against Lancashire on his debut in first-class cricket; and John made 94 and Brian 127 not out in the second against Sussex, but my own contributions were minimal. This made a difference because runs beget runs. In the next match I bowled 32 overs and pulled a muscle in the process, which left me with a problem, because our next fixture was against the Australians (minus Bradman), who made a far larger impact on the general public than any other subsequent touring party. Everybody wanted to see the Australians under Donald Bradman on their first tour after the war, and there was no television.

Australia had thrashed England in Australia and it was fairly obvious that any bowler who caused them any serious inconvenience could automatically claim a place in our national eleven. We were due to meet them at Fenner's. Did I play against them, although not completely recovered, or miss a game in which I desperately wanted to take part? I was unable to resist the temptation. Fully fit, I would have been lucky to have made any impression; bowling well within myself I sent down 15 innocuous overs while they amassed 414 for four. Although we lost by an innings, I did manage an undefeated 66 in the second innings, having been involved in a run out with Doug Insole during the first innings. We both found ourselves running hard for the same end and I made the mistake of asking Doug where we went from here. His reply has always been extremely fast and he merely said, 'You go back to the pavilion.' And he was completely right.

Having participated in this heavy defeat, I then displayed my naivety by taking part in the next game against the tourists at Southchurch Park over the Whitsun Bank Holiday weekend. This was the era of petrol rationing and I acquired a lift in the Australian coach to my home town, which proved an interesting experience. My admiration for them as cricketers was enormous, but individually they were so far removed from the Cambridge and Essex players I knew that they almost seemed to have come from a different planet.

In the Essex game I had further cause to admire and envy their skill. Although we bowled them out in one day, they did manage to amass the little matter of 721 runs. In the first half hour, fielding at backward slip, I made the elementary error of trying to catch a Sid Barnes hook, which broke a finger in my left hand. My fingers have always been too small and delicate for serious cricket and this break was only one of many, all done when fielding.

There were several intriguing features about that Southchurch massacre. First, the Australians never accelerated – they kept plodding along at just under 250 runs per session. Second, I bowled Keith Miller first ball for nought with an absolutely straight ball. I remarked to Don that Keith had not appeared interested, to which he replied with the cryptic, 'He'll learn'. Third, although the attendance of 32,000 for the two days was easily a ground record, I have met subsequently at least one million people who claim to have been present. Finally, we managed somehow to bowl 129 overs, which was remarkable in six hours of play considering the amount of time spent retrieving the ball from the boundary.

In retrospect my lack of success, injuries and the arrival of the Australians in 1948 were good for me because until then I had not thought sufficiently about my game, nor worked enough at it. There were no genuinely fast bowlers in England and until 1948, as one of the fastest around, I still cherished the hope that I would become a bowler of real pace who would be able to blast out the opposition. The arrival of Ray Lindwall and Keith Miller changed all that, as their pace was yards faster; while the third member of what was essentially a three-pronged pace attack, Bill Johnston, was not only a much better bowler than myself, but also quicker. The Australian batsmen also demonstrated a distinct partiality for my bowling. I bowled against Don Bradman in three matches, which gave me sufficient time to appreciate his technique as he made centuries on each occasion.

The first was against Essex, when he came in well before lunch with the total 145 for one. My initial reaction was of slight disappointment, because he did not produce a series of spectacular strokes. Indeed, he did not appear to be scoring especially quickly, until I happened to glance at the scoreboard after he had been at the crease for less than half an hour and he was already 30. He departed when the score was nearly 500 and after he had plundered an effortless 187. One reason for his prowess as a run accumulator was the unerring way he was able to put the bad ball away to the boundary.

During the South of England game at Hastings I did in fact trap Don with a long hop which he mishooked. However, I could hardly rate that as a personal success: not only had he acquired 143 runs, my two wickets cost 125 in only 21 overs. It made me thankful that I had not bowled against him in his prime. It also made me realize that I would have to make a careful reappraisal if I was to avoid ending up as just another county hack, meat and drink to any class player on a good pitch. The Australians had demonstrated very pointedly that my pace was not sufficient and my bowling not good enough. Something had to be done.

The transformation took time, thought and practice. First, I cut one whirl from my action, which eventually gave me greater smoothness and control. Second, I gradually grooved my action, angled my approach to be closer to the stumps, and improved my accuracy. Third, I extended my repertoire by varying my pace, angle, and place of delivery. I would run up to bowl and try to send down an outswinger, a nip-backer, or an inswinger. Although it often did not work, it made bowling much more interesting. Fourth, I began to study batsmen, notice the position of their hands, their initial movement, and where they scored most of their runs. I would then try to bowl accordingly. Fifth, and possibly most important of all, I made sure that I stationed my fieldsmen in the most effective way, depending on whether my main objective was attack or defence. From that moment no captain ever set a field for my bowling because I knew better than anyone what was likely to be the most effective deployment, although I was quite happy to listen to suggestions. It makes me shudder to think of some of those stereotype fields I used to employ in my early days. After tea against the Australians at Southchurch I was still bowling with two slips, a gulley and a leg slip.

My change from a lively tearaway into an accurate thinking seamer who knew exactly what he was trying to do, even if he was not always able to do it, took about five years. I knew for certain I was on the right track as early as 1949, when I found myself for the first time opening the bowling for England.

WE'RE A COUPLE OF SWELLS

We're a couple of swells
Who live in the best hotels
We put it on expenses
And we don't give a damn who tells
Insole-Bailey parody

My Essex debut was at Ilford against Derbyshire in 1946, when I opened both the batting and the bowling with reasonable success. Apart from those occasions when injury necessitated my playing purely as a batsman or bowler, I continued as an allrounder for the next twenty years. For most of that period we were a middle of the table club, never good enough to challenge seriously for the Championship. Although summer followed summer with no likelihood of our ever finishing with the title, we enjoyed our county matches and so did our followers, which says much for the three-day game, and especially the way it was played during that first decade after the war.

Some international players become bored with three-day cricket, but for a number of reasons it never had that effect on me. First, it was essentially fun, without which all games seem pointless. We played hard, but we also found time to laugh. It was rather like being a member of a civilized, exclusive club which consisted of essentially pleasant people who had standards which they both respected and obeyed. Throughout my career I encountered nobody on the county scene whom I actively disliked, and only three in international cricket, which really does say much for the game. I can think of no other group of people to which it could also apply.

Second, first-class cricket is totally unpredictable. A sudden hat-trick, rain at the wrong time, an infuriating run out, that totally unexpected last-wicket stand by two frightened rabbits, or a Denis Compton century on a difficult pitch – all these and more provided an ever-changing pattern to the game.

Third, as an allrounder I had the satisfaction of being very involved throughout most games. It might occasionally have been tiring, but it was certainly never boring.

Finally, in Essex, we lived a nomadic existence as we had no regular home and played in nine different centres spread throughout the county. These were Brentwood, Chelmsford, Clacton, Colchester, Ilford, Leyton, Romford, Southend and Westcliff. This had obvious snags, like no nets on any of our grounds, which meant that any Essex batsman out of form simply had to make runs in the middle. Each venue also had a different groundsman and pitches varied considerably. None was more baffling than Clacton, which tended to be green in the morning, ideal for batting throughout the afternoon and early evening, and then 'green up' for the last hour. It excelled its reputation for unpredictability in 1951. In the first match of the festival Nottinghamshire amassed 576 for 9 declared in a day and a half. We then followed the instructions of our captain, Doug Insole, by passing their total with fewer wickets down in extra time on the last day. Doug did not approve of teams batting on into the second day, unless they had an attack capable of dismissing the opposition twice. The next match, against Warwickshire, was played on a strip a few feet away and on which no rain fell. The wicket produced a definite and exciting result in which nobody hit a century and the highest total on either side was 216 – yet both wickets had looked identical.

I found a summer with Essex was not dissimilar to an overseas tour, except it was more strenuous, because we played six, often seven, days per week, drove considerable distances without the aid of motorways, and unlike a tour there were no rest periods. Moving round the county from ground to ground had its disadvantages, but there were also many advantages because one was always encountering new faces, new friends and new conditions. It was, of course, far more fun than having to play all one's home matches in a large, ugly stadium, which more often than not was only partially filled. A crowd of 4000 in Westcliff's Chalkwell Park was ideal, but would be lost at Old Trafford.

These then were some of the reasons why Essex cricket was and, I am glad to say, remains fun to play, and why our relationship with other counties has, over the years, been so harmonious. We have usually been able to avoid those petty inter-county squabbles which blow up on the circuit from time to time, and sometimes last for years.

The happy atmosphere at Essex has in part been derived from a remarkable continuity in the captaincy with only five leaders since the war. All five – Tom Pearce (1933–38, 1946–50), Doug Insole (1950–60), myself (1961–66), Brian Taylor (1967–73) and Keith Fletcher (1974–85) – have been fortunate in being blessed with a committee who have given them freedom of action. The County Committee, having selected a captain in whom they have confidence, have quite correctly left the cricket in his hands. Although a selection committee was appointed annually, it never met in the 21 years I was with Essex. The final decision on who was included in the team and, even more important, the way the cricket was played, was left entirely to the skipper, which is how it should be.

The five Essex captains had four advantages. First, all could justify their place in the side as a player. Although it is feasible to 'carry' a captain successfully in a powerful county, to have done so in Essex would simply have made a difficult job more difficult. Second, all gained considerable experience from their predecessors before taking over. Third, all were natural ball players and proficient in another team game. This interest in another sport gave them a broader outlook. Fourth, although their temperaments, backgrounds and approaches were very different, all possessed a sense of humour and a deep love for the game.

My big disappointment during my long association with Essex was that I never had the satisfaction of playing in a side which looked like winning a title. The extra challenge would have suited my own temperament, which was one of the reasons why I enjoyed Test cricket so much, and I sometimes think that Yorkshire would have been the ideal county for me, though not in recent years.

There was nothing surprising about our failure to win an honour. It took us over a hundred years to break our duck, then in 1979 we captured both the County Championship and Benson and Hedges Cup under Keith Fletcher, by which time the considerable gap which had once divided the top counties from the main body had narrowed. Whether this represented a levelling up or a levelling down remains a matter of opinion.

Although I regret never having the satisfaction of playing in a Championship-winning team, I have no regrets about when I played. However, two facets of the present day cricket scene appeal greatly to me. First, with four titles available each year it follows that it is at least four-times easier to finish with an honour, especially as it is not even necessary to be a particularly good team to carry off either the John Player League or the NatWest Trophy. The 1983 Yorkshire XI, arguably the worst in the history of the club, and led by a 51-year-old captain, still finished top of the John Player League, while the NatWest Trophy, formerly the Gillette Cup, has been won on several occasions by limited XIs. I would also have relished the excitement of the cup matches being played before a capacity crowd.

Second, I would certainly have liked the increased cash which is now coming into the game and into individual cricketers' bank accounts, both as a county secretary and as a player. Although inflation has greatly reduced the face value of money, it is still interesting that England cricketers were paid for one home Test against Sri Lanka more than seven times as much as I received for a six-month tour of Australia and New Zealand! The danger of cricket's new-found revenue is that it is not the outcome of increased interest in the game, membership or gates, but is entirely due to commercial sponsorship. Without commercial sponsorship, and its adjunct television, the game could not exist in its present form.

My career with Essex divides neatly into three distinct phases, the first under the captaincy of Tom Pearce, the second under the captaincy of Doug Insole and the third when I was both the captain and secretary of the club.

In my first three seasons with Essex I was an occasional, rather than a regular, member of the team. During 1946 I was available only in the holidays; and in 1947 and 1948, not until after the University Match in early July. It was an interesting and exciting period in which I had no responsibility. Nevertheless, although I was an amateur and playing entirely for enjoyment, I was fanatically keen, very determined to do well and intolerant of anybody with less enthusiasm. It would be fair to say that the game meant more to me than to most professionals.

Despite being a new boy to county cricket, I had no doubts about my ability to command a regular place in the Essex side. Not only had I played frequently with many of my colleagues during the hostilities, I had also done well in several representative matches. My approach would have been very different if I had gone into the team straight from school, which I believe would have happened if the war had not interfered. I was ready to be introduced into first-class cricket at 17 and as amateurs were often included in teams before the war, even when they were not as good as the professionals they displaced, I imagine I would have been given a run during the holidays, when there was always a large influx.

There were a number of reasons for this amateur invasion. It saved money. Each county was captained by an amateur, so it obviously helped to be able to appoint one who had had some previous experience in the county game. Some amateurs – Ken Farnes was a perfect example – strengthened the team, but not all. It was believed, not always correctly, that amateurs (batsmen for the most part) brought additional colour and excitement to the game because their livelihood did not depend upon figures at the end of the season. It will also be appreciated that by August the majority of the counties were no longer in contention for the Championship and cricket supporters primarily came to a game of cricket between two teams, especially if it gave them the opportunity to see an established star such as Wally Hammond, Patsy Hendren, Harold Larwood, or 'Tich' Freeman. In Essex it was also true that the average spectator would prefer the opportunity of watching a local amateur to an ordinary professional batsman, who might not be much better.

The years immediately following the war were a rewarding time in which to play county cricket. It is true that the standard was not high. Some of the pre-war players had died and the others were, understandably, a little rusty, while the new generation had not had the opportunity to play first-class cricket and it would take some time for them to develop. There was an absence of genuine fast bowling, but every county had at least one class spinner who expected to capture a hundred or more wickets during the summer. On the other hand, players and followers had been starved of first-class cricket for so long that the former were determined to enjoy and savour what they had been missing, and that approach satisfied the latter who turned up in their thousands.

The Essex team I first joined was led by Tom Pearce. It was sharply divided into those professionals who had been in the side before the war, Peter and Ray Smith, Tom Wade and Reg Taylor, or had been on the staff, like Sonny Avery; a couple of experienced amateurs, Harry Crabtree and Denys Wilcox, who headed the 1946 batting averages; and a handful of newcomers, both professional and amateur, who, in the main, were not good enough and never made the grade.

'Unflappable' is the adjective which best describes my first skipper, who was popular with his own side and opponents. It was nigh impossible to ruffle his composure and he made sure cricket never became too serious. Tom directed operations from his permanent position as a not-too-mobile first slip – still smiling amiably even when we walked off the field after that massacre by the Australian batsmen, or when more chances than usual had gone astray, or even when we had lost. As a young fast bowler who never appreciated anyone dropping catches, especially off my bowling, it took me some time to understand his calm. At Clacton I saw outside edges bisect my slips at catchable height on four occasions in my first spell. It was too much and I let out a plaintiff cry to the heavens, 'Through the b.....s again'. Tom, beaming broadly, merely suggested I bowl at the wicket.

Although not an outstanding tactician, he was seriously handicapped by often having what was virtually a two-man attack, Ray and Peter Smith. When I first came into the side I found myself opening the attack with Ray who, off his long run, bowled fast-medium inswingers. After five overs I would come off and Ray would simply put on his cap and bowl non-turning off-breaks off his short run with Peter Smith at the other end. Apart from a possible 'psychological' over before lunch from Frank Vigar or Reg Taylor, the Smith cousins simply carried on until the arrival of the next new ball, and sometimes well after it. At this juncture, Ray would remove his cap and revert to his long run and I would go on at the other end.

There were occasions when I found these tactics slightly confusing, as when Warwickshire made 284 runs. Ray bowled 52 overs and took one for 106, Peter sent down 46 overs and took four for 115, while my 13 overs brought me five for 27, which suggested it might have paid to have given me a few more overs. In contrast the Essex batting, though lacking an international-class bat, had resilience and depth, which was best illustrated by a match against Derbyshire in 1947 when our number eleven, Peter Smith, scored 163 in a record last-wicket partnership of 218 with Frank Vigar. In that match Dick Horsfall was number six, Denys Wilcox seven, myself eight, Doug Insole nine, and Ray Smith ten.

The social revolution which led to every cricketer becoming a professional could be said to have begun in 1946. Until then a professional cricketer, irrespective of his age or ability, addressed an amateur, even if he was still at school, as 'sir'. The amateurs and professionals used different accommodation during away matches, the former hotels, the latter frequently 'digs'. They changed in different dressing-rooms and even entered the playing area through different gates. The amateur was considered a gentleman in the Victorian sense; the professional was an artisan. On tour the two kinds were sharply divided, except on the field of play. It all seemed silly to me, as I had always considered it of no consequence whether a player was paid, unpaid, or paid indirectly. The only important thing was how well he played cricket, but when I started county cricket the amateur suffix still possessed considerable snob appeal.

Fortunately Essex were fairly democratic in this respect. Apart from Tom Pearce, who was called 'skipper' or 'Burly T', it was christian names all round and I could not imagine anything else. Ray Smith had been my captain when I had been playing for the British Empire XI, while Reg Taylor had been decorated in the war as a Flying Officer. There was never any question of separate dressing-rooms on Essex grounds, because in our little club pavilions there was seldom sufficient room for the two teams – Alec Bedser once asked me at Brentwood, before the extension was added, where the showers were and I pointed to one minute wash basin which just about took one of his very large hands. On one occasion at Old Trafford, our amateurs stayed at a different hotel, but this custom was quickly ended, though it lingered on in some other counties for many years.

Despite the social changes which were occurring in county cricket, certain differences, sometimes subtle, sometimes obvious, still existed between the amateur and the professional. The 1948 Essex annual, the first to be published since 1939, contains a picture of our team. Sitting in the front row is the captain, Tom Pearce, and the senior professional, Peter Smith . . . and four amateurs. On the scorecards in that book, the amateur had his initials in front of his name, the professional behind. More significantly, we were still very much in the era of the amateur captain, so that when Tom Pearce was unavailable the job was given to Len Clark. A reasonable club bat, he knew considerably less about the game than any of our senior professionals. During 1946 and 1947 Len made 24 appearances for Essex. When his services were no longer required, he was awarded his county cap as a reward . . . a professional was given one only on merit, as a cap not only made a considerable financial difference to him, but also marked the start of his qualification for a Benefit. This pre-war practice of giving caps to amateurs who had not merited them by their performances on the field was, I am glad to say, discontinued.

My first full season with Essex was 1949 and its outcome exceeded my most extravagant expectations. This considerable advance as a player began with my taking a wicket with the first ball of the season at Lord's and was underlined by the enormous improvement in my figures at the end of the summer. In the previous year I had bowled 646 overs and taken 63 wickets costing more than 31 apiece. In 1949 my 1020 overs brought a haul of 130 wickets costing just over 24, which was acceptable considering the amount of bowling I had to do in a heavy-scoring Test series and a very fine summer. More important than the figures was that from a promising county allrounder I had become one of the country's leading players. I was selected for all four Tests against New Zealand and opened the bowling for England; did the 'double', the first amateur, though that really did not matter, to have achieved this feat for many years; took all ten wickets in an innings; and was chosen as one of *Wisden*'s Five Cricketers of the Year.

In view of later developments it is amusing to quote *Wisden*'s comments on my batting. 'Bailey is a capable No 5 or 6 batsman. He would be quite content to play sound, steady cricket, but circumstances have tended to make him an aggressive player. He is an attractive stroke player with a fondness for the cut, but can score freely with the drive and leg-side strokes.'

What was my cricket like that summer? I was a fast-medium bowler – not fast in the Lindwall–Miller sense, but sharp enough to be able to send down a reasonable bouncer, to obtain the odd wicket through pace alone and to make the tailender slightly apprehensive. I relied largely on the outswinger and the 'nip-backer', but though I had gained greater smoothness through cutting out a whirl in my action, it was still not completely grooved and I had not yet attained the control required, nor had I sufficiently studied opposing batsmen. I was not yet a *thinking* bowler. As a result, there were occasions in both the Tests and county matches when I was too expensive. However, my striking rate was high, which was the main reason, apart from a lack of competition, why I opened the bowling for England.

As for my batting, I had become a dependable middle-order batsman with Essex, who expected to score more than 1000 runs in a full summer with an average of over 30. If, at this time, I had concentrated entirely on batting and claimed a permanent place higher in the Essex order I could have made more runs, but I would not have been picked to play against New Zealand. Anyway, I would never have found the game so satisfying if I had become only an occasional bowler.

In addition to being an allrounder, I was also an allround fieldsman. I have always enjoyed fielding, until one day at Leyton towards the end of my career when I stood at slip and dropped catch after catch off my two unfortunate spinners. However, in 1949 I was equally at home in the deep, the covers, the slips, or backward short leg, which was a useful asset, especially in international cricket.

To capture all ten wickets in an innings is a rarity in any form of the game, and to do it in a first-class match requires even more luck, because the bowling at the other end should be of a fairly high standard and one would expect at least one wicket to fall. The feat is normally achieved on a bad wicket, over a short period in a low-scoring contest, but my ten wickets came about in a very different manner, one which was, perhaps, rather typical of my county.

The wicket at Clacton was good. In the previous match on the adjacent wicket, Somerset had amassed 488, we had lost by an innings and I had taken one for 133, figures which hardly suggested picking up many wickets in the next game. Lancashire, having won the toss, elected to bat and scored 331, a reasonable total. Although I was delighted to take all ten, it did not do Essex much good as we lost the match by the considerable margin of ten wickets.

I did not bowl unchanged but I was decidedly weary when I collected my last wicket in my fortieth over, which was quite a number for a 'quickie' on a hot day. It never occurred to me, or to anybody else, that I would finish with all ten until very late on. At lunch, I was pleased at having taken three wickets and even more satisfied to have six when we came in for tea. It was not until two more had come my way after the interval that I realized I had a chance. But I could never have captured the final two without the active co-operation of Tom Pearce, who in the closing stages used two non-bowlers, including himself, whose purpose was not to get a wicket. His objective was to do everything possible to help me. The fact that the Lancashire tail scored rather more runs than they should have done he regarded as immaterial.

It was a generous, typically pre-war approach, which I appreciated at the time and afterwards, but I am sure that I would never have taken all ten if Tom's successor, Doug Insole, had been captain. Doug believed that records were of no importance and had to occur within the strict context of the game. A perfect example of his philosophy occurred earlier in the season when he had skippered Cambridge University against Essex. At the close of the first day Cambridge were 441 for one, the outcome of an unbroken stand between Hubert Doggart (219) and John Dewes (204) of 429. If he had allowed them to continue batting on the second day, they would probably have broken the world record second-wicket partnership as they were only 26 runs short of it. Instead he declared, much to the annoyance of the large crowd and the cameramen who had turned up to watch and film what would have been a remarkable feat.

1950 marked the end of my first era with Essex. We finished last in the table for the first time in the club's history. Tom Pearce resigned the captaincy in June because not only was the team doing badly, but he was also failing to produce his usual quota of runs. After his years of great service to the club, Tom deserved better than a mid-season resignation. Doug Insole became skipper but despite scoring heavily he was unable to prevent our downward plunge.

A combination of lack of success and changing horses in mid-stream upset some of the harmony which had always been one of the features of the county, but I remained largely oblivious to the nuances around me. I was too busy trying to establish myself as an England regular to worry about what other people thought and did. In fact, apart from finishing at the bottom and badly tearing muscles which prevented me from bowling and forced me to miss two Tests and a number of games for Essex, I enjoyed the season. The main reason was Doug, who had come down from Cambridge and had joined the George Wimpey Company. His firm had decided, logically, that it would be advantageous to have a well known sportsman in their promotional division. They therefore allowed him to play cricket throughout the first-class season. (Names have always helped to open doors and as an added incentive Doug, who had been a successful skipper at Cambridge, had been promised the Essex captaincy as soon as Tom retired.)

Doug's arrival gave me a boon companion for the whole of the summer, a permanent room-mate and another cinema addict. In addition, we had children of similar ages, both played football and held similar views on cricket and how it should be played. It was an extension of a sporting partnership and friendship which began at Cambridge and was to continue for a decade of Essex cricket.

The fact that Doug was made captain, though I was an international cricketer, did not worry me in the least because I was aware that at that time I was entirely unsuited for the job. I was too concerned with my own performance, intolerant of anyone who was unwilling, or unable, to give to the game the same devotion as myself, and too mercurial. Unlike Doug, I have never been a political animal and have always lacked discretion, because it has never worried me if what I said or did upset somebody who might be useful in the future. From a purely cricket angle, Doug also had one enormous advantage. He was a batsman, whereas I was an opening bowler cum batsman. Some things in cricket never change, which is perfectly illustrated by what the late Sir Pelham Warner had to say on captaincy some 75 years ago:

> The chief qualifications for a good captain are a sound knowledge of the game, calm judgement, power of observation and the ability to inspire others with confidence.
> Bad captains may be split into three classes:
> (1) Excitable men
> (2) Dull, apathetic men
> (3) Bowling captains, with an aversion to seeing anybody else bowl but themselves.

I possessed a good knowledge of the game, but lacked calm judgement, while any ability I may have possessed in inspiring confidence in others was reduced because I personally had never required motivation. As to Warner's three categories of bad captains, I was probably too excitable at that time, because I was liable to become too emotionally involved, and I was certainly a bowling captain. And, like all real bowlers, I loved bowling and wanted to bowl the whole time, even when the situation was totally unsuitable. I do not believe that I would have allowed this to interfere with my professional assessment of a situation, but all bowling captains are open to criticism for bowling too long even when completely unjustified. They also have to contend with the jealousy, naked or otherwise, from the other bowlers who also want, and should want, to be bowling. This especially applies when the tailenders arrive. The batsman captain, wanting to end the innings as quickly as possible, can bring on a quickie, or a spinner, in place of the bowler who has been doing the damage but is, perhaps, tired or lacks real penetration, without incurring more than a resigned and muted protest. Exactly the same move by a bowler captain, particularly if he brings himself on and then proceeds to gobble up the tail – or, probably more damaging, fails to achieve the objective – is viewed with suspicion.

In addition to the bowler captain who overbowls himself, with J. W. H. T. Douglas supplying a classic example, there is the captain who, for various reasons, does not bowl himself enough. I have always had a high regard for Ray Illingworth as a player, a tactician and a captain. Under his command England and Leicestershire prospered and, when over 50, he led a poor Yorkshire XI to the top of the John Player League in 1983. However, if one were to find fault with Ray as a tactician, and he was an exceptionally able one, it would be for when he failed to bowl himself sufficiently.

Very aware of the dangers of bowler captains, when I took charge of Essex I went to Gordon Barker, who knew his cricket, and told him – no, ordered him – to inform me the moment he felt I should come off or, just as important, bring myself on. I don't think I ever disobeyed his advice and it worked reasonably well, but it would not have done in 1950.

Doug also enjoyed another considerable advantage, he was not employed by the Committee, whereas I was a direct employee of the county club. This meant that he was in a position to tell the Committee exactly what they could do with the captaincy should the occasion have arisen. It was of course a two-edged weapon, because it meant that the Committee could dispense with his services without any serious problems. This freedom of action is one of the good things which were lost when it was decided to do away with the amateur.

The amateur system allowed someone like Doug, who was in his early twenties, to take command without upsetting too much the senior players in the side. If Doug had been a professional, the professional hierarchy of that time – the Smith cousins and Tom Wade – would have objected strongly.

Although pleased when Doug became captain of Essex, I was saddened by the manner of Tom's departure, which simply confirmed my view that it was stupid to trust any committee, or political body. It had been fun playing under Tom, but I preferred Doug's approach to the game, which was essentially 'post-war' – more realistic, professional and tighter, especially in the matter of field placing. In the process, some of that pre-war charm and laughter was lost. There was a greater emphasis on the importance of winning and rather less on simply participating.

In terms of results, it made no immediate difference as we finished bottom, but in the first complete year of Doug's reign we shot up to eighth place in the table with basically the same side. This was in no small measure due to Doug's insistence on daily fielding practice, which raised the standard considerably and was particularly appreciated by the bowlers who saw catches being taken that previously were being put down. Doug himself possessed an exceptionally safe pair of hands.

Doug brought to the job that burning enthusiasm one normally associated with University captains. It would be true to say that it took him a little time to appreciate the difference between leading Cambridge and leading a professional team of varying ages and outlooks. Although a shrewd and imaginative skipper whom opponents knew would set a reasonable target and never go back on a deal, Essex never seriously challenged for the title under Doug, for the simple reason that we possessed neither the ability nor the balance. In addition, we never experienced that long run of luck which occasionally allows a limited club, like Hampshire in 1961, to enjoy one golden summer.

It did not help that during this period Surrey, with a bowling attack which was considerably stronger and more varied than most international elevens and frequently operated on pitches which were below standard, as well as uncovered, won the Championship seven times on the trot. This made life difficult for counties like Essex.

During Doug's reign I reached my own peak as a player and established myself as the allrounder in the England team, reckoning to do the 'double' providing I was given sufficient bowling in the Tests. Although I opened the bowling for Essex, for England I became the recognized third seamer and middle-order batsman – except overseas, where I was pressed into service as an emergency opener with monotonous regularity. My own position with the county also changed, because Bob Patterson, the Essex secretary, resigned and went to take up a position in Scotland. Bob, who was a good club cricketer, had played for the county on a few occasions in 1946. At one time he had ideas of combining the job of secretary, player and possibly captain, but this became out of the question once I became his assistant. Quite naturally, he rather resented my appointment: as a cricketer I was capturing the headlines, while he was largely unsung, though doing most of the work. Bob's departure suited me, as it allowed me to supervise the general administration of the club, the signing of new players and the coaching, which I enjoyed. Initially, I had the assistance of an honorary secretary, a beaming, genial, Pickwickian character, Horace Clark, before becoming secretary in my own right.

The Essex batting throughout Doug's period of captaincy was above average, with considerable depth and the ability to score runs quickly, even though only Doug himself was a high quality batsman. Our weakness was the attack on anything but pitches that favoured seam. What we lacked was a match-winning spin bowler who was able to dismiss the opposition twice on a turning pitch. Peter Smith was nearing the end of his career when Doug became captain, while anyway he was a wrist-spinner and therefore more likely to take five for 100 on a good wicket than seven for 30 on a wet one. Neither did we ever possess a really fast bowler who was able to blast out the tail by sheer pace. We had to rely on myself, who missed a large number of matches through representative calls; the swerve of Ray Smith, who suddenly found a new lease of life when off a short run, swinging the ball either way more than anybody in the country; Ken Preston; Jack Bailey for a couple of seasons; Roy Ralph who, at little more than medium pace, proved remarkably effective; and, towards the end, Barry Knight, who originally bowled mainly inswingers at a decidedly lively pace, but became an outstanding bowler when he cut down and learned to run the ball away from the bat off the seam.

I took over from Doug with mixed feelings. I had lost my constant companion and the club had lost their best batsman. On the other hand I enjoyed captaincy and it provided me with a new challenge which I needed as my international career was over. The Test selectors had written me off as a Test cricketer and as Doug, who never changed his mind about anything, was one of them there was no chance of my recall.

The first thing to decide was what name the players should call me. The normal 'skipper' was obviously out, because not only had Doug been known as that for many years, but it was also bound to cause confusion when Doug himself was playing. After much thought we came up with 'Chief', or more often 'Chiefie', which was derived directly from my well known addiction for Westerns. It beat 'Sherriff' by a short head.

For the first few seasons all went well. Although my dream of lifting the County Championship never materialized, nor looked like doing so, we kept in the top half of the table and achieved some remarkable victories, including one over the 1964 Australians when it still meant something to both the players and their supporters to defeat the tourists. We also had a highly improbable win over Warwickshire at Edgbaston in 1962, where having been shot out for 85 we had to score 193 to make them bat again.

However, there were increasing financial problems. Gates, membership and Test match receipts were not producing sufficient revenue and serious sports sponsorship, without which professional cricket as we know it today would have died long since, had not arrived on the scale required. The Gillette Cup had started, but it was in its infancy and only drew large crowds in the later stages.

The problems were typified by our first Gillette Cup match – against Lancashire at Old Trafford. Most clubs, including Essex, simply could not afford the away expenses as, unlike the Championship matches, there was not a reciprocal fixture. As a result, for the first two years of the competition the home team players put up the other team. Essex had a long drive for that game and we arranged to meet the Lancashire secretary, Geoffrey Howard, and those players who were billeting us for the night at Altrincham police station at midnight. It was in the days before motorways and we did not arrive until 12.30, which I suppose was hardly the ideal preparation for a vital limited-overs game.

The lack of money forced Essex to reduce our staff to such an extent that eventually we had no reserve cover. Our performances suffered while, by this time, I had lost my ability to win matches. My pace was no more than medium and my 'nip-backer' was no longer gaining the lbw, merely finding that inside edge.

In retrospect I made three big mistakes, because I still enjoyed playing cricket so much. First, I should have retired two seasons before and obeyed that edict of the stage, always leave the audience wanting more. Second, I failed to realize that if I was to continue as a first-class cricketer it was necessary for me to train and forgo some of my business activities. Third, I continued playing when injured because we had no reserves. In a Gillette Cup fixture against Derbyshire I tore a muscle in my right thigh so badly that even today there is a big hole. I should not have played again that summer, but stupidly went back on parade within a week, carrying a leg, which not surprisingly had an adverse effect on my performances which, anyway, were on the decline.

Brian Taylor was appointed captain in 1967. I took a Testimonial which was arranged too quickly to produce much money, played the occasional match and resigned as secretary. This last decision took some time. I had been secretary of Essex for 13 years, the big question was whether I wanted to go on doing the same thing until I retired. It was an attractive life and though, at that time, not especially well paid, the Essex offer, considering the state of their finances, was very generous. Eventually I decided no, but there have been the odd occasions when I have wondered whether I should have stayed.

I enjoyed enormously my twenty years with Essex, which was hardly surprising as I passed most of my time doing things I liked in delightful surroundings and in very pleasant company. My summers were spent out of doors playing a game which never failed to interest me. If there were occasions when I became a little bored, there was always the prospect of the next innings, the next bowl, the next catch and the next match, which might prove very exciting, while I could always console myself with the thought that I much preferred spending 11.30 to 6.30 on a cricket field to working in an office or a factory. In addition to allowing me to play cricket throughout the summer months, I was in a position to accept tours overseas during the winter, which amounted to seeing the world in luxury.

I found the game's administration interesting, especially as I had the good fortune to have a Committee who were not only considerate, but were prepared to take my advice on most things. In Essex, the Committee has, at least since the war, been well above average, largely because a high percentage of its members had actually played cricket at a reasonable level, while those who had not were prepared to leave the running of the game to those who knew something about it. This happy state of affairs has not applied to a large number of counties. I have always believed that Lancashire would have been far more successful with an Essex-style Committee at their helm. Certainly we have managed to avoid the type of problems which have beset Yorkshire and Derbyshire in recent years.

I can think of only three occasions when the Committee chose to disregard my advice, two of them concerning the club's finances. The first was in the early 1950s when I went down to Worcestershire to find out how to run a Football Pool. It was such an obvious money spinner, especially in a county as big as Essex, that I knew it would be a winner. Nevertheless, the suggestion was overwhelmingly turned down by the Committee because the president, Sir Hubert Ashton, and vice-chairman did not want to see cricket turn to gambling for income. About ten years later, and ten years too late, they changed their minds. The second occasion was in the economic depression of the 1960s when the Committee decided to launch an appeal with professional help. It had worked well in Gloucestershire, but my Committee failed to appreciate the essential differences between the two counties, Gloucestershire essentially royalist and close knit, Essex Cromwellian without a figurehead and split into little, often hostile, groups. The outcome was a complete waste of time and money, neither of which we could really afford at that juncture.

The third time the Committee chose to ignore my advice was when it came to appointing my successor as captain. The Committee decided on Brian Taylor, who did an extremely able job in his own distinctive way, but my choice was Barry Knight, the most accomplished cricketer in the team. He might not have proved as successful as Brian, but we could ill afford to lose at that time our best player and I knew that Barry would not be prepared to play under Brian. Sure enough, Barry joined Leicestershire and then emigrated to Australia, where, when I was last out there, he was the oldest cricketer playing grade cricket in New South Wales.

One of my more interesting secretarial duties was attending the TCCB meetings at Lord's, which basically made the decisions controlling first-class cricket in this country and also enjoyed, along with the MCC, considerable control on what happened overseas. Although the decisions were invariably made with the best possible intentions, all too often, when put into practice, the outcome was very different from what was expected. The meetings also produced some moments which came close to pure farce. Derbyshire, who sat next to Essex, were represented by Wilf Taylor, a delightful man who had become secretary before the First World War and carried on for more than fifty years, and his chairman, Captain G. R. Jackson. They were close friends who frequently shot together, but on one memorable occasion both spoke with considerable passion for and against the same Derbyshire proposal, a performance which brought a round of applause from those present and left Tom Pearce and myself crying with laughter.

One winter when MCC were touring Pakistan, the papers carried the story of how some of the England players had given the 'water treatment' to a Pakistani umpire. This consisted of throwing a bucket of water over him in a hotel one evening, long after close of play. Had I been out there, I might have enjoyed that moment of the tour. It was a classic case of boisterous, fairly juvenile horse, or rather water, play which would never have hit the headlines if the umpire had not encountered one of the Pakistan team, which meant that he had lost face. I had a chuckle and forgot about it until I arrived at the TCCB meeting which was held on the following morning and was, as usual, chaired by the president of MCC.

The president is chosen by his predecessor and does not have to know much about cricket, though he generally does. At the time the MCC president was Earl Alexander, who began the session by informing the assembly that he had been on the phone to the President of Pakistan, a former army friend and colleague, and told him that he was prepared to bring back the England team and call the tour off. The President had, not surprisingly, refused to accept the offer. I regret to report that county representatives applauded an action which was much appreciated by the press as 'MCC president offers to cancel tour' made a fine lead news story. It was an occasion when 'Gubby' Allen and I were in complete agreement and rather supported the theory that soldiers do not make the best diplomats.

The most fascinating aspect of my job was looking at young prospects, trying to assess their potential and then, if they sufficiently impressed, offering them a summer engagement on the groundstaff. Although their weekly wages were no more than a pittance, the majority enjoyed the life enormously for which much of the credit must go to the Essex coach, Frank Rist, who was their guide, philosopher and friend. This point was brought home to me recently when I was in South Africa and ran into one of the many who never made the grade to the First XI, Ronnie Carr. Despite

Variations on a well known theme by Roy Ullyett

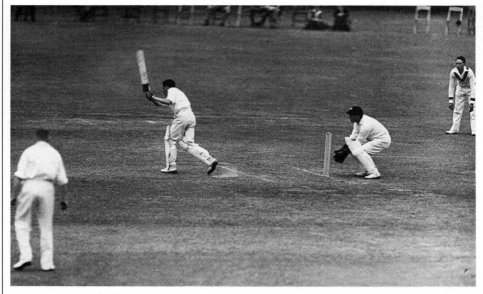

ABOVE Batting for Dulwich College against the Old Alleynians, 1940. Behind the stumps is S.C. 'Billy' Griffith. *Sport & General*

BELOW LEFT A somewhat scruffy Dulwich captain of 1941 with Horace Kiddle, who would have played county cricket and might well have gone to the very top if he had not been killed while flying during the war. *Sport & General*

BELOW RIGHT Leading out the Public Schools XI at Lord's, 1942. Alongside me is Tony Mallett, a colleague at Dulwich and later in the Marines, who was to play for Oxford University and Kent after the war. *Sport & General*

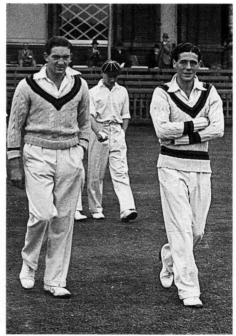

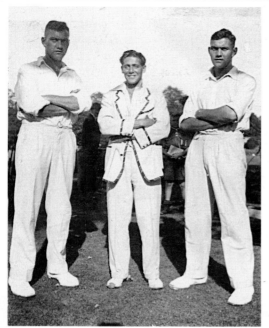

ABOVE LEFT A beefy Bedser sandwich — Eric and Alec, 1942…or is it Alec and Eric?
ABOVE RIGHT Lieutenant T.E. Bailey, Royal Marines, 1944

BELOW The Essex team that I joined in 1946. Left to right (standing) Harry Crabtree, Dickie Dodds, Frank Vigar, Bill Morris, Robert Patterson (sec), T.E.B., Ray Smith, 'Sonny' Avery, Norman Borrett; (sitting) Reg Taylor, Denys Wilcox, Tom Pearce (captain), Tom Wade. *H.L. Smerdon*

ABOVE Cambridge University v Warwickshire, 1947. Left to right (standing) Michael Earls-Davis, T.E.B., P.B. Datta, Hugh Watts, Richard Pearsall, Doug Insole; (sitting) John Pepper, Michael Mills, Guy Willatt (captain), Norman Mischler, Guy Shuttleworth. *A. Wilkes*

BELOW Trying to find the gap during my 66 not out for Cambridge against the 1948 Australians at Fenner's. Arthur Morris is the bowler, Ron Saggers the wicket-keeper and Keith Miller and Lindsay Hassett the fielders. *E.A. Wood*

TOP LEFT Going out to bat at Chalkwell Park against Gloucestershire, 1947. The worried look is probably due to a typical Essex collapse. *Barratt's*
TOP RIGHT Bowling in 1949 in Valentine's Park, normally sympathetic to the quicker bowler. *PA-Reuter*

BELOW Batting in 1949 at Chalkwell Park, always hard work on the lively wicket. *PA-Reuter*

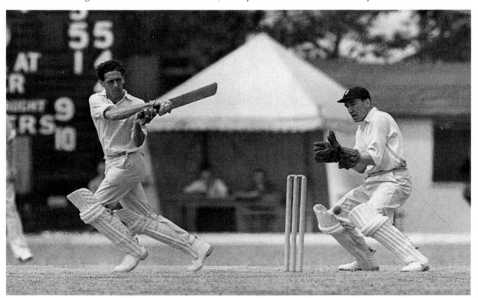

ABOVE Essex, Cambridge and England colleague Doug Insole, a fellow cinema enthusiast and a fine county captain. *J.B. Hood*

RIGHT Scorecard of my career-best allround performance, Essex v Hampshire, 1957

BELOW The Essex side in my final year as captain, 1966. Left to right (standing) Harold Dalton (physio), Graham Saville, Brian Edmeades, Rodney Cass, Tony Jorden, Robin Hobbs, Keith Fletcher, David Acfield, C.V. 'Jenks' Jenkinson (scorer); (sitting) Michael Bear, Gordon Barker, T.E.B., Brian Taylor, Barry Knight.

ESSEX V HAMPSHIRE.

AT GIDEA PARK, ROMFORD. 3D.

SAT, MON, TUES, MAY 25th 27th 29th, 1957.

Hours of play, 1st 2 Days, 11-30 to 7-0, 3rd Day, 11-30 to 5-0 or 5-30, Intervals- Lunch 1-30 to 2-10. Tea:- 4-30.

Umpires- C Corrall & N Oldfield. Scorers- C V Jenkinson & H Lovell.

ESSEX

	First Innings		Second Innings	
1 Barker G	lbw b Cannings	5	b Shackleton	0
2 R E Evans	b Shackleton	4	b Cannings	0
†3 Taylor B	lbw b Heath	35	run out	17
*4 D J Insole	b Heath	14	b Shackleton	0
5 T E Bailey	b Heath	59	not out	71
6 Bear M	b Cannings	2	c Sainsbury b Shackleton	1
7 Smith G	c Harrison b Shackleton	5	lbw b Shackleton	4
8 Durley A	b Heath	4	c Eagar b Cannings	11
9 R Ralph	b Sainsbury	1	b Sainsbury	16
10 Preston K C	b Sainsbury	1	b Shackleton	0
11 King J	not out	0	c Eagar b Heath	9
Extras	b- lb- w- nb-		b-5 lb-7 w- nb-	12
*Captain	Total	130	Total	141

Fall of Wickets

	First Innings										Second Innings									
	1	2	3	4	5	6	7	8	9	10	1	2	3	4	5	6	7	8	9	10
	9	9	40	87	94	105	117	118	120	130	0	0	0	38	44	48	75	105	112	141

Bowling Analysis	O	M	R	W	Wd	Nb	O	M	R	W	Wd	Nb
Shackleton	16	6	37	2			26	6	47	5		
Cannings	16	10	15	2			27	14	30	2		
Sainsbury	24	10	41	2			4	3	4	1		
Heath	24,1	9	37	4			15.4	1	48	1		

HAMPSHIRE

	First Innings		Second Innings	
1 Marshall R E	b Bailey	4	c Taylor b Bailey	6
2 Gray J R	lbw b Bailey	2	c King b Bailey	40
3 Horton H	run out	1	c Taylor b Bailey	7
4 Sainsbury P J	b Ralph	5	lbw b Preston	3
5 Barnard H M	c King b Insole	26	b Bailey	15
6 A C Ingleby-Mackenzie	not out	37	c Taylor b Bailey	23
†7 Harrison L	b Insole	8	b Bailey	5
*8 E D R Eagar	c Taylor b Bailey	0	c Insole b King	3
9 Shackleton D	lbw b Bailey	5	not out	2
10 Cannings V H	b Bailey	7	c Taylor b Bailey	2
11 Heath M	c Insole b Bailey	0	c Taylor b Bailey	0
Extras	b-4 lb-10 w- nb-	14	b-4 lb-1 w- nb-	5
†W Kpr,	Total	109	Total	116

Fall of Wickets

	First Innings										Second Innings									
	1	2	3	4	5	6	7	8	9	10	1	2	3	4	5	6	7	8	9	10
	5	8	9	27	72	82	83	89	109	109	6	26	34	62	95	100	103	103	116	116

Bowling Analysis	O	M	R	W	Wd	Nb	O	M	R	W	Wd	Nb
Bailey	17	5	32	6			23.5	7	49	8		
Preston	14	5	30	0			17	6	31	1		
Ralph	9	2	19	1			8	1	21	0		
Insole	7	1	14	2			4	1	3	0		
King							6	3	7	1		

-ESSEX WON by 46 RUNS

RAIN STOPS PLAY
ABOVE The floods at Southchurch Park, Southend, 1953.

BELOW LEFT The trials of a county secretary during a typical summer, Colchester 1958.
BELOW RIGHT Bill Greensmith, Barry Knight, Ken Preston, myself and (on haunches) Brian Taylor taking cover in April 1961 in the pre-tracksuit era.

ABOVE LEFT Greta, Kim and I indulge in a bit of 'product endorsement' for Lucozade.
ABOVE RIGHT England v Australia, Lord's, Second Test, 1953. A rare attacking stroke during
the Watson-Bailey stand.

BELOW England v Australia, Headingley, Fourth Test, 1953. Laker is caught Benaud bowled
Davidson to end a vital stand of 57, of which Jim's contribution was a dashing 48. I am in my
normal role of non-striker.

that, and the shortage of cash, he reckoned the two years he spent with Essex were among the happiest in his life.

Before the beginning of each season I held trials for anybody who requested one, though normally I would already have heard about the best prospects from school, or club, while any senior club cricketers who were likely to prove useful would already have scored so many runs, or taken so many wickets, that I could hardly have missed them. Also, Frank Rist would have seen the best of them and invited them to play in our Second XI.

A high percentage of those who came for trial were nowhere near the required standard, though I never experienced the problem that the Warwickshire coach had encountered when giving a trial to a young lad. The boy produced the strokes but never made any contact with the ball. It transpired that he had been taught in the attic at home by his father, who had never used a ball. I do remember a youth wearing a dashing Teddy boy outfit who came for a trial to Chalkwell Park as a fast bowler. He removed his jacket, put on a pair of pumps, paced out an impressive long run-up and left his comb as his marker. His first delivery was somewhat disconcerting as it travelled over the top of the very high nets and hit the Ladies in the background full toss.

The whole time I was at Essex, it was one continual financial battle to keep out of the red. We could usually afford a First XI squad of about 14, and to run a Second XI and Club and Ground XI. These two teams were filled by First XI players who were out of form or could not command a regular place; our reserve wicket-keeper; capped Second XI players serving their apprenticeship; possible recruits from another county; chosen trialists; the young lads on our groundstaff; and amateurs.

The size of our groundstaff depended largely on the state of the county's coffers. The majority I signed on when they had just left school at 15 or 16. I engaged about two per season. They did not cost much money, which was vital, as we simply could not afford a mature married man unless he was good enough to play regularly in the First XI. A high percentage of the trialists were also promising footballers and my advice to the father was that unless his son was an outstanding soccer player – this was in the era of the maximum and minimum wages – he would, if he reached the top, do rather better at cricket as he would have a longer and more enjoyable career, while there was the added attraction of a tax-free Benefit.

It is a gamble taking on a boy at 15 who has had little, or no, coaching and played only a limited amount of cricket and to be sure that he will develop into a first-class cricketer, and quite impossible if he happens to be a spinner. Inevitably a number failed to make it: some possessed the ability but lacked application, whereas others surprised me and did better than my first look at them had suggested. On only three occasions was I able to sign on a player absolutely convinced that he would go on to play not only for Essex but also, given the necessary health, for England.

The first was Barry Knight, who had an outstanding record in school and local cricket. I asked him along to a pre-season First XI practice on the Chelmsford ground. Barry, who was 16, batted so impressively that I offered him a contract immediately, before I even bothered to see him bowl.

The second was Keith Fletcher, who came from a village school in Cambridgeshire. A conscientious careers officer visiting Keith's school was surprised to hear that Keith wanted to become a professional cricketer. It was the first time he had encountered this and he took the trouble to inform Harry Crabtree, the sports education officer for Essex and also on the Committee. Harry alerted me and I arranged for Keith to play in an Essex Club and Ground match at the end of the summer and took part myself. I was impressed, not only by his obvious potential but also because he had what I term a cricket brain. Throughout the winter Keith came to the Ilford indoor cricket school for nets. The way he was able to drive off the back foot on the up convinced me further that he would be challenging for a place in the First XI before he was 18. He was also one of the few players whom one could teach to hook without concern, because his initial reactions were so quick.

The third was much easier, because the player concerned was older and had played some serious cricket in Barbados, where they do not take the game lightly. I was captaining the Rothman Cavaliers in the Caribbean. After our first match against Barbados, a high percentage of their side went off to Jamaica for the First Test against Australia. As a result our second match was with virtually a Bajaan Second XI, which included Keith Boyce whom I had never seen nor heard of before. He proceeded to bowl fast (if not by some West Indian standards, at least by ours), hit the ball with exceptional power, field beautifully, and throw with sufficient velocity to have a flat trajectory from boundary to stumps.

I have always believed that if you intend to bring an overseas player into county cricket, unless he is an established international star he should be a spectacular performer who will automatically excite spectators. Consequently, before the end of the game I had signed on Keith Boyce for Essex and informed my club of my decision.

Keith was a natural. He was a fast bowler who was quick enough to unsettle the apprehensive; a ferocious, distinctly unconventional hitter with a marvellous eye, who could transform a game in a matter of minutes and was ideally suited to the needs of the limited-overs game; and a world class fielder, with a beautiful pair of hands and an exceptional arm, and possessing a graceful, lithe and athletic physique. He epitomized crowd appeal, but before making up my mind to bring him to Essex, where he was an enormous success, I checked with great care what he was like as a person, as whatever his ability I would never have signed on somebody who I felt would prove a disruptive influence to what has, and still is, an essentially pleasant county.

Taking on young players could be very rewarding, but at times disappointing, particularly with slow bowlers. I signed David Daniels in his teens, when he could bowl a 'Chinaman' with a disconcerting loop, which turned on even good pitches and at a pace which troubled all my first team players in the nets. He looked so good that I even considered playing him for the county, but a few years later, when he finished his national service, he had grown and all the magic had gone. One of the few spinners who was good as a schoolboy and retained his ability has been David Acfield.

When engaging a young Essex player, my first prayer was that he did not have that dangerous menace, the all-knowing, overdemanding dad who is trying to recapture his own youth through his son's success and is forever complaining when things are not going well. Unfortunately, it so often has the reverse effect. I have always maintained that it helps for the boy's dad and family to be very interested in his career, but he does need to breathe and too often I have seen talent smothered. There is only one thing worse than an overpossessive dad and that is an overpossessive mum.

The prime objective of the Second XI and Club and Ground is to develop players for the First XI and one of the weaknesses of the Essex set-up in the days when we did not have a headquarters ground was that I saw little of the boys on the groundstaff, except

67

during the pre-season practice and at indoor nets in the winter, because I was invariably playing myself.

If engaging players was one of the most positive features of my job, telling players that they were not being re-engaged was unquestionably one of the saddest. It was bad enough having to inform a 17-year-old that he was never going to make it and explaining why, but far worse when I had to tell a capped player, who had become a personal friend, that his contract was not being renewed by the Committee, especially as it was nearly always the outcome of my recommendation.

Essex cricket has provided a rich and varied kaleidoscope of memories. Brentwood always seemed to me to be not only the most picturesque first-class ground in the county, but also one of the most attractive in the country. It was beautifully maintained by one splendid groundsman, plus the best dog in the busines. I was always fascinated by the number of batsmen unable to resi ie very short boundary at one end (where even I could mishit a six) and holing out.

It was at Brentwood that I enjoyed what was probably the most spectacular spell of bowling in my life – seven wickets for three runs in 5.1 overs against Glamorgan – but it was also the scene of my most stupid shout. Against Somerset in 1951, the pitch was lively and slightly muddy, my field was ultra-attacking and I finished with seven wickets. In the course of my spell somebody top-edged a hook which could have been comfortably caught by nine fielders and the keeper. While Doug Insole was deciding whose name to call, I shouted 'mine' in a voice which brooked no interference and continued down the pitch. I finished full length and dirty about a yard past the stumps at the far end, while the ball landed safely another three feet further on and my colleagues dissolved into laughter.

All our players liked the Clacton Festival which took place in August. The club treated the week as two away fixtures because there was so much holiday traffic on the narrow congested roads that it took too long to reach the seaside town. We were booked in at one of the local hotels and in our short stay saw all the local shows and invariably paid one visit to Butlins. Unlike most grounds the biggest attendance was never on the Saturday, that being the change-over day.

It was at Clacton against Yorkshire that I achieved my only 'pair' in county cricket: caught behind chasing a wide one in the first innings, and plumb lbw sweeping Norman Yardley in the second. It was also against Yorkshire, but many years later, that I used a runner for the first time, having pulled a muscle in my leg. For about half an hour I enjoyed myself immensely, obtaining the odd single and stroking the occasional four, while Brian Taylor, who had come to my aid full of confidence and saying 'Leave it all to me, Chief', took over the calling and running. It seemed to me this was the way to play cricket, until Brian decided to take one to silly mid-off and we both returned to the pavilion.

It was about nine o'clock on a Sunday morning when my phone rang at home to inform me that the Colchester ground, where there had been no play on the previous day due to rain, was under water because the river had overflowed. I arrived to find the entire outfield covered by at least a foot of water and we literally pushed our wooden benches to dry land. There was clearly no chance of further play so with the cooperation of the army, and the agreement of Notts and the TCCB, we transferred the game to the Garrison ground, which I like to think showed some initiative, and we started on time on the Monday.

I was never too enthusiastic about the Gentlemen v Players fixture at Lord's, unlike those which were part of the frivolities in the Scarborough Festival. I preferred a normal county game. In 1957 I had pulled a muscle in my groin, which was sufficient to stop me bowling in the first match of the Colchester Week, though I played against Somerset as a batsman. Doug Insole had been picked for Lord's, but I withdrew from the Gentlemen to take part in the second Colchester match as a batsman. Our opponents were Sussex and, much to my amusement and Robin Marlar's annoyance, Robin (their captain) was chosen in my place. Although I scored some runs, I did not bowl in Sussex's first innings, but by Tuesday I thought I might have an exploratory trundle. It produced five wickets for 14 runs and some rather strong comments from Marlar.

Occasionally when frustrated I would resort to my 'Alfred Mynn' ball, a roundarm slinger, which I used once against Denis Compton who looked destined to score a hundred well before lunch on the first day at Colchester. To my amazement, and his consternation, it bowled him round his legs. It was the only time I have ever taken a wicket with that particular delivery and it was not a bad one.

It is open to doubt who was the worst batsman I have seen, but certainly high on the list was West Indian Lance Pierre, who averaged 0.33 on their 1950 tour to England. Ray Smith wanted only one wicket to reach his 100 for the season when Lance arrived at the crease at Southchurch Park with 'Sonny' Ramadhin at the other end. Ray asked me to let him have a go at one or the other and I willingly agreed, but I failed to appreciate the impossibility of not getting Lance out. I deliberately bowled very wide outside his off stump, yet he still managed to tickle the ball to the keeper, almost rupturing himself in the process.

Year in and year out I found the Ilford pitch at Valentine's Park to be the fastest in the county and I normally enjoyed bowling down the considerable slope. It was here in 1957 that we at one time looked like beating the West Indians after bowling them out for 115 in their first innings, which would have been considerably less, but for a splendid fifty of authority from Clyde Walcott. It was here in 1951 that we also almost beat the South Africans who had asked us to score an unlikely 280 runs in a mere 135 minutes with no compulsory 20 overs in the final hour. We went close, because Ray Smith produced his most spectacular innings, 147 out of 204 in 94 minutes and in the process struck the fastest hundred of the year. Jim Laker made his return to first-class cricket at Ilford in 1962 as a genuine amateur after several years in the wilderness. He immediately showed his skill with a ball of perfect length which turned, lifted, took the inside edge and Gordon Barker, who had volunteered for the backward short leg position, promptly put it down.

I was delighted that Jim agreed to play a certain amount for Essex between 1962 and 1964. He was still a great bowler and a big attraction and he cost us nothing. Nevertheless, some of my Committee were not in favour, which made me smile, especially when I noticed what some football clubs were prepared to pay to disenchanted footballers, providing they had ability and a name.

Unquestionably Leyton was our ugliest ground. It had once been the club's headquarters, when we had been the poor relation of Surrey and Middlesex. Unable to pay the mortgage before the First World War, the Essex Committee turned for help to the father of J. W. H. T. Douglas. He agreed to supply the money, providing his son was made captain instead of Percy Perrin, who, though wealthy, had not been willing to put up the money – a somewhat unusual way to acquire the captaincy, suggesting cricket was not always whiter than white even in the Golden Age.

Financially, our return to Leyton in 1957 proved a success and the old stone encircled wall and old style pavilion did give it a certain gnarled charm. I could easily picture the days which Horace Clark, the former Essex honorary secretary, had often told me about, when the Australians arrived there in hansom-cabs and his father had run the bar in the pavilion. I certainly enjoyed playing there and never more so than in 1958 when we beat Surrey by an innings, having shot them out twice for well under 100.

A considerable difference exists between metropolitan, cosmopolitan and rural Essex, as shown in this little Leyton cameo. Alan Hurd, a good off-spinner who had gained a Blue at Cambridge, was brought into the team there on a pitch which was not sympathetic to spin. In consequence, Alan only bowled a few overs, occupied his normal place in any batting order without distinction, and had the misfortune to allow a ball which had bounced awkwardly to go through his legs to the boundary. This was too much for a spectator on the public side.

'He can't bloody well bowl, he can't bloody well bat and he can't bloody well field. What are you playing him for?'

Fortunately our members usually have a quick comeback and on this occasion it was: 'But, he's terribly kind to his mother.'

My first visit to the Chelmsford cricket ground was by bike to see Essex play the Australians in 1938. When I started to work for the county the club office was in a little back alley called Crane Court, straight out of a Dickens novel. We did not own the Chelmsford ground, simply used it for the Festival week and at one period for nets and pre-season practice.

As secretary I attended the dinner given by Worcestershire to celebrate winning the County Championship in 1965. During the reception I met several close Warwickshire friends, both from the county and their wealthy supporters association, who asked me how things were down in Essex. I explained that as usual we were short of money and that this was especially unfortunate because we had the opportunity to purchase the freehold of the Chelmsford ground which would give us a base. This would mean that in future the secretary would not have to go to the office at Chelmsford, have nets on the Old Blues Ground at Fairlop or hold trials at the Ilford indoor cricket school.

They asked me what I wanted and I said an interest-free loan to enable Essex to buy the ground. By the end of that memorable dinner I had received the Warwickshire assurance that they would supply the loan and they were the type of people who would never go back on a promise. I informed my Committee and that is how Essex came to own the Chelmsford ground. It was easily my most important contribution to the club.

It does not always pay to make the opposition follow on and Essex discovered that it could be a big mistake at Romford in 1951 against Derbyshire. On the second day we dismissed them for 125. I had bowled throughout their innings, sending down 24.1 overs and picking up six for 44. Not surprisingly this had taken a little out of me, so that I was completely against asking the visitors to bat again, a view which was not shared by our captain, Doug Insole, or our batsmen, some of whom I suspect were only too pleased not to have to go out and face Jackson and Gladwin. I bowled a further eight overs on the trot and limped off, and did not bowl again in the match which we only just avoided losing.

On one occasion having won the toss at Romford I asked Jim Laker whether he felt we should bat or insert our opponents. He went out to have a look and was missing for a very long time. I asked Jim where he had been and he said that he had been looking for the pitch and was still not sure whether he had found it. The pitches at Gallows Corner were inclined to be a little on the green side.

Chalkwell Park was naturally my favourite festival week because it has been my home ground throughout my life. I cycled through it on my way to school as a child, lost a friend in it by removing some of his teeth with a fast ball which rose sharply from the rough outfield when we were enjoying a pick-up game, and played cricket for Westcliff CC there, both before the war and after I had retired from the first-class scene. Because I have always had a tendency to forget things when I leave home, it was handy to be able to go back and collect in a matter of minutes such minor items as cricket trousers, boots or even a shirt.

As secretary, Chalkwell Park had the appeal of being one place which for years never showed a loss, mainly because it was compact, central and had sufficient capacity for the three-day game, although it ran into the problem of being too small for the bigger crowds which come on Sunday when the club is doing well in the John Player League. I enjoyed batting and bowling in Chalkwell Park as it had atmosphere, usually provided plenty of runs (because the outfield was small and fast) and wickets (because the pitch had to be well grassed to prevent the top going), and provided a definite result on the third day, without recourse to declarations, which is one important criterion of a good cricket wicket. I have even played there on one occasion in a midweek limited-overs club match when it was so dark that my appeal for lbw was turned down by the visiting team's umpire because it was too dark for him to see!

One of the big attractions of Chalkwell Park back in the mid-1940s and early 1950s, when food was in short supply and meals on cricket grounds were inclined to be unimaginative, undistinguished and minute, were Garon's lunches. These were served in a big tent and those for the two teams were paid for by the owner of the many tents on the ground, an early form of commercial sponsorship. It was here that I was an enthralled spectator at the most remarkable lunch I have seen consumed during a cricket match.

The executioner was our wicketkeeper, Paul Gibb, who, though small and slight, did possess a Gargantuan appetite. On this occasion we were in the field and Paul quickly disposed of the soup before moving into the serious business. Having acquired a double helping of chicken and ham, he surrounded this base with 14 new potatoes, which were not especially small. He next covered the plate, which was already heavily overladen, with a large bowl of salad plus lashings of mayonnaise. His sweet, and I should mention that Paul was rather partial to ice-cream, consisted of a double helping of fruit salad bedecked by six ice-creams. He washed it all down with a cup of coffee before taking up his place behind the timbers for the rest of the afternoon.

Unlike a footballer or athlete who trains to a peak, a cricketer is able to reach the top of his profession and still enjoy a normal life style. He can in moderation afford to drink, to smoke and to enjoy a good party. I once attended a very lavish twenty-first during the Southchurch week. It was still swinging at 5.00 a.m. and some of the guests arranged to meet me at the ground before start of play, but predictably nobody arrived until the tea interval. They were surprised, as I was also, to find me in the seventies and batting grimly on a 'green-top'. I remembered to keep my head down that morning, as it was necessary.

I'VE BEEN EVERYWHERE, MAN

This just about sums up my first-class career as I played on no fewer than 61 different grounds in the UK.

DERBYSHIRE

Derbyshire has always seemed to me to be the natural habitat of the English seamer and there can be no doubt that the dominating feature of Derbyshire cricket since the war, and indeed immediately prior to it, has been the power of their pace attack. Although dangerous to generalize, and there have been exceptions, I tend to think of a Derbyshire seamer as a hard, rawboned undemonstrative character. Taciturn by nature, he might permit himself a few pungent phrases if a batsman took some unpardonable liberty, or the ball pierced the slips off the edge on three occasions, but in the main he simply kept on bowling. He was essentially a miser who begrudged every run.

His detestation of sending down anything resembling a half-volley was sometimes a weakness because it meant that he was inclined to bowl a fraction too short on occasions, when a slightly fuller length would bring wickets more quickly, even if the cost in terms of runs was higher. This is probably why Mike Hendrick, who was an invariably economical and fine fast-medium bowler, never captured five wickets in an innings, despite 30 Test appearances, some against limited opposition, while at the same time Ian Botham repeatedly gobbled up five or more.

I always treasure my memories of one particular Essex match against Derbyshire, in 1957, which illustrated why, on a green wicket at Burton, they were such a formidable side. Doug Insole was playing for MCC, and to make matters worse we had been badly hit by injuries, so I captained a side which was forced to include two from the Second XI and a young amateur, Graham Horrex, who had been scoring heavily in club cricket.

Having won the toss on a damp pitch which might become worse, I decided to bat, even though life against Les Jackson and Cliff Gladwin was bound to be, at best, problematical. Graham opened the innings with Gordon Barker and discovered the biggest difference between club and county cricket, the shortage of loose deliveries. Through a combination of skill, luck and unusual generosity by the Derbyshire close catchers, who normally missed little but managed to put him down a couple of times, Graham managed to exist for over an hour, by which time our innings was in tatters. But for some hearty blows from Roy Ralph and Ken Preston, we would have been pushed to reach 50, instead of the comparative respectability of 80.

When Graham returned to the pavilion with the riches of 20 runs to his credit, which had come mainly via the edge, he was apologetic for not scoring more quickly. What baffled him was that Messrs Jackson and Gladwin never served up anything remotely resembling a half-volley, full toss or long hop, which, if not a staple diet in club cricket, do occur with reasonable regularity. It is hard work scoring runs against that remorseless Derbyshire length at any time, but when it is aided by a pitch on which the ball seams, as well as swinging in the air, it does present serious problems for even the most accomplished players.

The two from our Second XI were Barry Knight and Tony Durley. At that time Barry's appearances were limited by his duties in the RAF. He was a lively, if distinctly erratic, inswing bowler, an attractive strokemaker, though not especially impressive against pace, and a brilliant fieldsman. Although plainly destined to become an outstanding cricketer, he was then hardly the ideal player to be brought in on a seamer's wicket, where accuracy was essential and the opportunities for brilliant strokes few.

In that summer with our Second XI, Tony scored some 650 runs for an average of about 27, figures which indicated a good club, rather than a county, batsman, but our Second XI captain, Arnold Quick, was most enthusiastic about his slip catching, which appealed to me. Unfortunately Arnold made the fatal mistake of saying, 'Tony never drops a catch', instead of 'he hardly ever drops one'.

As expected, the Burton pitch remained ideal for seam bowling

WICKETS, CATCHES AND THE ODD RUN

and at 63 for five they were struggling. It was at this moment that Alan Revill edged a catch off my bowling straight to the unfortunate Tony at slip and inevitably down it went. Alan then decided to chance his arm, rode his luck and made 86, which was more than sufficient to give his side a comfortable win. Although I had the personal satisfaction of taking seven for 61, their total of 199 was too high as they should not have made more than 100. We again had problems in our second innings and were all out for 112, which was about par for that particular pitch, but things were not helped by a sharply lifting ball from Derek Morgan cracking my right knuckle bone and forcing retirement. However, my abiding memory of the game was the look of sheer despair on Tony Durley's face when that catch went down, which, coming on top of a duck in his first first-class match, illustrated what a cruel game cricket can be.

Our two chief executioners on that occasion, and many others, were Les Jackson and Cliff Gladwin, who for more than a decade were the most feared and effective opening attack in county cricket. There was never an argument over ends, because the former made the ball leave the bat, sometimes in the air, and sometimes off the wicket, and had a 'nip-backer' which brought him numerous lbws and very painful, direct hits on the inside of the right thigh of opposing batsmen; while the latter was essentially an inswinger, who was invariably supported by a gaggle of short legs, possessed quite exceptional control and later acquired a very good leg-cutter.

Fred Trueman reckoned Les was the best six-days-a-week, day-in-and-day-out paceman in county cricket since the war. Why he only played twice for England will always remain a mystery. The looks of disbelief on the faces of his colleagues – we were playing them at Southend – when they heard that John Warr had been chosen for the 1950–51 tour of Australia ahead of 'Big Les' were unforgettable. The abiding memory I have of Cliff is the way he invariably knew, at any stage in an innings, exactly how many runs had been hit off him, how many overs he had bowled and, if you wanted to know and were prepared to listen, exactly how each delivery had fared.

GLAMORGAN

Glamorgan are different from the other counties because they are virtually the national side of Wales, who, when playing away from home, will attract the many exiled Welshmen. They were the last county to be admitted to the Championship and until the last war were very much looked upon as a club destined to finish near the bottom of the table, alongside Leicestershire and Northamptonshire.

Since then, things have greatly improved and in 1948 they carried off the County Championship. Their advance was due to a number of different factors, increased gates, membership and an early realization that a large and active supporters association, with a football pool, could make the club financially sound for the first time. Unfortunately, during the last decade Glamorgan have suffered a number of setbacks which have been due mainly to poor management, a remarkable number of bad signings, and more elementary mistakes than even the most stupid – and there are some very stupid – county committees would expect to perpetrate.

The dominating figure in Welsh cricket has been Wilf Wooller. As captain then secretary between 1947 and 1978, Wilf supplied the force, the enthusiasm and the drive which lifted Glamorgan from an also-ran into a power in the game. He ruled club, committee, and game as autocratically as a medieval emperor, convinced that he was always right and that everything he did was in the best interests of Glamorgan, which it usually was. Outspoken and fearless, it was inevitable that he would upset plenty of people, including other counties, players, umpires and the media – but not Essex. In fact, we enjoyed our battles with Wilf and his Welshmen. We had disagreements, but no fights.

The Welsh are correctly famed for their singing and their bowlers and fielders have never been averse to using their vocal chords with the same passion. On one occasion I felt they were rather overdoing the appeals. I was attempting to play out time on a turning pitch and every time I was struck on my front pad by a sharply spun off-break shouts rang out. My counter was to appeal every time I hit the ball in the middle of my bat, which helped to enliven a chatty session.

Although Wilf was a brilliant rugby player, he was not an outstanding cricketer. By sheer determination he turned himself into a useful county allrounder, a medium-pace bowler who could swing the ball, an obdurate batsman who invariably had to be dug out, a very fine fieldsman, and a shrewd ruthless captain. He was one of the first county skippers to concentrate on fielding. It was this feature, especially the close to the wicket catching, which more than anything else was responsible for their triumph in 1948.

A highly controversial character, incidents and Wilf went together like bread and jam. Midway through (a rather nondescript) Cardiff afternoon, Barry Knight produced a creditable bouncer which flicked Wilf's glove and was caught by Brian Taylor. Wilf began making his way back to the pavilion and Doug Insole remarked to me that it was the first time he had seen Wilf walk. As we discussed this phenomenon sitting on the grass, at first and second slip, Wilf turned round and, to our amusement, came back to the wicket claiming that it had hit him on the chest. From a prone position we quietly asked the umpire, Paul Gibb, 'How's that?' After a slight delay, slowly, very slowly, he raised his finger and Wilf, slowly, very slowly, began his second walk towards the pavilion.

One of the oddest matches against Glamorgan took place at Colchester. On the third day, the only possible result was a draw and Doug Insole, with the agreement of Wilf, made a declaration of convenience which allowed our opponents to change, apart from a few batsmen, pack their bags and catch the one train which would enable them to reach Wales before midnight. There was no chance of bowling them out on a very good hard wicket; to save money we did not even bother to use a new ball and they opened with a couple of tailenders. A short, sharp shower reduced the time available still further, but livened up the pitch to such an extent that wickets began falling at an alarming rate. Bound by his agreement, Doug did not claim the extra half hour and led us off the field to the accompaniment of boos from our own supporters who felt, with some justification, that we might even have snatched a sensational victory.

The Glamorgan pitches have tended to be slow and receptive to spin so that their match-winning bowlers have, in the main, been spinners, especially off-spinners, the first of whom was Johnny Clay, a member of the team when they acquired first-class status and also when they carried off the title for the first time. He was followed by Len Muncer whom they acquired from Middlesex and proved a fine investment. Then came Jim McConnon who had a pleasantly curving trajectory and spun the ball considerably, but was rather too sensitive. Day in and day out the best of them was John Shepherd, who began life as a quickie and became a very accurate medium-pace off-cutter, who normally had his keeper standing back. 'Shep' gave nothing away, was a complete professional and could be devastating on any wicket which gave him a little help. I have always thought that he was unlucky never to have been picked for England. Admittedly he was faster and flatter than the conventional off-break bowler, but think how many Test wickets his lefthanded counterpart, Derek Underwood, secured.

The quality and the quantity of their off-break bowlers was one of the reasons I invariably found runs hard to acquire against Glamorgan, because I always preferred batting against those who made the ball leave the bat. Conversely, I usually fancied my chances bowling against Glamorgan, particularly in Essex, and it was against them at Newport that I secured my one and only first-class hat-trick, Pleass, Hever and Shepherd, not a very distinguished trio, and Essex lost by an innings.

One Glamorgan wicket I do recall very clearly was Wilf Wooller's at Ilford. After the age of 30 I began to find my first delivery of the day, as my muscles creaked and groaned, a painful experience. It was inevitably of gentle pace and not infrequently badly directed which tended to bring forth a couple of expletives and became known as my 'Oh Christ' ball. Why Wilf should be opening I never discovered, but my first ball was an inviting long hop which was so slow that he slashed well to the right of my cover, Gordon Barker. My curses simply flowed on into a 'Oh, well caught "Bark"' as he dived to his right to bring off a quite remarkable catch. As Gordon had recently been run out backing up by Wilf (though, let me add, he had been warned), he was especially pleased with his acrobatics.

GLOUCESTERSHIRE

In the days before Gloucestershire changed into 'Proctershire' and such a high proportion of the key players were imports from overseas, two characteristics stood out: the number and quality of their off-spinners, and the number of batsmen who looked like inferior copies of Tom Graveney.

Their surfeit of off-break bowlers stemmed from the slow sandy Bristol wickets and a tradition which really started with Tom Goddard, one of the very few of his kind to have his ability recognized before the war. In addition to being a big spinner with enormous hands and a teasing flight, Tom was one of the loudest and most optimistic appealers I ever encountered. I discovered this during a hundred against Gloucestershire on Tom's first, and last, visit to Fenner's. His comments on that easy-paced pitch were also powerful.

Tom Goddard was followed by 'Bomber' Wells, John Mortimer

and David Allen. The 'Bomber' was essentially a village cricketer in approach, action, build, humour and character, but he happened to be a first-class bowler. He drifted from very minor cricket straight on to the county scene and had the shortest run-up I have ever seen. When batting, but never for long, he swung optimistically and on those occasions when he made contact the ball would travel, though where was anyone's guess, but he did once hit me for a couple of sixes in an over which amused everybody apart from myself.

I preferred batting against David Allen to John Mortimer, because he was not quite so accurate. So saying, I thought that David, especially on very good pitches, was a better bowler as he spun the ball more, had a teasing flight and was less mechanical.

The strength of the Gloucestershire batting immediately after the war revolved around four distinguished pre-war cricketers, Wally Hammond, Charlie Barnett, George Emmett and Jack Crapp. I had the distinction of sharing in a century partnership with Wally in a wartime match. Even though my contribution was only 13, it was a marvellous experience as I had the opportunity to watch and admire a master at work. What impressed me most was the way he punched the lifting ball along the ground through the covers off his back foot.

Charlie Barnett was one of the most spectacular opening batsmen I have bowled against. He never believed that the main objective of an opener was to provide a solid foundation and a sound start. He wanted a hundred before lunch and attacked the bowling from the outset, which I found disconcerting, especially as he had the unpleasant habit of dismissing a highly respectable delivery to the boundary. He was also not afraid to lift the ball back over the bowler's head. I have always liked his description of facing very fast bowling on a lively wicket as being similar to the challenge of jumping those dark black hedges in a steeplechase.

George Emmett was a dapper little player who not only possessed a complete vocabulary of strokes, but also used them. I sometimes felt that he would have made more runs with a smaller repertoire. Jack Crapp provided the solid sensible graft to support the more spectacular efforts of his colleagues. He was the imperturbable lefthander who simply chugged steadily along.

Tom Graveney was easily the finest of their post-war batsmen. I first played against him in 1948, but it was our second encounter at Cheltenham which I shall always cherish. In this match I had the considerable pleasure of having Tom caught behind, hooking my bouncer which had risen too high for the stroke. Also, I was witness to one of the most unusual speeches I have heard during the luncheon interval.

Speeches during cricket matches are mercifully rare, but this was special both for its length and its content. It was delivered with all the confidence and lack of ability which has been such a feature of so many Mayoral addresses over the years. I happened to be sitting next to Basil Allen, the Gloucestershire skipper, who only two seasons earlier had failed to win the County Championship by the narrowest of margins. He was not too pleased when the speaker started by saying that the outstanding feature of both sides was their mediocrity. The speaker then went on to welcome 'the men from Exeter' before suggesting there were signs that things might improve for Gloucestershire and 'the brothers Gravity' had showed some promise. I still automatically think of Tom as 'Gravity'.

Subsequently, I was to play with and against Tom on many occasions and I cannot think of any post-war English batsman who has given more pleasure. A few – but only a few – may have been fractionally better players, but none could match him for elegance and style. When he left Gloucestershire because his Committee removed him as captain, he probably became a more effective, and certainly sounder, batsman. This unhappy affair left its mark, causing him to lose some of his casualness, and his batting became a more serious business.

Unlike the majority of the greats, Tom was essentially a forward player, even paddle-hooking the very fast bowlers off his left leg. This had an advantage in certain conditions, as was perfectly illustrated by an Essex v Gloucestershire match on a Romford 'green top'. We dismissed them in their first innings for 153, of which Tom contributed 100. In their second innings they managed 107, of which 67 came from Tom. Only two of his colleagues managed to reach double figures in either innings, the ball deviating sharply off the track as well as swinging in the air. Tom's two knocks were a classic exhibition of high-class batsmanship. Throughout, he never looked in any particular trouble.

Tom's top-of-the-handle, high-back-lift, front-foot conscientious-ness was particularly suited to Bristol pitches, or indeed to 'green' wickets. It resulted in many imitations by Gloucestershire batsmen, but one who did not fall under his spell was Arthur Milton, who favoured the back foot. If Arthur had had a slightly less amiable and relaxed temperament, he would have made more international appearances for England at both cricket and football.

The worst feature of Gloucestershire cricket has always seemed to me to be the Bristol wicket which, even when it did not turn, could be described as slow and low. It was the type of pitch on which a batsman struggled to score runs quickly, but could stay there, and it gave bowlers no encouragement. Towards the end of my career I deliberately demonstrated this point for about an hour on the first morning of a match by bowling line and length at the middle stump to a ringed field all saving one. My nine overs cost about six runs, because the ball did not come on to the bat and there was no chance to hit it on the rise as the ball never rose. My brief demonstration was to convince the officers of the club that the pitch was not in the interests of the game, or their spectators, a dwindling breed, and something should be done. I was interested to learn some twenty years later that this problem is being investigated, but in 1985 with D. V. Lawrence, C. A. Walsh and K. M. Curran available it appears to have been solved!

HAMPSHIRE

The Hampshire teams I encountered tended to be workmanlike, hard to beat and rather lacking in sparkle. During the immediate post-war years, this was due to their having a couple of match-winning spinners, Charlie Knott and Jim Bailey, and adequate seamers but, apart from John Arnold, their batting was weak so they usually struggled to put together a reasonable total. In later years there was no shortage of runs – Roy Marshall, Henry Horton and Jimmy Gray were consistent and affluent with the bat – and there was an abundance of quality seam bowling, especially from Derek Shackleton, but they did not possess a penetrative slow bowler. This meant that their seamers were often forced to bowl tightly for long periods to defensive fields, which was unexciting though frequently effective.

Except when in contention for the Championship, which they carried off in 1961 under the flamboyant captaincy of Colin Ingleby-Mackenzie, Hampshire were not a side to draw big crowds. They lacked the glamour of star international players, though this did give them the advantage of not being weakened by Test duty calls.

It would be difficult to imagine two more contrasting captains than the Hampshire pair, Desmond Eagar (1946 to 1957) and Colin Ingleby-Mackenzie (1958 to 1965). Desmond, who combined the role of secretary and captain and devoted his life to the betterment of Hampshire cricket, was a serious, conscientious, somewhat diffident and rather unadventurous captain who seemed to worry in case his action failed to produce the intended result.

I remember one match in which Essex came off the field at 4.15 on the last day, because if Hampshire intended to make any game of it the declaration was already overdue. We arrived in the pavilion, when Desmond came dashing down to inform us that he intended to continue batting for another couple of overs or so, which turned a dying match into a dead one. For the first nine years of his captaincy Desmond had a decidedly limited team, which normally finished in the bottom half of the table and made his caution understandable, but he had the satisfaction of leading his county to third place in 1955. The big improvement in the make up of his side was in no small way due to his efforts as secretary. What I found particularly refreshing about him was his enormous enthusiasm for the game, his county and his players, which never wavered.

My abiding memory of Desmond is of spending the night with him and his wife Marjorie. I had come down to speak and make the draw for a car which was the main prize in a large raffle for club funds at a time when survival for counties like Hampshire was the first priority and the salary of a secretary was small. Much to my delight I drew Marjorie's ticket. We had some celebration drinks when we returned to Desmond's home and, quite rightly, Marjorie cooked me a very special breakfast on the following morning.

It always seemed to me that Colin was a throw-back to those independent amateur captains of Edwardian England who played their cricket for fun in between the more important social engagements, like the commencement of the grouse shooting season, the Derby, or a country house party. He brought a refreshing approach, which he had initially acquired at Eton, to the rather staid first-class game, but he was fortunate to have inherited from Desmond a by now well above average Hampshire side. Even his exuberant leadership could not have transformed their immediate post-war teams into Championship contenders.

Colin is by nature a gambler and something of an expert, or so he tells me, on horse racing. Much of his success as a captain stemmed from his willingness to take a chance. Unlike some of his brethren he was prepared to risk losing a game in order to win, but like every shrewd gambler he only bet on reasonable cards, not tram tickets. The outcome was that Hampshire, with no more than a limited team, won the Championship in 1961 through a combination of luck, sensible declarations, brilliant batting by Marshall, solid contributions from Horton and Gray, occasional flashes of brilliance from Colin and, above all, some excellent seam bowling.

As Colin was both persuasive and a good talker, opposing captains were less inclined to be suspicious of a Hampshire declaration than one by Yorkshire or Surrey, while they would also set a smaller total to chase. Colin was, in fact, a rather less generous skipper than he first appeared, as shown by the tight, defensive fields he used most of the time, but he looked a cavalier.

Colin's great season was summed up for me by my only visit to Cowes. Having won the toss, Essex batted for most of the first day and I enjoyed a lengthy fourth-wicket partnership with our South African, Joe Milner. This was not to the liking of 'Gubby' Allen, the Chairman of Selectors, who had come down to have a look at Barry Knight – why he should have picked Cowes as the place to judge a quick bowler I never did discover. Worse was to come. Barry, keen to impress 'Gubby', came charging up to bowl after my declaration, pulled a muscle in his second over and was unable to bowl again in that match.

Ken Preston and I spent Saturday evening with Colin and, as one would expect, he knew the best pubs and clubs. Around 11 p.m. we ran into one of his vast collection of acquaintances, who are to be found in the best places throughout the world. He suggested that we might like a few drinks on his yacht in the harbour. Having been rowed out to the yacht, Ken and I sipped a beer on deck while our host went back to fetch Colin in the dinghy.

It was then that we witnessed one of those sequences which seem to happen in slow motion and are the basis of the best visual comedy. We watched as Colin prepared to step aboard the yacht at exactly the same moment as the dinghy, unnoticed by Colin, decided to move slowly in the other direction. We knew exactly what was about to happen but could do nothing about it, not that we would have wanted to. What annoyed Colin was not our hysterical laughter, but our inability to assist him aboard when he eventually reappeared, because we were still rolling helplessly on the deck.

On the Monday we bowled out Hampshire on a pitch which was taking a little spin and gained a handsome lead of 90 which we increased. On the final day I declared for the second time at 150 for five, rather pleased with life as another decent score suggested that I had ended what had been something of a bad patch with the bat. I set them 241 to score in about three and a half hours. Later in the season when they were in serious contention for the title I might have given them a stiffer target, but it seemed just about right at the time, especially when they were 35 for four. It was then that Colin gained ample revenge for his involuntary swim as he hit a lively and frequently improbable 132 not out which won them the match. If 'Gubby' Allen had not come down to see Barry Knight, if Barry Knight had not tried to bowl too fast too soon, if Colin had not been put down a couple of times, it might have been a different story. Instead it was Ingleby's summer, when fortune quite rightly favoured the brave. In retrospect it always seems rather sad to me that a few years later their laughing captain lost the job to which he had brought both gaiety and success.

I saw more of Derek Shackleton than anybody else in the Hampshire team, because every time I went to the crease he seemed to be bowling, which rather supports the story that he was wound up at the commencement of the season and permanently took over at one end for the whole of the summer. Originally a fast-medium inswinger with a high, fairly open action, he developed into a great seam bowler at just above medium pace. His control was exceptional and he had the ability 'to do a little' both in the air and off the pitch. To me he epitomized the perfect mean seam machine, who considered a couple of long hops in his daily stint of 25 to 35 overs was overgenerous. I cannot remember him ever bowling a full toss.

In order to upset his habit of dropping ball after ball on exactly the same good-length spot, I normally took my guard about a foot down the wicket, especially on a seamer's pitch. This meant that either he had to bring his keeper up – which automatically gave me a point, because he preferred to have him standing back – or he had to vary his length a little. I sometimes wonder how many times I employed a forward defensive stroke against him and how many hours he bowled at me.

In 1957 I enjoyed my best-ever allround county match against Hampshire. I was on the field for all but one hour of the contest, which, considering I batted at number five, was unusual. The game was played at Gallows Corner at Gidea Park, not one of the county's more attractive grounds; indeed, I often thought that the odd gibbet dotted around the boundary would not have been out of place, but the pitch, as on this occasion, was usually green.

Essex were bowled out for 130, about par for the course as the ball deviated sharply off the seam. It was fatal to play back on it, which I did not find difficult, while the longer I stayed the more negotiable it became. I was well content with my 59, but even more satisfied when we shot them out for 109. I had the satisfaction of taking six for 32, giving us a useful lead in what was clearly destined to be a low-scoring contest.

Although well accustomed to Essex collapses, I did not expect to be walking out to the middle for the second time with the scoreboard reading 0 for three, with those two well known executioners, Shackleton and Cannings, having done the damage. After that start we did well to reach 141, especially as we were 112 for nine and Ian King was not a noted tailender. I was therefore delighted to be undefeated on 71.

This meant that Hampshire had to make the highest score of the match to win which was never likely on that pitch, especially as Roy Marshall departed cheaply for the second time. They mustered 116 at their second attempt and I walked off the field with the knowledge that, having taken eight wickets for 49, I would never dominate another first-class match to that extent again. Rather disappointingly, I cannot remember any of my 14 wickets or 130 runs, but at least they are in the book.

KENT

I have always felt an affinity with Kent. As well as having lived for over a decade in a house called Kentview, I can indeed see it from my bedroom. Both Essex and Kent use a number of grounds spread throughout the respective counties. Both link up with London without being like Surrey and Middlesex, which are really London clubs. Both have bred some of the best and most civilized supporters in the land, who welcome success for their own side, but are prepared to recognize and applaud good performances by the opposition. Both have instilled in their players acceptable standards of behaviour, on and off the field. Both have done much better in terms of results since the introduction of the limited-overs competitions, because until recently neither possessed the balance needed to carry off the Championship, and rather lacked the stamina and the ruthless efficiency to press home an advantage or, when on top, grind the opposition into the ground.

In general, Kent pitches were, and probably still are, though not to the same extent, more sympathetic to batting than those in Essex. This is rather supported by my own experience over the years as I have scored a considerable number of runs in Kent, but usually found taking wickets far more difficult. It always seemed to me that the Kent batsman who averaged a highly respectable 40 over a ten-year period would probably average about 30 if he was playing for Yorkshire or Derbyshire.

Although one tends therefore to remember Kent batsmen more than their bowlers, two world class spinners have played for the county since the war. Both have owed much to the fact that their methods were essentially different from other bowlers of their era, which therefore made them more difficult and unusual to bat against.

Doug Wright was that rarity – a fast leg-break and googly bowler. He had the run-up of a quick bowler, with a high arm action, and was liable to send down more than his share of no balls, while his faster ball was distinctly sharp. He bowled his leg-breaks if anything a shade quicker than Chandrasekhar. This is what I wrote about Doug Wright, who incidently was one of the nicest, quietest, and most unassuming people to have ever played cricket for England, more than thirty years ago, when describing the MCC match against Western Australia in 1950–51.

During that game I fully realized what a great bowler Doug Wright of Kent can be. I suppose that Doug will go down to posterity as one of the unluckiest bowlers in cricket history. Many people who judge performances from records and the newspapers have told me he is overrated. All I can say is that the Doug Wright I saw perform in Perth was a bowler of the highest possible calibre. On a very fast pitch he sent down leg-breaks and googlies which came off the pitch at what would have been nearly fast-medium in England. As he was also turning the ball appreciably both ways and none of the batsmen and few of the fieldsmen, could pick the googly, he was as close as anyone I have ever seen to being *unplayable under ideal batting conditions*.

If we had held our catches Doug's figures would have been classic, instead of merely very good. Troubled by fibrositis he unfortunately never again that tour looked the world-beater he was in Perth.

I first saw Derek Underwood bowl at Maidstone against Essex and was immediately impressed by this 18-year-old for three different reasons. First, he was accurate, effective and difficult to score off, which was reflected by his figures of 35–12–77–4 in an Essex total of 293 for eight declared. Second, he had the advantage of being unusual in that he was a genuine over-the-wicket left-arm medium-pace seamer who automatically moved the ball in the air into the righthander. He had not yet become the 'deadly' left-arm spinner who was destined to take hundreds of wickets in all types of cricket and on all types of pitches. Third, he had me lbw for nought and, though I did have the satisfaction of bowling him out when he batted, he was clearly one up. I did manage to have a much longer look at the new Kent bowler during the return match at Leyton, while the reason my 75 took four and a half hours was in no small way due to Derek, who also eventually ended my vigil to the relief of the slumbering spectators.

I captained Derek during a somewhat improbable tour to Cyprus undertaken by the Cricketers Club of London. On the mat laid on concrete, Derek, who by this time had become a recognized spinner, did not achieve as much turn as expected, so I suggested that he experiment with a slower ball. This failed to produce the intended result, simply because he was more of a cutter than a spinner, obtaining more break at medium than at a slower pace.

On a wet wicket Derek was unquestionably one of the most formidable bowlers I have ever faced. What I found so difficult – quite apart from his pace, accuracy, lift, turn, and the additional menace of Alan Knott behind the stumps – was that it was almost impossible for a righthander to cut him because the ball came in such a long way with his arm. Conversely, he was less effective against lefthanders who could afford to play the shot against him.

Derek is the type of bowler every captain wants to have in his team. Calm and assured, he is not only a match winner and a stock bowler, but over the years has also been in limited-overs cricket just about the best 'brake-bowler' in the business.

Of all the Kent players I encountered, the one I disliked bowling against most was undoubtedly Arthur Fagg, who seemed positively to worship the Essex attack. He was a beautiful hooker, put away the bad ball with the calm assurance of a master and loved batting. Although Colin Cowdrey was a more accomplished player at international level, in a county match I preferred seeing the back of Arthur to Colin, though I was always pleased to see either returning to the pavilion.

Canterbury is a famous, beautiful, well equipped ground and the club headquarters, but Essex seldom played there, which gave me the opportunity to sample their other venues. All had their attractions, apart from Blackheath, which had little to recommend apart from what was normally a friendly batting wicket. I have always had a special affection for Tunbridge Wells, which has a delightful setting and a pleasing atmosphere stemming from a long history of cricket. My fondness was unquestionably influenced by the fact that on my first visit Essex won by an innings and 143 runs, Arthur Fagg failed to make many runs in either innings, I scored an undefeated 153, and put on 183 with Colin Griffiths, whose century was the fastest of the season. For me, Kent's most attractive ground was Dover, while a game at Dartford, since the arrival of the Tunnel, is almost a home match for Essex supporters and players. Before then we had the delights of a sea trip on the Tilbury ferry, which could cause awkward delays during the holiday season.

In many respects the oddest match I took part in against Kent occurred at Clacton in 1950 on a typical Essex 'green top' with plenty of life and lift. In his first over Fred Ridgway, a small quickie who was lively rather than fast in the Graham Dilley sense, happened to drop one short in his first over and saw it fly over the head of a somewhat startled Dickie Dodds. Fred's eyes opened wide with delight and he proceeded to unleash a barrage of bouncers, which were answered by a series of probable, and improbable, shots from Dickie, who often hooked by instinct without watching the ball on to the bat, sometimes with his eyes closed, possibly in prayer. On this occasion the Lord was certainly with him, because when Fred, after a short spell, was withdrawn from the firing line, he had taken no wickets and conceded 60 runs. Dickie departed, having struck 57 in 41 minutes, and Fred was eventually brought back, forgot about the bouncer, bowled accurately and took eight wickets for 112 out of an Essex total of 324, which was at least 100 more than it should have been.

In these circumstances, I expected to pick up some wickets but failed to take one, while Peter Smith, bowling leg-breaks, captured seven for 44 and Kent followed on. In their second innings, Arthur Fagg scored his customary century, Peter the destroyer in their previous innings had to settle for one wicket in 17 overs, I ended up with eight wickets for 70, and we won by ten wickets. It underlined the unpredictability of cricket as three bowlers cannot often have captured 23 of the 30 wickets to fall in a completed match.

It is impossible to talk about Kent without mentioning their extraordinary capacity to produce outstanding wicketkeepers. After the war Les Ames had given up keeping, but I saw sufficient of his batting to convince me that he was probably the finest wicketkeeper-batsman of them all. In his prime he was probably good enough to have been picked for a strong England XI purely as a batsman. As one might expect from a former keeper, his reactions were very fast, as shown by one shot Les invented against Ken Preston who, at that time, was distinctly lively, while Les was in his forties. Ken dropped a short ball which really bounced and would have passed safely over the head of Les, if he had not played a two-handed overhead smash which sent it back past the astonished bowler for four. It was one of the most remarkable strokes I have seen in serious cricket.

Godfrey Evans, who took over from Les, was at his best the finest wicketkeeper, both standing up and standing back, I have encountered. Not only that, he camouflaged deficiencies in the field with his own activity and exuberance by sprinting out to meet an indifferent return and taking it on the full pitch. He made wicketkeeping look exciting and with him behind the stumps it was. A natural showman, he thrived on the big occasion – the bigger the better, so it would be true to say that he did not always keep as well for Kent as he did for England. It was not that he kept poorly for his county, but for Kent he was sometimes mortal, while for England he was seldom less than 'superhuman'.

Godfrey's successor, whom I took as a teenager on a Rothman Cavaliers tour to the Caribbean, was Alan Knott. He was less boisterous and extravagant than Godfrey, but even more dedicated to his chosen craft, a 101 per cent professional. He was very agile and obsessed with physical exercises, which obviously helped him enormously because, right up to his retirement at the end of the 1985 season at the age of 39, he could still look the best wicketkeeper in the world. I came to that conclusion on a bitterly cold day at Canterbury during a rather indifferent Benson and Hedges zonal match against Glamorgan. First, Alan improvized brilliantly with the bat to provide a much needed acceleration in the closing overs. Next, he brought off two breathtaking full length catches in front of second slip, if there had been one, and which few keepers would have touched, let alone caught. Then he executed a stumping without flourish but so quickly that I almost missed it. Finally, the way he removed the bails to achieve a run out could not have been bettered.

This long line of great Kent keepers has made life hard for the number two, many of whom have been brilliant, like 'Hopper' Levett, who toured with MCC and played in one Test match, and Paul Downton, who was selected for England after he joined Middlesex. Although Tony Catt, who was understudy to Godfrey Evans for several years, never came into that category, he accepted his difficult role cheerfully and philosophically, and was also a useful, hard-hitting tailender. On one occasion he came to the crease against Essex, when I was bowling, picking up wickets and hoping to wrap the game up. In my first over at Tony, he went for the big hit over mid-off and though mid-off was underneath it he failed to hold the catch, a little matter which did not please me. An exact replica, except the catch was easier, in my next over was even less to my taste and also induced an elementary mistake. I moved my mid-off to mid-on. The result was all too predictable. In my next over Tony's big hit provided mid-on with another chance to make amends. He grassed it with a certainty that caused me to go through my full repertoire at least twice before consigning the unfortunate culprit to third man, where I reckoned he could do no more damage, and only wishing it could have been Hades.

LANCASHIRE

Apart from a brief period of success in limited-overs cricket, Lancashire have not done as well as their playing ability and resources have warranted. Their failure to make the best use of the considerable amount of talent they have had since the war, indicates indifferent leadership. Malcolm Hilton, Roy Tattersall, Peter Marner, Tommy Greenhough, David Lloyd, Frank Hayes, Bob Barber, and a seemingly endless list of wicketkeepers and seam bowlers are just a few of their players who promised, and indeed achieved, so much in their early days with the club, but then fell away. Many of them departed to other counties.

There have, of course, been exceptions, like Cyril Washbrook, Brian Statham, Ken Higgs, Peter Lever and Jack Simmons, but not nearly as many as there should have been. Cyril was a Test-class opener and the best player I have seen on a bad wicket after Hutton, Compton and Graveney. He loved to hook, so we invariably stationed fine leg squarer; had a devastating cut; and was a very shrewd captain who was inclined towards caution. Brian Statham was the fast bowler every skipper dreams about having in his side. He was very accurate and, unlike most of his clan, not temperamental. His philosophy could be summed up as being, 'If the batsman misses the ball it will hit the stumps.'

I am continually asked how Brian Statham compared as a bowler with Fred Trueman, who together formed the best new-ball pair England has had since the war. Personally, I preferred to face Fred, because I could never see where or how I was going to score a run off Brian. He never seemed to serve up anything remotely resembling a half-volley, just a non-stop diet of balls pitching just outside the off stump, which were fractionally short and would hit the stumps, interspersed with the occasional yorker. Fred did more with the ball, but at least he did occasionally, and often deliberately, send down a half-volley. Class batsmen like Tom Graveney and Colin Cowdrey preferred facing Brian because the unexpected was less likely to occur, whereas Fred was more volatile and aggressive and always liable to produce that late away-swinger, which only outstanding players touch and I simply missed.

Ken Higgs had a short, sensible run-up and, with the aid of a powerful body action, was able to generate more pace than the receiver normally expected. I found that after batting against Ken for any length of time the inside of my right hand would be bruised from the jar of the bat handle, just as had been the case with Alec Bedser. He also had the disconcerting knack of making the odd ball lift from a length to hit the gloves. Peter Lever was an honest seam bowler with a marathon run-up, who could move the ball and was a great trier. In addition to having a record breaking Benefit of £128,000, which represents an enormous tribute to a good county allrounder, Jack Simmons would have made a splendid Lancashire captain, a fact which apparently was known only by everybody outside the club.

My first visit to Old Trafford was in 1946 and I was impressed not only by the ground and the atmosphere, but also by the behaviour of the crowd throughout what was a very exciting game, which Essex won by 15 runs in the penultimate over, having set Lancashire a target of 299 runs in just over three hours.

Cyril Washbrook and Winston Place had 120 runs on the board in 45 minutes and I was the main sufferer. It was treatment which I neither expected nor relished, but it made me appreciate that there was much more to bowling than hurling the ball down as quickly as possible. Once during the hectic run-chase the ball was lofted near the boundary line and we were not sure whether it was a six or a four. The Lancashire spectators, almost in unison, shouted 'four'. They showed exceptional impartiality and doled out their applause according to performance, not team. When we eventually walked off the field, having just won a fine match, the pavilion rose to us, and I left the ground convinced that Lancashire had the most appreciative and fairest spectators in the land.

My next game at Old Trafford was with Cambridge University. It confirmed my belief that, in the days of austerity and rationing, the Lancashire Committee's dining room was easily the finest luncheon club in the game; indeed, it produced meals which were superior to most West End restaurants.

Apart from Tests, when the crowd treated me with kind tolerance, I did not return to Old Trafford for a county game until the 1950s and was sorry to note how the attitude of their supporters had changed. Nigel Howard, who was then captain, was jeered all the way out to the wicket, not just by the paying spectators but also by members whose Committee had appointed him. My opinion of Lancashire crowds dropped still further when they barracked Cyril Washbrook for no specified reason, while my wicketkeeper, Brian Taylor, one of the fairest of all cricketers, was called a cheat by a member as we made our way through the pavilion and had to be restrained from hitting him. Standards of crowd behaviour have sunk these days, and sadly I would now place the Lancashire spectators among the worst in the land.

Lancashire's Committee has also done some peculiar things. In my first appearance at Old Trafford I kicked away a ball and Essex were credited with one leg-bye by the umpire. To our considerable surprise this single was removed by the scorers on the orders of the Lancashire chairman, but later countermanded by the Essex captain. What amused me even more was the telegram received by their skipper at Clacton which told him exactly who was to open their bowling. On another occasion I found myself travelling down to Southend on the same train as Nigel Howard. I asked him where he and the team were staying and I was somewhat surprised to find that he was in a different hotel, which though common practice before the war was hardly the ideal way to produce team spirit.

They say that the weather in Manchester is not as bad as it is made out, but I must confess that I have always considered a raincoat an essential piece of equipment for Mancunian cricket watchers, a view which is somewhat influenced by memories of the time I endured almost a fortnight there in 1954. During the Pakistan Test I spent considerably more time in the pavilion playing bridge than on the field playing cricket. It was only heroic efforts by the groundstaff that allowed any cricket, which was largely academic because the game was reduced to under 13 hours and there was no chance of a result. I remained in Manchester to await the arrival of Essex for the weekend game, by which time I had seen every film in the area at least twice. The county match commenced after tea on the Saturday, but that was that, as it rained throughout Monday and Tuesday.

LEICESTERSHIRE

In the 1950s, when discussing diabolical punishments for heinous cricket crimes, the Essex players reckoned that one of the worst would be to sentence the guilty party to playing all his cricket at Grace Road, which in those days was desperately short of aesthetic appeal, spectators and success. It reminded me of a remand home. Regularly performing before a handful of supporters and a dog in a dull setting does not normally bring out the best in players, and Leicestershire surprised everybody, including themselves, when they finished equal-third in 1953. But in the main they were among the weaker counties when I was playing and the glory days under Tony Lock and Ray Illingworth were a long way off.

Despite their headquarters, some colourless teams and the fact that my personal performances with bat and ball were seldom more than adequate, I have more memories about Leicestershire than practically any other county. Here are fragments from some forty long-forgotten battles which still make me smile.

Jack Walsh spun the ball more prodigiously than any other bowler I have encountered and was able to turn his Chinaman and googly on any wicket. My first encounter with this mischievous Australian was at Clacton in the mid-1940s. At that time I had no idea what the ball was going to do. Remembering the maxim 'when in doubt, push out', I played forward and was hit on my front pad by his first two deliveries, which both pitched around my off stump. The third was on my leg stump and without even considering, let alone picking, the googly I played an instinctive leg glance off my front foot. I made no contact and found myself looking into the face of 'Paddy' Corrall, their wicketkeeper, who was attempting to take the Chinaman and intercept my intended stroke. I am not sure which of us was more surprised, as the ball went over the top of my off stump for four byes.

Assuming one was allowed to return to this world as a cricketer, I would choose to come back as a wrist-spinner like Jack. There have been better spinners, but I have never come across any Australian who enjoyed cricket more, while it must have been enormous fun to have the ability to make batsmen look quite so silly. It used to be said that he had three different googlies: one he deliberately showed to give a misplaced sense of security; the other two were very well concealed, acting as a double double-bluff. The one person who always knew which way the ball would turn before it had pitched was his team-mate and fellow Australian, Vic Jackson, who stood at first slip. Vic would frequently move across to leg slip if the Chinaman was dropped around middle and leg; this not only prevented a number of byes but also produced the occasional wicket. I still treasure the amazed consternation on Harry Crabtree's face as he started to run for an unintentional snick down the leg side only to discover he had been caught by Vic.

In addition to his fielding, Vic, like so many of his race, was a useful, highly competitive allrounder. An off-break bowler with a low arm action, he at times introduced a roundarm delivery which was the nearest thing to underarm I ever faced.

It always seemed to me that Charlie Palmer was one of the more unlikely looking cricketers. Small, slightly built, bespectacled, with thinning hair and a soft, almost apologetic voice, he seemed a natural for the role of hen-pecked bank clerk in a farce. Yet he was a highly accomplished county batsman with a most attractive style, and I would rate the 127 he scored for the Gents against the Players in 1955 as an outstanding innings by any standards. Charlie was also a medium-pace bowler, who was not quite the harmless 'phantom seamer' he at first sight appeared. What delighted me most about his bowling was his genuine high 'donkey drop' which he introduced from time to time. His intention was for the ball to drop on top of the stumps from some 15 feet above the batsman's head. I did have the satisfaction of seeing him dismiss Gordon Barker with it. Gordon began by deciding to smash the ball to mid-wicket, switched his aim to square leg and ended up trying to blast it to fine leg, but failed to make contact and was bowled. The look of utter disbelief on Gordon's face was pure pantomime.

During my two decades in first-class cricket, the pitch at Grace Road was usually flat, rather slow and very true, which, combined with a fast outfield, tended to make bowling painful and a rather unproductive occupation. However, I did obtain one wicket there in 1949 which was entirely due to the docility of the pitch. At that time I still tended to imagine that I was a real fast bowler and, more in frustration than anything else, I hurled down a bouncer which just about reached bail height. As I walked back to my mark thinking what a waste of time and effort that had been, I noticed that their diminutive opening batsman had nipped down the pitch and was, rather ostentatiously, patting it down close to the end of my follow-through. This was tantamount to a challenge to pistols at dawn. I immediately responded with a bouncer, charging up, giving it everything, and a little more. To my delight, and considerable surprise, I managed to make the ball lift to about five feet, the height of my protagonist, who, knowing exactly what would happen, executed a full-blooded hook. He made one mistake. He miscalculated the speed of the ball which rose so slowly that he had completed his stroke and swung round by the time it arrived. The ball hit him on the back of his head, knocking him unconscious over his stumps.

Our captain, Tom Pearce, with the ideal sense of humour for that type of situation, lifted him on to his back and carried him to the dressing-room, going via the old scoreboard to make sure that the scorers had put it down as hit wicket bowled Bailey.

Years later, when Mike Turner's plans to transform both Leicestershire cricket and Grace Road were already under way, I arrived from Scarborough to find a pitch which was far removed from anything I had encountered there before; indeed, my pre-match inspection suggested I had never left the seaside town. There was so much sand on the wicket that I settled down on the pitch in a deckchair with my daily newspaper and asked Mike if he could also provide a bucket and spade. The ball turned from the outset and it took only four overs for the sand and grit to rip the shine to pieces.

I have clear memories of three other Leicestershire grounds; Coalville, where white flannels seemed pointless because of the continual downpour of coal dust; Ashby-de-la-Zouch, where I was able to pad up in my bedroom, as our hotel adjoined this delightful spot; and Hinckley, where the town turned on for Essex, only the second first-class county to visit them, a genuine festival. Ashby-de-la-Zouch provided an atmosphere which was rather closer to country house cricket than county cricket. It was here that we experienced one of our longest tea intervals. Having bowled out Leicestershire on a turning pitch I naturally requested their heavy roller, but it refused to budge. The alternative was too light for a garden, so their captain, Willie Watson, whom I always rated as the most accomplished Leicestershire batsman I bowled against, handed the problem over to an upset groundsman, a perplexed motor mechanic and two worried umpires, while the tea interval looked like lasting until stumps.

In many respects the most exciting of the Midlander's batsmen was Maurice Tompkin. Blond, tall and lean with a top-of-the-handle grip and a full follow-through, he hit the ball back so hard and straight that slow bowlers sometimes wanted to take refuge behind the umpire. Once at Colchester, on the third day when we were cruising to victory, Maurice represented the only serious threat. I dropped him a bouncer which he top-edged to 'Chick' Gray at mid-off. It all seemed so simple until 'Chick' managed to trip over his feet and put down a catch he would have held 99 times out of 100. Never keen on seeing dropped catches, especially off my own bowling, I had some pertinent things to say. At the end of my tirade I mentioned to Tom Pearce, rather forcibly, that 'Chick' could have caught it in his adjectivally emblazoned mouth. Tom merely chuckled and came out with, 'The trouble was he tried to use his hands' – to which there was no reply.

Who were the other Leicestershire batsmen I remember most? Although past his peak and with the extra responsibility of having to captain (1946 to 1948) a rather poor team in an era when professional skippers were almost unique, I was impressed by the batting of Les Berry. It might have been described as soundly organized; indeed, it had to be to have topped 1000 runs in a season on no fewer than 18 occasions. Maurice Hallam, who was also an opening bat and also led the county for three years (1963 to 1965), possessed more elegance though he was less impressive against excessive pace. Both Les and Maurice were superior to numerous England openers. However, before the levelling up among the counties, or possibly the levelling down if one removes the domination of our domestic game by overseas internationals, a player had to be considerably better than the other candidates if he came from an unfashionable county like Leicestershire.

Until the arrival of the explosive Brian Davison, I would rate the lefthander Clive Inman as the most difficult to contain, on a good wicket; while the player who gives me the greatest pleasure when scoring runs is David Gower. Despite a technique which one could query, including a tendency to play so many strokes from that over-the-crease no-man's land, David can strike two boundaries with a casual effortless grace which are more memorable and give me more pleasure than most fifties. This gift also applied to Frank Woolley and Gary Sobers. Perhaps their lefthandedness had something to do with their appeal.

Although cricket is a beautiful game, it has always contained a brutal, primitive streak which was typified by the beamer, the deliberate head-high full toss which bowlers of my era employed from time to time to liven up the proceedings. This was far more lethal than the bouncer. Quite a number of fast bowlers objected strongly if a batsman starting walking towards them and would warn the culprit with, 'I will let one go straight at your head if you do that anymore'. John Warr had the right action for a very useful beamer, but it never came easily to me because my rocking style of delivery was unsuitable. However, I did employ the occasional beamer, until a match against Leicestershire at Romford. Vic Munden, a perky allrounder, was scoring runs off my bowling rather too easily for comfort so I slipped him my beamer, which not only hit him but also fractured his cheekbone. I saw Vic in hospital and never bowled another in my life. A few years later, it was correctly outlawed.

MIDDLESEX

The County Championship is almost invariably carried off by a club with a balanced, penetrative attack, good catching and the ability to score sufficient runs, but this was not the case in 1947 when Middlesex took the title largely through the brilliance of their batting. It is, of course, a very different story in the limited-overs game, when one big innings from an outstanding strokemaker plus steady bowling will more often than not win the match – one cannot help thinking how effective that 1947 Middlesex team would have been in one-day cricket.

The first four in the batting order during that golden summer were Jack Robertson, Sid Brown, Bill Edrich and Denis Compton. The two openers each scored over 2000 runs, while Denis and Bill both easily topped 3000 runs and broke record after record in the process. It was not just a case of amassing vast quantities of runs, it was the speed with which they were acquired which proved the decisive factor. Their captain R. W. V. Robins's instructions were 400 on the board by tea time and the fact that this was so often achieved emphasizes the high quality of the batting, even though the majority of county attacks were decidedly insipid.

Jack Robertson was a text-book batsman, because he played all the strokes correctly and with style, a perfect model for any aspiring youngster. Although clearly unlucky not to have made more appearances for England, especially if one thinks of some of our openers in the past twenty years, I always thought he looked a shade vulnerable against excessive pace. I remember how unhappy he was against Cuan McCarthy on one occasion in a Gents–Players, even though he did score fifty. Sid Brown was an efficient workman, with an open stance and a penchant for the on side.

When I first encountered the Middlesex twins I was a naive, erratic quickie and it proved to be a somewhat chastening experience, as I began to believe that I was bowling for run outs. Denis and Bill had much in common. Both had been left wingers, the former with Arsenal and the latter with Spurs. Both possessed an enormous enthusiasm and stamina for all the good things in life, like the opposite sex, gambling, drinking, horses, cards and big parties. In addition, both were fine fielders and useful change bowlers. They did however have entirely different temperaments, which were not dissimilar to their bowling styles, Denis a gloriously unreliable wrist-spinner and Bill an uncomplicated, fast and decidedly erratic quickie.

How did they compare as batsmen? In his prime Bill was a top-class international batsman. Like so many pugnacious little men he was a ferocious hooker and very quick on his feet. As one might expect with his distinguished RAF record, he was not afraid of fast bowling. On one occasion after he had been hit a painful blow by Ray Lindwall, which he had not bothered to rub, I made the mistake of going down the pitch and asking him how he was. His reply was pure, predictable Edrich: 'Of course I'm all right. Let's get on with the game.'

Denis was quite simply a genius with a sound defence, a wide range of attacking strokes and the ability to improvize. He was never spoilt by the adulation. In fact, I very much doubt whether he ever quite realized just how very special he was. Having toured with Denis on many occasions; shared a room with him and at last discovered someone who is more untidy than myself; gone racing with him; been run out by him, not unusual; spent five holidays with him and his family; and, most remarkable of all, had him cook my breakfast, admittedly not too complicated, a hard-boiled egg and toast – I can claim to know just a little about the golden boy.

I will never forget encountering the Compton sweep for the first time. I was fielding at square leg to Peter Smith and Denis played his first shot too fine for me to stop so I was moved to a position midway between square and fine leg. His second shot was even finer and I was shifted again. His third shot sent the ball skidding along the ground to the boundary through the very same spot I had just vacated. The whole experience was quite an education!

When the members of this remarkably affluent-run quartet departed from the county circuit they inevitably left an irreplaceable gap which, not surprisingly, has never been completely filled. Nevertheless, they produced some fine post-war batsmen prior to the arrival of Mike Gatting. Probably the three best have been Eric Russell, a sound, unspectacular opener; Peter Parfitt, a cheerful and fairly inventive lefthander; and the ever dependable Clive Radley with his ugly, yet effective style. All three have first-class career averages in the mid-30s, which indicates competent rather than outstanding performers. Rather surprisingly, Peter has a higher average in his 37 Tests than in first-class cricket, but he acquired many of his runs off Pakistan, whose attack at that time was less than lethal.

Mike Gatting has been a fine batsman for a considerable period, but until the 1984–85 Indian tour had been unable to translate his immense potential into runs at Test match level. In fact, one wonders whether he would have been granted quite so many opportunities if he had played for one of the less fashionable clubs. There are certain definite advantages to being a Middlesex player as anything you do will be seen by somebody with influence.

With their fine practice facilities, excellent net pitches, above-average coaches and the opportunity to engage any outstanding young cricketer on the MCC groundstaff, it is hardly surprising that over the years the Middlesex batting has tended to be more impressive than the bowling, especially if one ignores their imported bowlers of recent years.

The best of their English pace bowlers was Alan Moss, tall, fast, accurate and, most important, prepared and able to keep going for long spells. His misfortune was to be around in an era when there was no shortage of quickies. In his prime he would have been an automatic Test choice for the last two decades. Of similar pace to Alan was John Price, who began his very long, half circular run from about five pitches away. He did not achieve as much bounce, or movement, but made more Test appearances.

Until the arrival of the highly talented, but enigmatic and unpredictable Phil Edmonds, Jack Young was their most accomplished slow left-arm spinner. Small, with a rather flat trajectory, Jack was never less than economical, which brings me to, in many respects, the most remarkable of all Middlesex slow bowlers, Fred Titmus. He played in five decades of first-class cricket, lost four toes in an accident in the West Indies, but came back to play more Tests and completed the 'double' on four occasions. Although many would label him an allrounder, rather than an international-class off-spinner, I always think of Fred at international level as a bowler who scored runs, but as an allrounder in county cricket. This is rather supported by a career batting average of 23, which might have been higher if his county had required more runs from him. It also seemed to me that Fred was more of a genuine slow bowler than the normal off-spinner, claiming numerous wickets with his changes of pace, deceptive flight and deadly arm-ball, as he did with break, which was why he did so well overseas.

The Middlesex Cricket Committee has always contained more distinguished former players than any other county. Nearly all have their own firmly held views on the game and how it should be played, which are frequently at variance with the views of others. To make things rather more difficult they are invariably convinced that they are correct. This is probably one of the main reasons why there have been 15 captaincy changes since the war; while the quality most required by a Middlesex secretary must surely be diplomacy, a knowlege of cricket probably being a distinct disadvantage.

However, over the years Middlesex have produced some exceptionally able skippers, starting with the effervescent R. W. V. Robins, whom I found very stimulating once I realized his ability to laugh at himself. I loved his story of the 1930 Lord's Test, when he was hammered all over the field by the Australians, and especially Don Bradman, yet the only time he did not have a silly mid-off was when his captain, Percy Chapman, was off the field with an injured ankle.

His own captaincy was always lively. It contained adventure, realism, gamesmanship, impatience, imagination and the willingness to take a calculated risk. In 1948, when the Australians were routing England with the same contemptuous ease shown by the West Indies in 1984, there was a move to bring back Robins, as he was certainly the most spectacular of the county skippers. He wisely resisted the temptation. That season I played under him for the Gentlemen against Sir Donald Bradman and company. Shortly after 'Robbie' had reached the crease Ray Lindwall produced a delicious bouncer which skimmed over his head as he flung himself on to the ground. At the end of the day Don came to our dressing-room, poked his head round the door and, with a smile on his face, said: 'It's a good thing you didn't attempt that comeback, Robbie. We'd have dropped you.'

Robbie was succeeded by George Mann, who did a splendid job for England on the 1948–49 tour of South Africa. Rather like Mike Brearley many years later, as a batsman he was never quite good enough at international level, but I would rate Goerge as the most inspiring captain I played under, and certainly one of the most charming.

John Warr took charge of Middlesex after Compton and Edrich had retired, which was rather like being asked to produce *Robinson Crusoe* as a pantomime without Robinson and Friday. John soon realized that he had no batting personalities who even approached that illustrious pair. He concentrated therefore on the fielding of what was a young and enthusiastic side. His leadership, combined with a useful attack, turned Middlesex into a more formidable team than they really were. Although not as quick as when he was a surprise choice for Australia in 1950–51, John became a very good county seamer, who had the comparatively rare ability of being able to swing the ball away from the extreme edge of the crease.

Considering the number of MCC members on the Middlesex

Committee, it was inevitable that they would try to maintain the tradition of amateur captains and there were short, not very successful spells under Ian Bedford and Colin Drybrough, before they turned to first Fred Titmus and then Peter Parfitt. In 1971 Mike Brearley made himself available for the full season and reigned until 1982, soon establishing himself as the most astute captain on the circuit. In this period he was also entrusted with the England captaincy and did extremely well, though it must be admitted that he is somewhat flattered by his record, which was achieved almost entirely against teams who had been denuded by World Series Cricket. He never encountered the big test, the West Indies, and lost when he took England to Australia after their Packerites, about 80 per cent of their team, were back on duty.

Although Lord's has always been one of my favourite grounds, I have suffered rather more than my share of injuries there, which began in some long forgotten wartime match with R. W. V. Robins as my captain. I spent most of the contest chasing the ball round the outfield and, keen to impress, hurling it back. Until that contest I had a strong, accurate throw of just under a hundred yards, but I threw my arm out and my throw was never quite the same again.

My second injury was against Middlesex, when I found myself at silly mid-off to Denis during a spell from Peter Smith. I think silly was the operative word, because there was no truth in the story that Denis could not off-drive. To make matters worse, I have always been handicapped by very small hands and delicate fingers. Denis went down the pitch and drove the ball towards me at catchable height and I made the mistake in trying to hold it instead of taking evasive action. As the ball beat extra cover I glanced at my right hand and was horrified by the sight of blood pouring fourth. I hurried quickly from the field without another look, as I am sensitive about blood, especially my own, and after a request for a doctor over the tannoy, a Harley Street specialist – only the best patronize Lord's – put ten stitches in the webbing between my third and fourth fingers of my right hand. In due course it healed, but it was to trouble me for the rest of my career and eventually I had to keep the two fingers permanently strapped while fielding, apart from when I was bowling.

My third injury at Lord's occurred when I was batting in 1953 in a game which contained two far more interesting features: Bill Edrich played a masterful knock in a first-innings total of 343 for eight declared, his double hundred emphasizing yet again the stupidity of not taking him to Australia in 1950–51; and Doug Insole, who has a tremendous record against Middlesex, as indeed he has against most counties, bagged a 'pair'. In my seventies, in our first innings, I was facing Alan Moss from the pavilion end. He dug one in short and it followed me down the hill while I was attempting to negotiate it from my normal half-cock position over the crease without giving a chance round the corner. At the last moment I avoided contact with my bat, made the mistake of taking my eye off the ball, and played it with the point of my elbow, which is not to be recommended, particularly against anybody as fast as Alan. Ice and running repairs enabled me to continue batting until I repeated my error against an identical delivery, which was to put me out of action for the rest of that game and the next.

The one county who can never be accused of doctoring their pitches to suit themselves are Middlesex, because these are left entirely to MCC. On the other hand, it could be argued that over the course of a summer it is not really necessary, because, with the square so heavily employed, it would not be feasible to provide absolutely plumb pitches for all Middlesex matches which automatically increases the chances of definite results. In addition, there is also that pronounced slope, which, as a bowler, was much to my taste.

In recent years Middlesex have been one of the strongest clubs, and have possessed a powerful and balanced attack with the pace of Van der Bijl and company, later Wayne Daniel and company, supported by the spin of Emburey and Edmonds. It is interesting to note how, in the early months, their seamers do most of the damage and the combined haul of their spin pair is small. Then in late July and August, on pitches which usually have retained the scars of previous battles, the offspinner and the lefthander frequently become the match winners, even though often handicapped by a minute boundary on one side of the wicket, when a chip shot can produce a six.

NORTHAMPTONSHIRE

As a small boy I used to feel pity for Northamptonshire. What must it be like to play for an entire season without winning a single match? When this disastrous sequence continued still further they became a music hall joke and I wondered how their players approached each game when the best they could expect was a struggling draw, or to make their match with Yorkshire last into the third day. The answer I suppose lay in the fact that eventually you become used to anything and even the unacceptable becomes acceptable.

In 'Nobby' Clarke they did at least have a genuine fast bowler with a very hostile bouncer and temperament to match. In a wartime game my colleague Tony Mallett had the temerity to smash 'Nobby', who by now was no more than fast-medium, to the boundary. This act brought forth the inevitable bumper plus a heartfelt lament that if he had only been a few years younger he would have pinned him to the sightscreen.

Northants crowds, never large, dwindled still further during their bleak years in the 1930s, while their ground, which they shared with the football club, was decidedly drab and completely lacking aesthetic appeal. The shortage of money meant that they were unable to bring in outside talent, but fortunately for them spectators before, and for a time after, the war came to watch the cricket and the other side. If the current attitude of success being all important had applied, they would have folded.

In the immediate post-war period, Northants remained a chopping block for the other counties and their cricketing depression continued. Things started changing when their supporters association began to produce money, which allowed their Committee to import players from overseas and other clubs. The new-found ability of the less fashionable and wealthy clubs to increase their playing power with the revenue acquired through extra-curricular activities has lessened the gap between the top and bottom, and is one of the main differences between pre- and post-war cricket, while the introduction of big commercial sponsorships and limited-overs cricket has made the gap still smaller. In recent years, Northants have possessed probably the strongest batting line-up in county cricket, but have not experienced as much success as expected because their bowling has lacked penetration.

The Northants revival really began with their importation of three experienced and competent Lancastrians: 'Buddy' Oldfield, an outstanding cutter and hooker; Albert Nutter, an accomplished seamer; and Gordon Garlick, a useful off-spinner. Their next requirement was to find someone able to mould together a diverse group of players and in 1949 Freddie Brown was appointed captain. It was an inspired choice, underlined in his first season when his club rose from bottom to a highly respectable sixth place in the table.

Their new skipper was still a fine allround cricketer. A forceful bat, a wrist-spinner and a useful medium-pace seamer, he would have been a big asset to any county purely as a player. More important, however, was that he had a powerful robust character which enabled him to instil that confidence which had been missing for so long. He was a straightforward leader rather than a subtle tactician, but he could inspire by his personal performances and approach, which was exactly what Northants needed.

Three Australians also had a major part in the county's renaissance, George Tribe, Jock Livingston and Jack Manning. George arrived in the 1950s, and was the most consistent allrounder on the county circuit throughout the decade, completing the double on seven occasions. He was a top class wrist-spinner who, like most Australians, spun the ball more than his English counterparts. He was unlucky to have gained only three caps back in 1946–47, these before he was anything near his peak.

I spent many hours batting against George and had particular difficulty in picking his googly – I always found it harder to spot the 'wrong-un' of a Chinaman bowler than that of a right-hand wrist-spinner. As their leading wicket-taker, as well as a more than useful middle order batsman, he was more responsible than anyone else for Northants doing so well between 1956 and 1958. He was especially effective against Yorkshire, looking, on more than one occasion, as if he might beat them on his own.

Jock Livingston was one of the finest players of slow bowling I have seen, small, neat and very quick on his feet. Once on the little Wellingborough ground, Jock was heading for the fastest hundred of the season which was held at the time by Ray Smith. Ray asked me to try to reduce Jock's gallop, which I did, but I seem to remember that he cantered to a double hundred.

Jack Manning was the only Australian orthodox left-arm spin bowler I have seen who has provided a serious threat to batsmen in England, probably because he had sufficient time to adapt to the different conditions. He was considerably faster than most of his breed, really spun the ball and swung it more than any slow bowler I faced. On the slow often-receptive-to-spin pitches so frequently encountered in Northamptonshire, he was the ideal foil to Tribe.

Even when doing well, Northants were always short on glamour, because their side did not contain players with big box-office appeal.

The one exception was Frank Tyson who, for a few seasons, was the fastest bowler in the world. It was his exceptional speed which was mainly responsible for England retaining the Ashes in Australia in 1954–55. Everybody wanted to see him in action. Strangely, he was considered a distinct gamble when originally chosen for that tour, as his record in county cricket was not as impressive as several of his rivals, including Fred Trueman who had captured many more wickets and been more economical.

The Northants pitch, which so often represented paradise for spin and purgatory for seam, helped to explain why Frank's haul of wickets for his county was not as high as expected, while it is true that he relied almost entirely on sheer pace, because he seldom moved the ball in the air or off the pitch.

In my opinion Frank never produced as much speed in England as he did 'down under', although he could still be very fast, as I used to discover when facing him. He made Bob Clarke, their chunky left-arm quickie, appear no more than slow-medium. Frank once sent down a long hop well outside my off stump which invited the cut, a shot I reckoned to play well. I was still executing the stroke when the ball was in the elegant hands of Keith Andrew. Some 15 years after he had retired from first-class cricket, I played with Frank in a Rothman Cavaliers match. He was still as fast as anybody in England, if not quicker.

I recall a morning in Chalkwell Park when Dickie Dodds secured an instinctive single off the edge to third man in Frank's opening over and then proceeded to hammer Kelleher at the other end all over the ground. At the other end Gordon Barker weaved, ducked and negotiated the 'typhoon'. With the scoreboard registering about 25 for nought and Gordon still not off the mark, our little opener went down the wicket and asked, very politely, if Dickie, a disciple of Moral Rearmament and a very committed Christian, could arrange for some of that divine assistance at Frank's end.

NOTTINGHAMSHIRE

When I first played at Trent Bridge in the 1940s, it was generally considered the best batting wicket in the country and far removed from the square on which Notts won the Championship in 1981. It used to be so good that the chances of obtaining a result between two teams of similar ability were remote without the aid of declarations, or bad weather.

Our captain's intention was to win the toss and bat for three days. It was a splendid idea, upholding my contention that it is possible to prepare a pitch which is too good, but it never materialized because Essex never possessed batting of the calibre required for a gesture of that nature. It was an operation which would have suited Geoff Boycott.

What is the ideal wicket for a three-day match? My criterion would be a pitch with an even bounce, sufficient pace to encourage both batsmen and the quicker bowlers, and would start taking a modicum of spin after tea on the second day.

The playing record of Notts since the war has been disappointing for a county which used to be one of the strongest in the land. The main reason has stemmed from their inability to produce bowlers of the quality needed to win sufficient matches, which is strange when one remembers that they produced Harold Larwood and Bill Voce. It is also most noticeable that when the club have done well, wicket-taking imports from overseas have played a major role, Bruce Dooland in the early 1950s, and latterly Richard Hadlee and Clive Rice.

I have always rated the transformation which Bruce Dooland achieved at Notts as one of the most remarkable individual feats in county cricket. In 1951 Notts had been bottom of the Championship table and in 1952 only one place off it. The following year Bruce arrived. Despite his county being without their best pace bowler, Harold Butler, for most of the season, owing to injury, and their most experienced batsman, Joe Hardstaff, suffering a very lean spell, Notts finished a highly respectable eighth in the table; in the following year they were fifth.

How much the club depended upon Bruce's bowling is illustrated by a look at the Notts bowling averages for those two summers. In 1953 Bruce captured 160 wickets at 16.33 and his next most successful colleague took 78 wickets at 25.43. His figures for 1954 were even more incredible and explained why the club was sometimes known as 'Doolandshire'. His 181 wickets cost a mere 14.96 each – wrist-spinners are reckoned to be expensive! The nearest to him in the club's bowling averages collected 67 wickets at 29.88. In addition to his devastating bowling, Bruce was a decidedly useful middle-order batsman.

It is difficult to think of any other cricketer apart from Gary Sobers who could have done as much for Notts as Bruce did during those two great years. Their present hero, Richard Hadlee, is a possibility, but I do not think he would have taken so many wickets on the Trent Bridge pitches of 1954. Gary certainly could have done so in his prime in 1961, when he achieved the Australian 'double', and it should be remembered that in his first summer with Notts in 1968 Gary transformed them from a struggling club to fourth place in the table. However, a combination of Test duties and injury subsequently reduced Gary's personal influence.

For those two years Bruce was unquestionably the finest leg-break and googly bowler I have ever encountered. He arrived at a time when the pre-war exponents were retiring and wrist-spin was going out of fashion. His performance at Trent Bridge in 1954 when he mesmerized Essex on a lovely batting wicket represented the most complete and sustained exhibition of wrist-spin I have ever witnessed. In our first innings we made 154, Sonny Avery carrying his bat for an immaculate 92 and Bruce taking eight for 39. Notts replied with 359 and Bruce completed the rout in our second innings by capturing eight for 44.

Without sufficient support, Bruce was inevitably overbowled and lost some of his magic, but for those two years he was superb. I have always maintained that if Bruce Dooland had been picked to tour England with Australia in 1953, instead of joining Notts, we would never have won the Ashes.

Although over the years the Notts attack has lacked high class bowlers, they have turned out several outstanding batsmen and some unconventional ones.

Joe Hardstaff was a member of that great quartet of young professional batsmen which England discovered just before the war, the others being Len Hutton, Denis Compton and Bill Edrich. When cricket was resumed, Hutton, Compton and Edrich were the three best batsmen in the country and everything suggested that Joe would join them. He was extremely graceful, with a classic stance and a top-of-the-handle grip, and scored heavily and stylishly for Notts without ever quite making the impact at international level which his ability warranted. Perhaps he was a shade too casual. He did experience rather too many bad patches. You knew immediately if Joe was out of form because he would then slip his hands down the handle, supporting my theory that most sound defensive players favour a low grip.

Reg Simpson succeeded Joe as the most accomplished batsman in the county. Reg was an especially fine player of fast bowling which he negotiated off his back foot with an ease and an elegance which at times bordered upon the disdainful. He did not duck, he did not hook. He merely watched the ball go by as he swayed to and fro. We toured together on several occasions and underwent several experiences, including visiting Honolulu for the first time; racing down the runway in the snow in Chicago to catch a plane which had decided to leave us behind; waking up over the Pacific to see that one of the propellers was not rotating; and going to the wrong airport in New York to catch the plane home.

I found taking the new ball against the Notts opening pair immediately after the war an unprofitable experience for a young fast bowler. Walter Keeton was a neat compact player with a distinct partiality for the on side, a 1500 to 2000 runs per year man. At the other end there was the one and only Charlie Harris. I never believed I could bowl out Charlie if he had decided he wanted to remain at the crease. It all depended upon his mood. He might block for two hours and then cut loose with a series of unconventional strokes, before another siesta. He had the habit of sometimes deciding to hit a boundary before the ball had been delivered. In fact, Charlie often seemed to regard batting as a personal duel with the bowler. Whether batting, fielding or in the dressing-room, he never stopped talking. One of his favourites was to say to the batsman as the bowler was starting to run: 'Skipper's just brought up another gulley' – out of the corner of your eye you could just see Charlie's false teeth smiling up at you from the turf.

With a different temperament Charlie might have been a great player, while another Notts batsman who should have done even better at Test level is the entertaining Derek Randall. If Derek had only learned to remain still, instead of giving his celebrated imitation of a cat on hot bricks as each ball is bowled, he would never have been out of the England side, especially if one also takes into account his enormous value in the field.

Probably because it was usually easier to score runs against Notts than getting them out, I tend to remember batting rather than bowling incidents. On one occasion at Southend we had been put into bat on a sodden pitch against what was a fairly limited attack, so as our opening pair walked out to the wicket I decided to have a complete massage. Although in the altogether, I was not especially disturbed or surprised when Arthur Jepson claimed a wicket in his opening over, but panic set in when Arthur proceeded to take another two wickets in the same over. That I managed to go in at number five was entirely due to the combined efforts of the rest of the team, who literally strapped on my pads and laced up my boots while I was trying to tuck a shirt into a frantically donned pair of trousers. I joined Gordon Barker, Arthur pulled a muscle and normality returned.

An even more unusual, not to say unlikely, event also occurred at Southend, when Doug Insole and I both scored hundreds before lunch on the third day of a Notts match. That highly improbable achievement has won me several pints over the years.

I have always had a big affection for Trent Bridge and Notts supporters, which to some extent is due to the high quality of the hospitality. It is one of the few grounds when both sides tend to stay behind after the game for a drink. That applies even today at Tests as well as county matches.

SOMERSET

At the commencement of the 1985 season, which was to be one of the wettest and most exciting on record, Middlesex at full strength, captained by Mike Gatting, looked to be the best balanced team and therefore could be expected to do well in the Britannic County Championship. Essex, the holders of both the County Championship and the John Player League, obviously had a fine chance to carry off one of the limited-overs competitions, as in addition to an experienced team they were led by Keith Fletcher, generally agreed to be the most astute captain on the county circuit. Any county which boasts three world class players, one in contention for the title of the best batsman in the world, one in contention for the title of the best bowler and one in contention for the title of the best allrounder – Vivian Richards, Joel Garner and Ian Botham – must be very strongly fancied to capture at least one of the knockout tournaments, especially as Somerset, captained by Botham, also has some other good cricketers, including Vic Marks and Peter Roebuck.

At the end of the summer Middlesex had won the most important and most demanding of the four honours available, the Britannic Championship, Essex had enjoyed the most successful year in their history, winning the NatWest Trophy for the first time, retaining their John Player title, being losing finalists in the Benson and Hedges Cup and finishing a respectable, though perhaps slightly fortunate, fourth in the Championship. In sharp contrast, Somerset not only won nothing, but finished bottom of the Championship table and were eleventh in the John Player League, with the result that Ian Botham resigned the county captaincy, as he did the England captaincy in 1981 after a short and disastrous spell in command.

These two failures might suggest that Ian is a poor captain, a view to which I do not subscribe, but as he is an allrounder, the biggest single draw in the game, is not a master diplomat and enjoys an extravagant life style, it was probably asking too much. He was given the England job at least five years too soon, and at the wrong time, as the opposition was so strong and England so weak that failure (in terms of results) was almost a certainty. In the right set of circumstances and with a good team manager I think Ian could prove a colourful captain who would lead from the front. He knows far more about the game than many people appreciate and would be extremely positive, always prepared to accept or lay down a challenge.

The Somerset situation emphasizes a view I have held for thirty years. The job of a county captain is very similar to that of a player-manager at football, but rather more demanding. Even the most stupid board of directors would never appoint a player-manager whom they knew would be unable to play about half of the fixtures, yet this is exactly what a county committee does when they make an England regular their captain. Without any doubt the best and most efficient county captains are those who are able to concentrate entirely on their job without the inevitable distraction caused by the Tests. Of course, the Test selectors will argue that an England captain will never gain experience in the art of captaincy if he does not do the job for his county and there is some truth in that argument, but looking at the problem from a domestic angle, it was noticeable how much better Leicestershire fared as a county after Ray Illingworth had given up the England captaincy. In 1986 Somerset under Peter Roebuck should manage to reach one of the finals, but whether Essex, led by Graham Gooch, who will presumably be missing with England for much of the summer, will do as well as they have done for the past two years is open to doubt, despite the arrival of the talented Allan Border.

In my era the main similarity between Essex and Somerset was a glorious and often infuriating unpredictability, plus the certainty that they would not win the Championship which, of course, was the only honour available. As a result the Somerset and Essex supporters had to be tolerant and possess a sense of humour, preferably for the macabre. Today, I cannot help feeling things have changed, and not entirely for the better. Essex followers have remained lovers of the game; but judging by their recent behaviour both at Taunton and at Lord's, some Somerset fans have displayed all the unpleasant tendencies usually associated with football and possessed a similar knowledge of the game, which makes microscopic an exaggeration. Could it be that the lack of a quality football club in the county has forced that mindless, moronic minority who have to associate themselves, even very indirectly, with a successful concern to focus their attention on Somerset cricket?

It has always fascinated me how adults can march down a street singing, usually out of tune, 'We are the greatest', even though they might never have kicked a football in their lives. If they chanted that their club was the greatest it would be different, but they seem to need to be more directly involved. In football they are not worried that the players in the team usually have no association with the town or city which they represent. They are quite happy to identify themselves with what are essentially a number of talented mercenaries. In the same way, Botham from the North East, Richards from Antigua, and Garner from Barbados are hardly representative of the lovely, largely rural county of Somerset.

However, there is nothing new about this importation of talent from outside the county which began shortly after the war. The list is long and varied and includes numerous rejects and dissatisfied players from other clubs as well as players from overseas. Here are just a few of them: Peter Wight, Geoff Lomax, Yawar Saeed, Colin McCool, Fred Rumsey, Bill Alley and Ellis Robinson. Back in the 1950s, Somerset were known as the last of the British colonies.

Although it is necessary these days for a county to bring in cricketers from other lands and clubs if it is to make a serious impression in the few domestic competitions, this was not initially the case with Somerset. It was the result of circumstances.

When the game was resumed after hostilities, Somerset were able to call upon far more experienced pre-war cricketers than most clubs with the result that they finished fourth in the Championship, their highest position since 1892. This success, much appreciated by their long-suffering supporters, was achieved by a side largely made up of 'has beens', whereas the other county teams included plenty of young post-war cricketers on whom, ultimately, all would depend. By 1952 Somerset were bottom of the table and that is where they stayed for another three summers. Something had to be done. The early formation of a supporters association provided them with the necessary cash and the Committee set out to buy success. In so doing they lost some of that benevolent, lazy cider charm which was a characteristic of Somerset cricket in the 1920s and 1930s.

Although Vivian Richards is the greatest batsman to play for Somerset, Joel Garner the greatest bowler and Ian Botham the greatest allrounder, they have always had some fine players, but as a club they have usually suffered from a lack of balance, while some of their captains have been distinctly limited. These have included a brilliant eccentric, a blimp, and a club cricketer who never quite appreciated that he was dealing in a school where you do not win with a pair of Jacks or a busted Flush.

The best Somerset batsman I played against was Harold Gimblett. Why he was selected on only three occasions for England and never chosen for a tour, where he would have revelled in the hard firm pitches, remains a mystery. As a bowler I found Harold's batting philosophy disconcerting. Anything very short he hooked or cut. Anything overpitched he belted. Anything fractionally short he drove off his back foot. And anything fractionally overpitched he drove off his front. He also enjoyed hitting seamers back over their head.

The next best of their batsmen born in England was the delightful Maurice Tremlett, who was surprisingly chosen to join the 1947–48 West Indies tour on the evidence of a first season in which his 63 wickets had cost 29 apiece and his batting average was 17. That he failed to prosper in the Caribbean was hardly surprising, but it was difficult to understand how he came to be chosen the following winter for South Africa. His lack of success with the ball on both these trips was probably responsible for his psychological breakdown as a bowler a couple of years later. I faced Maurice during this difficult period. It was an unnerving experience. His first ball was wide outside the off stump, the second a long hop, the third a wide down the leg side, the fourth almost bowled me, the fifth was a full toss. Occurrences like this made Maurice abandon bowling, but he then proceeded to make a great many runs, mainly with drives off his front foot. He also captained Somerset in 1958 to their highest ever position of third in the Championship.

Somerset's batting owed much to the efforts of three very different overseas cricketers, Colin McCool, Bill Alley and Peter Wight. Originally a slow, flighty wrist-spinner, Colin developed into a run-getter with a fine cut. Like so many Australians he was a born fighter. Bill came to the county from the Lancashire League primarily as a hard hitting left-hand batsman, but established himself as a genuine allrounder with his very accurate medium-pace bowling and his work in the gulley. A rugged, chatty, ageless Australian, he was still scoring runs and taking wickets in first-class cricket when most cricketers would have qualified for their old age pension. Peter Wight, who learned his cricket in British Guiana, was a destroyer of slow, medium and fast-medium bowling on a good wicket, but I always fancied my chance on a 'green' or lively pitch. It was interesting that he never seemed to score many runs against Yorkshire – until Brian Close decided to leave out Fred Trueman and Peter celebrated with a double hundred. In style he reminded me of Zaheer Abbas.

Over the years Somerset have fielded more than their share of characters. Bertie Buse was one of the more unlikely first-class cricketers. Invariably beaming, he reminded me of the story-book ploughman who lived in a cottage, drank in the local and played rustic cricket seriously, yet never forgot it was a game. His pace, a steady medium, angled zig-zag run-up and utilitarian action would not have been out of place in a village match, but his control and big 'banana' awayswinger would have been too devastating. As a batsman he nibbled some useful runs in the middle order.

Then there was the diminutive Johnny Lawrence whose pads seemed to protect his thighs and chest as well as his legs. A ball that rose stump high was almost a bouncer to Johnny. He was a purveyor of ultra-slow wrist-spin against which it was essential to use one's feet. His flight forced batsmen to think, which was often too much for them.

The cheerful chubby Horace Hazell was another whose avuncular appearance never remotely suggested a professional sportsman. He would win two or three matches per season with his left-arm orthodox spin, and on good pitches was employed as a dependable stock bowler. I once asked hm what he did in the winter and he came back with the perfect answer: 'I never get up before twelve.'

In general the Somerset spinners were more formidable than their seamers. I always felt that Brian Langford, who captured 26 wickets in three matches on his debut in the Bath Festival, ought to have done even better in his long career. He was, for example, a considerably better off-spinner than Vic Marks, but he was never even seriously considered for international cricket because there were so many quality operators around. Another good, somewhat temperamental off-break bowler was their Yorkshire import, Ellis Robinson, complete with a woebegone face, stoop and the conviction that the gods were not on his side, even though in his day he was a high class performer.

My abiding memory of Ellis was batting against him on the third day of a match at Taunton shortly before our declaration. I lofted him to long on, was dropped and we ran three. Ray Smith applied the lap to his next ball which square leg not only put down but in the process also managed to knock over the boundary for a six. When Ray proceeded to snick the following delivery through the gloves of the keeper for four Ellis was speechless, until I reminded him that he might have had a hat-trick and asked him what he intended doing with a new contract which Somerset had offered him that day!

SURREY

Surrey cricket during my era fell into three distinct phases, the first one being the immediate post-war period up until the early 1950s. Despite a series of captains of varying tactical and playing ability, they were among the stronger clubs and shared the Championship in 1950. Second came the halcyon days between 1952 and 1958 under Stuart Surridge, and later Peter May, when they carried all before them. Finally came the inevitable decline which might be said to have continued until today. Although they once finished as Champions and won the occasional limited-overs competition, the Surrey teams of the 1960s to 1980s have seldom consistently played to their above-average potential and have never approached the brilliance of those vintage years.

On an Oval wicket which was usually plumb the Surrey batting with rather more pre-war players than most was more formidable than their bowling, even though Alec Bedser immediately established himself as the best, indeed the only high class seamer in the country, and Jim Laker was developing into a quality off-spinner. I discovered bowling against Laurie Fishlock a most unrewarding occupation, especially as in those days on a rough outfield the shine soon departed.

Between 1952 and 1958 Surrey won the Championship seven times on the trot, illustrating that they were not only the best team by a large margin but also probably the finest in the entire history of county cricket. The three main reasons for their success were: first, they had the players, particularly the bowlers; second, they had the balance and this applied especially to an attack which was effective on all types of pitch; third, in Stuart Surridge, captain from 1952 to 1956, they had the ideal person to blend together the high class material.

Stuart himself was no more than a useful 'bits and pieces' cricketer – a handy third seamer who swung the ball, a hitter in the lower order and an exceptionally good catch – but he would not have commanded a regular place in a strong county XI as a player. However, he proved to be exactly the right person to lead that Surrey side. He brought to the task drive, infectious enthusiasm and the ability to motivate. His position as both a successful captain and an independent amateur meant that his rule was as near absolute as made no difference. His approach was positive and he had a supreme confidence in his ability to obtain results, and he knew how to get the best out of his bowlers.

Of course, the advantage of leading a team which contained four world class bowlers was enormous. The quartet of Alec Bedser, Peter Loader, Jim Laker and Tony Lock were capable of dismissing an international team, so shooting out county sides was usually not too difficult. It was made even easier because it was the era of 'sporting' wickets which were deliberately provided at the Oval and elsewhere. The objective was to obtain a result in three days without having to resort to declarations and run-chases.

If there was a stand Stuart would try his famed 'Surrey switch', which simply consisted of his two spinners Laker and Lock changing ends. Stuart himself – an unexceptional bowler, but very determined and confident of his own ability – provided cover for Alec Bedser and Loader; while in Eric Bedser he had an off-spinner who would have done the double with almost any other county.

The power of the Surrey attack meant that they did not require a very strong batting line-up, because they were not often required to make too many runs. Nonetheless, in Peter May they had a player of the highest class.

I have always maintained that Stuart's chief contribution to that Surrey run was his emphasis on that all-important department, fielding. He occupied with distinction those suicidal positions which most captains avoid, though not David Gower. This meant that in the field he led by personal example and courage.

One of the odd features of those fabulous seven years was it disproved the theory that crowds will always follow a winning team, because their gates went down. Perhaps their supporters, unlike those at Anfield, became satiated with their club's success.

After that long successful reign, Surrey's performances have been something of an anticlimax, even though they remained one of the stronger counties and provided England with many fine players, including Ken Barrington and John Edrich. In the 1960s I would unhesitatingly select Ken and John as the two most difficult batsmen to bowl against in county cricket. Both possessed a sound, well organized defence and had an insatiable appetite for runs, but occasionally Ken's run hunger caused him to forget the match itself.

By lunch on the third day of the Essex game at the Oval in 1964, Surrey had already acquired a handsome lead on a reliable pitch, and lost only two wickets in the process, Ken being one of the not-out batsmen. The only chance of a Surrey victory lay in an early declaration and bowling us out as we chased a large total against the clock. I used Robin Hobbs and Paddy Phelan after lunch and though this was clearly the time for quick runs my two spinners were allowed to operate for 45 minutes to normal fields without a single shot in anger being used against them. It was an incomprehensible piece of cricket and I enjoyed the look of utter bewilderment on Barry Knight's face as he came up to me from where he was having a restful time in the covers and said, 'What the hell is going on, Chief?'

Ken's tactics forced Micky Stewart to delay his declaration, which cost him the match. If they had had another half hour they would have bowled us out.

This did not mean that Ken was short of strokes. Indeed, when he was a young member of the great Surrey side I particularly remember a partnership with Peter May in which his driving off his back foot did not suffer in comparison with Peter. He was probably brought into the England side before he was quite ready. Dropped and forgotten for several years, Ken adopted a two-eyed stance, cut out some of his more flamboyant strokes and became a remarkable accumulator of runs.

I have always thought that John Edrich has been underrated as a batsman because he lacked the elegance of somebody like Tom Graveney. He was essentially a player's player, rather than a spectator's, who was less impressed by his judgement of exactly where his off stump was and what to leave alone, or his angled run down through the gulley, than those who had to bowl at him. However, John could, and occasionally did, throw the bat in a most spectacular fashion.

My opening spell against John was usually a sedate, watchful session. I would try to find his outside edge and he would content himself with the odd single down to third man and a nudge off his legs. As a result, when in 1965 he hit me for two fours in my first over and another two in my second over, including one over the top of mid-off, and all from good length balls, I was taken by surprise and forced to remonstrate. He then informed me that he had decided 'to give it a bit of a go that summer'. And he certainly did.

Batting against Surrey in their purple period was usually a battle for survival. Their attack was formidable even on an easy-paced pitch, while on one which provided assistance it came close to being impossible. On the other hand, making runs against Surrey provided the supreme test in county cricket and Essex did rather better than most. It was not that we won many games, but we often struggled to a highly respectable 180 to 200 on a 'turner' which gave them a contest, rather than surrendering in under two days. There were also occasions when we employed the 'defensive insertion'. We would invite Surrey to bat first, not because we expected to bowl them out cheaply on a wet pitch, as we lacked the ammunition, but because we were quite sure that that was just what they would do to us.

Of their two pacemen, I found Alec Bedser the most difficult and Peter Loader the most disconcerting. Batting against Alec represented a fascinating challenge. If I was lucky enough to stay at the crease I would be left well aware that I had been in a battle, because my right hand would be bruised and sore from the constant jarring when the ball hit my bat. Although he was not fast, he certainly made the ball hurry off the wicket. His inswinger went very late, his leg-cutter was the finest I encountered by a very long way and he was very, very accurate. 'Big Al' was unquestionably the greatest bowler of his type since the war. I would classify him with Maurice Tate and only just behind Sydney Barnes.

119

Peter was a lively fast-medium with an especially good outswinger, but what made him so unpleasant to face was that he had in his armoury a bouncer that was genuinely fast, and a perfectly disguised slower ball which he really spun. I reckoned I could normally pick the bouncer and the slower ball of most bowlers, but not Peter's – not even on tour when in the slips.

The Surrey spin twins, Jim Laker and Tony Lock, were the ideal pair, especially for the English conditions of the 1950s – off-break and left-hand orthodox. The contrast of styles, one turning into a right-hand batsman and the other turning away, applied equally to their characters. Jim was quiet, laconic and undemonstrative, at times appearing to be slightly bored with the whole business, whereas Tony was a boisterous, theatrical and demonstrative extrovert who became totally involved in everything.

Tony's bowling career had three distinct phases: first, as an orthodox slow left-armer with flight and a flowing action; second, as a flat spinner whose pace was closer to medium than slow, whose faster ball would send a stump flying out of the ground and whose action would not be permitted today; and finally, after he had seen films of his bowling action in 1960, he made the necessary adjustments and straightened his bowling arm. Although he was not as devastating in this final stage as in the middle period, he was still the best left-arm bowler in the country, while overseas he was more effective because he rediscovered his flight and started thinking batsmen out, instead of aiming to pitch leg stump and knock out the off at about the same pace as the average third or fourth county seamer.

As I have always preferred playing the ball that left the bat to the one coming into it, I found Jim harder to play than Tony. Tony was also more volatile and occasionally would drop one short outside my off stump, thus allowing me to indulge in my favourite stroke, the square cut. Because he was so quick through the air, edges tended to go to the boundary and it never worried me how the runs came providing they went down in the book.

My early encounters with Jim were a nightmare. I was a Laker 'bunny'. I would go to the crease, play forward with my bat a long way in front of my left pad. Everything would be fine until Jim made one lift and turn. The ball would take my inside edge and be caught by one of his short legs. This all became so unpleasantly predictable that on a 'sticky' at the Oval I decided to alter my tactics, and occasionally go down the pitch to him. This meant that he could not afford to drop every ball on the same spot and it also allowed me to play some on the half-volley. As a result, batting against Jim was no longer completely impossible, just very difficult, and I did sometimes, though not often, score some runs against him.

The most enjoyable occasion was undoubtedly a hundred against Surrey at Southend. I was in the seventies when I was joined by our number 11, 'Gerry' Jerman, a good club seamer making his debut in first-class cricket. I had the satisfaction of not only making sure that Gerry did not face one ball, but also taking my own score into the nineties. It was then that I lost the strike and had rather given up hope as my partner prepared to receive his first ball in county cricket from Jim. He unleashed a massive mow which sent the ball sailing into the lake outside the ground and left me wondering whether he really had needed my protection!

SUSSEX

I have always had a great affection for Sussex and have enjoyed enormously the cricket I have played and seen at Hove and Eastbourne. The club reminds me of a close friend of mine who was invariably kind, hospitable and very generous. He should have been able to live in style for the whole of his days and indeed might have become 'filthy, stinking, rich', but unfortunately he lacked business acumen. It seems to me that this same basic weakness has hampered Sussex, who own an excellent ground and command well-above-average support.

Although I am aware of how much it costs to run a county club and how difficult it can be to produce a profit, I must confess I find it hard to understand how one could lose money on squash courts when the demand for the game was at its peak; and, even harder, why a good, well situated pub suffered the same fate. Yet that was allowed to happen at Sussex. Could it be that the club would have been more successful both on the field and financially if their committee had contained fewer charming gentlemen and more former first-class cricketers and astute businessmen.

It has always seemed to me that the three most outstanding features of Sussex have been their batting; the family atmosphere resulting from having so many players with relatives who also have played for the club; and the high percentage of their captains since the war who have come from Cambridge or Oxford, a Blue thus appearing to be an almost essential requisite.

Until the amateur departed from the first-class game, Sussex were able to field an unusually high number of high-class amateur batsmen. Since the war these have included Hugh Bartlett, Hubert Doggart, Nawab of Pataudi, David Sheppard and Ted Dexter. Not surprisingly these players exerted a considerable influence on their professional colleagues who appeared to divide into two distinct categories. First came the solid variety who acquired their runs carefully and were thrifty with their strokes, suggesting that they were descendants from dependable yeoman farming stock. John and James Langridge provided two perfect examples. The second type of professional batsman suggested the background of a gentleman farmer. He dressed more fashionably, often spoke better and not infrequently batted with greater charm and freedom than his amateur counterpart. Those who immediately spring to my mind in this category are George Cox, Don Smith and, if you ignore that South African accent, Tony Greig.

This combination of good amateur batsmen with support from both a solid and a dashing professional core meant that Sussex were seldom short of runs. Their problem was that their attacks have usually lacked the penetration and variety required to win the County Championship, though they have had their moments in limited-overs cricket.

Prior to the war, and immediately afterwards, the Sussex team was very much a family affair with John and James Langridge, Harry and Jim Parks, Charlie and Jack Oakes. They have been followed up by two 'Omni-Busses', Tony and Ian Greig, and Colin and Alan Wells. There is nothing new about this trend as the Gilligan brothers were an outstanding feature of Sussex cricket throughout the 1920s, while the county has also had a happy knack of producing players who have been able to transmit their ability to their sons and, in the case of the Parks, their son and grandson. The following have all had two generations playing first-class cricket for the county: Langridge, Doggart, Griffith, Tate, the most famous, and Lenham, the most recent.

The two brothers who contributed most to Sussex cricket in my era were James and John Langridge, two down-to-earth characters who provided their club with that essential stability. James was the ideal county allrounder, an accurate, dependable slow left-arm spinner who gave nothing away on a good wicket and could be deadly on a 'turner', and a sound middle-order lefthander with the technique and the temperament which was ideal for conducting a rescue operation after an early collapse. Not surprisingly, I detested bowling against him. Like most of the seamers, I was even more delighted to see the back of John, with his ugly open stance and an effective technique which was all shuffle, push and dab. John was a very consistent opener and had a distinguished record against Derbyshire in particular, despite their pace attack. He was also a very unspectacular, deep-standing but extremely dependable first slip.

The great days of the Parks brothers belonged to the 1930s, but Harry continued afterwards and I saw his nephew, Jim, carry on the name with even more panache. Originally a spectacular attacking batsman, Jim was better against spin than pace – he tended to move over so far that he was caught too often down the leg side. He turned himself into a useful wicketkeeper, both for his county and England, and was happier standing back, which was hardly surprising as Sussex relied mainly on seam.

The first of the Cambridge captains was S. C. 'Billy' Griffith, who was disgracefully discarded after the 1946 season because the club finished bottom. He was followed by Hugh Bartlett who, like Billy and myself, had been to Dulwich College, where I bowled against him for the first time in a school match during the war. He was only playing occasional games and it showed; indeed, he scratched around so uncomfortably at the start of his innings that I found it difficult to believe that he had produced some of the most spectacular innings in first-class cricket. The Cambridge trend was broken by three years of Jim Langridge and followed by one highly successful season under David Sheppard, who had done extremely well as skipper of Cambridge University. By that time I had already visualized his pads becoming gaiters. David was a fine batsman and a good, though I thought somewhat intolerant, leader – indeed, ideal Bishop material. His Cambridge side was certainly the most unpopular since the war, which to some extent was due to an overliberal use by the standards of that period of bouncers and beamers, plus a captain who plainly believed in ruling by divine right.

I have always maintained that it was unfortunate for cricket that David should have retired after that memorable summer in 1953 in which he hit seven hundreds and scored over 2000 runs as well as fielding brilliantly, while Sussex finished in second place, because he had much to offer to the game. I also believe he should never have been chosen for Australia in 1962–63. His place ought to have gone to a batsman who would benefit from the tour as a player, instead of simply providing him with extra publicity. It must help in the ecclesiastical profession to be a bishop who is known to the general public and for reasons unlike those of the Durham incumbent.

David was followed by three more Cantabs, Hubert Doggart (1954), Robin Marlar (1955 to 1959) and Ted Dexter (1960 to 1965), but Robin was quite different from the other two. Indeed, he was very different from all the other post-war Sussex skippers as he was the only pure bowler. He was intelligent, occasionally brilliant, argumentative and often somewhat irrational, as on the occasion when sent in as a nightwatchman for the Rest against the Champion county: he was out stumped having hit the previous delivery for a distinctly fortuitous six. I always enjoyed clashes with Sussex when Robin was at the helm. Strange things were liable to occur to disrupt the run of the mill normality of the first-class game, like the time when he joined George Cox at Chelmsford and I was bowling. George was about 70 not out and Robin in his rightful place, next to the roller. The Sussex skipper summoned George for a whispered midwicket conference, when subterfuge of Machiavellian cunning was obviously planned.

Robin took guard and then, as I ran up to bowl my first ball to him and the second of the over, he started running down the off side of the pitch, while George sprinted hard for the other end. The object of the ploy was to give George the strike by taking a single to the keeper who was standing well back. The intention was excellent, but Robin had overlooked the possibility that I might bowl one straight. It was the only occasion in my career that I have knocked a stump out of the ground just as the two batsmen were about to cross in the middle of the pitch.

Ted Dexter possessed all the qualities which should have made him the perfect Sussex captain. He had a Cambridge background, was a splendid allround athlete who thought about the game, had a considerable personality and was the best, certainly the most spectacular, batsman to have played for his county since the war. He quickly appreciated the requirements for limited-overs cricket and his team twice won the Gillette Cup, but he never did quite as well as

124

he possibly should have done, perhaps because he was given the England captaincy at 26. This caused him to lose some enthusiasm for county cricket rather more quickly than if he had had to wait longer for the prime post. He tended to give the impression of being somewhat aloof and relatively speaking he was not as successful a player for Sussex as he was for England.

When Ted came in to bat against Essex I would set an attacking field for the first 15 minutes and, if he was still there, I would then try to make the acquisition of runs a difficult and lengthy business. Faced by this situation in a county match, as distinct from a Test match, Ted was inclined to accept the challenge. Although this attitude would produce the occasional dashing innings, he never registered against Essex the scores his ability warranted. In addition to his dislike of being restrained, Ted did sometimes become bored with the county game.

The Nawab of Pataudi, Jim Parks, Mike Griffith, Arnold Long and, currently, John Barclay have all led the club with varying degrees of success and skill. What has always seemed to me to be the basic weakness of Sussex captaincy has had nothing to do with the ability of the individual as a skipper or a player. It has stemmed from the Committee, who never seem sure for any length of time that they have made the correct appointment. They have tended to chop and change too much and thus have failed to achieve continuity, which can be such an enormous advantage.

Over the years it has been their batting and their batsmen that I have remembered most, but they have produced some fine bowlers, though strangely the majority have had ugly, or at best utilitarian, actions. This applied as much to their spinners, James Langridge, Alan Oakman and Robin Marlar, as to their seamers. Ian Thomson was an outstanding medium-pace seamer, but neither his shuffling approach nor basic action were remotely beautiful. Don Bates had a laboured run-up. There was nothing special about the action of Tony Buss. Even today, although their two imported pacemen, Imran Khan and Garth le Roux, are genuine international-class bowlers, they lack the aesthetic appeal of Dennis Lillee, Michael Holding or Wes Hall. There was, however, one exception to this generalization, John Snow, whom I first encountered in his early days with Sussex when he was keen to bowl, which did not always apply later in his career. The match was played on a slow, rather soft Essex pitch. From a short, delightfully relaxed run-up and classical rocking action, John was able to make the odd delivery lift sharply from just short of a length and bring the odd one back off the seam – I immediately knew that I was watching a potential international bowler.

I have three abiding memories of Hove: bowling downhill in the morning on a firm green pitch and trying to control the amount of movement; explaining to Sussex members on the third day how, by delaying my declaration by one minute, I had saved nine minutes because the break between innings would occur during the tea interval; and watching Gary Sobers from the other end in a Rothman Cavaliers game as he hit a leg-cutter from Tony Buss. It bit and turned into the lefthander, yet Gary hit it on the rise through the covers for four.

It was on the Saffrons at Eastbourne where I recorded my highest score in first-class cricket. My 205 in 1947 was the result of Frank Vigar and Chick Gray failing to reach the ground in time. Their car broke down and I was promoted. Frank was scheduled to bat at five and Chick at four, but I went to the crease when the scoreboard read 80 for three at, I suppose, about 12.45 and I was out before the close. Although the pitch was a batsman's dream and the bowling not too formidable, I would never have made a double hundred if Billy Griffith had not been behind the stumps. Having reached my hundred, I was more than satisfied. I indulged in some fairly flamboyant strokes so that the next fifty arrived before I realized what was happening. It was then that Billy asked me whether I had ever scored 200 and I suddenly realized that it was there for the taking, providing I did not throw it away.

WARWICKSHIRE

Until the substantial injections of cash into the first-class game from commercial sponsorship, the majority of the first-class counties had difficulty in existing on gate receipts, membership and share of Test receipts, because the costs of maintaining a ground, a professional staff and administrators are considerable. Warwickshire solved the problem and became a wealthy club, not through the cricket, which could never have provided sufficient revenue for their particular requirements, but by creating the largest and most successful supporters association in the land.

The money raised by their highly successful and well organized football pool was ploughed back into the ground and has transformed Edgbaston, once the poor relation of our international venues, into the best equipped in the country. The fact that the money was used in this practical fashion was one of the reasons why the relationship between the club and the supporters association remained so amicable. The facilities for players, spectators, practice, both indoor and outdoor, car parking and catering are excellent. If the enormous improvements had not been made, Edgbaston would never again have been allocated Tests, which now occur on a regular basis. It can therefore be said that the Warwickshire Supporters Association were directly responsible for bringing international cricket back to Birmingham.

A difficulty which confronts all major cricket and football grounds is how to capitalize on something which, for most of the year, will remain in magnificent emptiness. Even during the summer, Edgbaston is much too big for Warwickshire's requirements and, apart from the one Test (and even then only for Australia and the West Indies), the ground is never full. The Warwickshire Committee gave considerable thought to the problem posed by the unproductivity of their major asset and under the guidance of Leslie Deakins, the most hardworking and conscientious county cricket secretary I encountered, they have made many of their improvements dual-purpose, so that in winter and summer Edgbaston has become a social centre for an ever increasing number of people. It always seemed to me that Leslie and his wife, Nora, whom I have often stayed with, loved Warwickshire rather like a child and revolved their own life around its continued health and prosperity.

In the late 1950s and early 1960s, when Warwickshire were one of the few clubs without financial problems, their committee showed a most praiseworthy concern and interest in those counties who were less fortunate. They have always gone out of their way to help cricket at every level, providing not only money but also practical aid, which is one reason why I have such a high regard for the club.

In general, supporters from the Midlands were inclined to put a higher value upon the success of their team than their southern counterparts. When Warwickshire won the County Championship in 1951, large crowds flocked to see them, but these quickly disappeared in the leaner years which followed. Considering the wealth of the county, which has enabled them to maintain a large staff, pay well above average wages, provide top class facilities and attract star cricketers, it has always seemed rather odd to me that they have only twice managed to carry off the Championship since the war, in 1951 and 1972.

On the first occasion Warwickshire were led by Tom Dollery, an outstanding professional captain in an era when most clubs were led by amateurs. Tom was a natural leader, liked and respected by his side, an extremely able tactician, and a master batsman who could attack or defend according to the requirements of the situation. There is no doubt that he extracted the utmost from the far from exceptional talent at his disposal, which is the number one requirement for any skipper. He was assisted by being able to keep the same side together as none of his players were required for the Test matches.

In that summer, Tom and his wicketkeeper, Dick Spooner, had averages of over 40, while his other four batsmen averaged more than 30. He therefore had six players in form, and these were backed up by the brilliant, if somewhat unpredictable, allround talents of Alan Townsend. His attack was basically a four-man affair: Tom Pritchard, who was distinctly sharp rather than genuinely fast; Charlie Grove, an outstanding seamer whose ability to obtain movement, either in or away, was determined by the position of his left foot; the remarkable Eric Hollies; and an orthodox slow left-arm spinner, Ray Weeks, who promised so much at 21 but quickly faded from the first-class scene.

Tom was a New Zealander with a consuming passion for cricket, whether he was simply hurling the ball down as fast as he could or trying to hit it into the next parish. His new-ball partner, Charlie, provided the accuracy and that nasty, nagging length which has been the hallmark of every good English seamer. However, the key member of the Warwickshire attack was Eric Hollies, who was both their chief match winner and stock bowler, an unusual combination for a wrist-spinner. Very early in my career I discovered the hard way – lbw bowled Hollies – that it was fatal to play back to him, because he possessed a very good top-spinner which would pitch on off stump, hurry through and hit around middle and leg. This is the reason why so many batsmen returned to the pavilion wrongly thinking they were a victim of the Hollies googly, which was in fact easy to pick.

Until the arrival of their West Indian imports, Rohan Kanhai and Alvin Kallicharran, the best and most prolific of the Warwickshire batsmen was Mike Smith, who captained them with distinction and quite exceptional charm from 1957 to 1967 and was also probably the most delightfully relaxed of all England skippers. Mike was inclined to be rather seam conscious, but this was understandable as it was the only bowling of quality he had under his command at Warwickshire. He enjoyed a particularly successful season in 1959, both as captain and as a batsman. His team finished fourth, having been sixteenth in 1958, while he scored over 3000 runs. In that summer they attacked targets set by other counties to such good effect that they rather ruined the declaration market. In 1962 they were third in the table, in 1963 fourth and in 1964 second, also reaching the final of the Gillette Cup.

Not surprisingly Warwickshire, with a good seam attack and plenty of fast-scoring batsmen, were well equipped for limited-overs cricket, though they were well beaten at Lord's by Sussex, because the ball moved about in the morning session after Mike had decided to bat. One of his committee members condemned him for not inserting Sussex, saying that there had been mist on the M1 at 7 a.m. when he had been driving down from Birmingham and it was obvious that there would be moisture in the wicket. It seems to me that it is hard enough captaining a side without being expected to drive along the motorway in the early hours of the morning to ascertain the behaviour of the pitch!

The one outstanding bowler in Mike's team was Tom Cartwright, the best genuine medium-pace seamer, as distinct from fast-medium, I faced in county cricket. He had the ability to obtain some movement off even a very plumb pitch, while on a crumbling wicket he was often more effective and more accurate than a genuine spinner. However, he was not responsible for the most improbable piece of Warwickshire seam bowling against Essex, which surely belongs to A. C. Smith at Clacton in 1965.

I have always thought that A.C., who succeeded Mike in 1968 as the Warwickshire captain, looked the untidiest keeper in first-class cricket. His pads flapped and never seemed to fit properly, his walk between the wickets appeared clumsy, his stance behind the stumps lacked style and his gloves looked too large. Although A.C. was never an outstanding keeper, and I never fully understood how he came to keep for England, he was far better and more effective than many people realized and he did not miss many chances. He was underrated because he never quite looked the part.

On this occasion at Clacton, Essex required 203 to win in a

low-scoring match on a pitch which gave the seam bowlers some assistance. It was a tough target, but as Rudi Webster was injured we fancied our chances. Then A.C. took off his pads and started to bowl seamers off the wrong foot. He secured a most impressive hat-trick of Barker, G. Smith and Fletcher and then had me caught, his fourth victim in 34 deliveries without conceding a run, a little matter which he has never allowed me to forget.

WORCESTERSHIRE

In the days before commercial sponsorship, the Bank Holiday match, apart from the Tourist fixture, was for the majority of counties the most important game of the season. A fine Saturday, Monday and Tuesday often meant the difference between profit and loss in the club's balance sheet.

Our annual opponents were Worcestershire which meant that I spent every other August Bank holiday at Worcester on what I have always thought to be one of the most attractive grounds in the country. In fine weather the wicket would be fast and true and this, combined with a quick outfield, made batting a delight. Neither team, until the great Worcestershire period in the 1960s, possessed a sufficiently penetrating attack for these ideal run-getting conditions, the result being that most of the games ended up as high-scoring draws, with declarations seldom achieving their objective. As a result the Essex crowds became a little tired of seeing Worcestershire on either Whit or August Bank holiday and eventually a rota system with other counties was introduced.

When I first played against Worcestershire their attack revolved mainly around four interesting and contrasting pre-war bowlers, Reg Perks, Dick Howorth, Percy Jackson and 'Roly' Jenkins.

Reg was one of the most consistent of all seam bowlers, which is shown by the fact that when he retired at 43, 27 years after he had joined Worcester, he had claimed 100 wickets for the sixteenth season. For a quick bowler to capture 100 wickets so often, especially when the home pitch was so amicable, was remarkable. Only 'Tich' Freeman, the Kent spinner, has beaten that figure. Reg had a high, somewhat open-chested action so that his stock ball was the inswinger. Although he lost a little of his pace after the war, he was still lively and, more important, had become a thinking bowler and quick to spot any batsman's weakness.

Reg was one of my favourite cricketers and he helped me

enormously. When I first encountered him I was a slightly built, tearaway quickie who was forever pulling muscles, especially in my back. I discussed my problem with Reg, who never appeared to break down, and he suggested that I follow his example and wear a vest and then a 'roll on' under my shirt. Although the sight of me donning my wife's black roll-on (I did cut off the suspenders) did cause a certain amount of comment in the dressing-room, it certainly paid off. I was never seriously troubled by torn muscles in my back from the moment I began to wear a girdle for bowling.

Dick Howorth was the ideal slow left-arm spinner. He could be a match winner on a helpful pitch and could be employed effectively as a stock bowler on a plumb track as he demonstrated so often at Worcester and in the West Indies.

I always felt that Percy Jackson could have been an outstanding off-break bowler instead of merely a competent one. He spun the ball viciously, but was unable to accept with sufficient equanimity the setbacks which befall every spinner.

The most fascinating of the Worcestershire quartet was unquestionably Roly Jenkins who was that rarity, a very slow wrist-spinner who gave the ball air so that he could beat batsmen both in the flight and off the pitch. Roly flourished on fast pitches and I have always felt that he was unlucky to have had only one tour, against South Africa. On that occasion he not only headed the bowling averages but also took far more wickets than anybody else. In England, on a slow pitch, it was often possible to adjust one's stroke, but unlike most good slow bowlers you could not afford to play him entirely from the crease, you had to venture down the wicket from time to time.

Roly was about the keenest cricketer I have known. When dissatisfied with his bowling, which often happened, he would sometimes spend the entire luncheon interval trying to correct some minor fault. He was also something of a comedian, who never stopped talking and was enormous value in Benefit matches against club sides – we used to provide their beneficiary with some players during our Bank Holiday Sunday in Worcester and they reciprocated in Essex. In a Benefit match Roly had the ability to finish off the game whenever it was felt necessary, because his blend of spin and flight hypnotized the average club batsman. In addition he had one or two little party tricks with which to enliven the proceedings.

The first time I saw Roly do his cricket striptease before a big

Essex crowd, he brought the house down. His timing was perfect. The Essex beneficiary (I have a feeling it was Ray Smith) asked Roly to bowl. Although a hot day, Roly slowly peeled off three sweaters which he handed to the slightly surprised umpire. He marked out his run, then returned to the wicket and proceeded to remove his first pair of trousers, which he handed over to the umpire who was beginning to resemble a human clothes-horse. Eventually he started on his over.

In the late 1950s and 1960s, Jack Flavell and Len Coldwell combined to form one of the best post-war county opening attacks. 'Jolting' Jack bowled outswingers and 'nip-backers' and Len bowled inswingers. Originally, Jack had been genuinely fast, but he was too erratic and proved expensive. When he reduced his run-up and grooved his powerful body action, with his left foot invariably landing in front of the middle stump, he became a high class attacking bowler, much feared and respected by batsmen everywhere.

Batsmen often have a partiality for the bowling of a particular county or counties. When two from the same XI have this liking and open the innings, it tends to become rather monotonous. I hate to think of the hours I spent in the field watching Don Kenyon and Peter Richardson make merry at our expense. This accomplished pair were entirely dissimilar in style and technique. Don was a complete batsman, one of the most prolific and efficient players in the country for more than a decade. In contrast Peter was utilitarian, a lefthander with a penchant for the back foot. He had a small backlift and acquired most of his runs by unspectacular pushes, nudges and deflections on both sides of the wicket.

Seeing them together, one would unhesitatingly choose Don as the established international batsman and Peter as the competent county opener, yet the reverse applied. Don was one of the unlucky ones: quite simply, he was unable to transfer his expertise to the Test arena. In his 15 innings for England, apart from an 87 against South Africa, Don was totally unrecognizable as the Worcester run-machine. In contrast Peter, despite a limited range of strokes, enjoyed a most distinguished Test career. He thrived on the big occasion, possessed plenty of determination, was never worried when beaten by a ball and kept within his limitations.

Our August Bank holiday fixture at Worcester used to coincide with a large Conservative party fête, which was held on the Saturday on the adjoining school cricket ground. One year Diana Dors was scheduled to open it, but her train was delayed. For well over an hour, and at five-minute intervals, apologies were broadcast over a most efficient loudspeaker system. Eventually, the great lady arrived just as I was about to bowl. The applause was deafening and, though I was credited with the wicket, Miss Dors was really responsible for it.

Of the many games against Worcestershire, and I never missed any because Tests were not played during the Bank holidays, three stand out in my mind. The first was in 1950, when I arrived at the ground with the news that my wife had given birth to our first son, Kim. I received a generous ovation on going out to bat, celebrated with a distinctly frivolous fifty and drove home that night. In those days it took a long time, so it was well after midnight when I finally arrived.

The second was in 1953 at Chelmsford on a pitch which was as unpredictable as the game itself. If it had not rained the match could easily have ended in one day. I reckoned that 20 on that particular wicket would be an achievement and I regard my 75 as probably the best innings I ever played, certainly in county cricket.

The third game took place in 1963 at Leyton and provided a classic example of how collaboration between two captains (not allowed at that time) could rescue a match for players and spectators. The whole of the August Bank holiday Saturday was lost through bad weather, so that when Martin Horton, a strangely underrated allrounder, went out with me to toss up it had become a two-day match. We agreed that whoever batted first should receive 55 overs before declaring or being bowled out, and the side batting second should receive 50 overs.

Essex declared at 190 for one and Worcestershire then presented me with a slightly unusual captaincy problem. Barry Knight and Ken Preston were bowling so well on a pitch assisting seam that it was going to be difficult for me to reach my pledged target of overs. I solved the problem by bringing on Paddy Phelan and Robin Hobbs in conditions they would never normally have bowled on and the last wicket fell for 181 at stumps. Everybody had had an absorbing day's cricket!

The following day I declared our second innings closed at 210 for four. Essex eventually won the game by 31 runs with five minutes remaining, but for most of the chase Worcestershire had looked to be much better placed. Certainly nobody, least of all myself, expected their last four wickets to fall for nought at their final score of 188.

At the end of what had proved to be a very entertaining contest one of my committee members came up and said, in all seriousness, that we ought to revert to two-day matches because they provided more exciting cricket than the three-day ones. The game did illustrate what can be achieved by a good declaration. It has always been my belief that the essential factor in a contrived finish through a declaration or declarations is that both teams must consider it feasible to win the match. I reckoned that if a match finished in the last ten minutes, or ideally in the last over as indeed it did on numerous occasions, I had got the formula exactly right.

YORKSHIRE

I have a great love for Yorkshire, the people and their cricket. Outside my native Essex, my wife and I have more friends in Yorkshire than anywhere else. My affection goes back a long way and stems from a mutual understanding, appreciation and respect. As a player I found the Yorkshire crowd exceptionally generous, while I would have enjoyed playing for Yorkshire as their competitive streak combined with their success would have appealed. Also, we both detest bad cricket.

I batted and bowled against Yorkshire more than any other county. In addition to the annual two county fixtures they always came to Fenner's, and for twenty wonderful years I took part in the Scarborough Festival, when the three matches included the MCC v Yorkshire fixture.

It must surely have been a Yorkshireman who first remarked, 'Look after the pennies and the pounds will take care of themselves.' This does not mean that the average Yorkshireman is mean; he is merely careful. Money takes time and effort to accumulate, so it is therefore foolish to use it rashly. The Yorkshire attitude to cricket was summed up by the remark Len Hutton once made to a young Peter May who was just starting his international career: 'Remember, Peter, you don't play cricket for fun.'

This basic Yorkshire approach helps to explain that long running farce known as the Geoff Boycott Saga, which has done so much harm to the county and cost them so much money.

For more than seventy years Yorkshire were the most important and powerful county. Although there were occasional pretenders, when the likes of Lancashire, Surrey, Middlesex or Nottinghamshire would win the Championship, Yorkshire would always be near the top and playing hard, efficient cricket, while an England XI which did not contain several of their players was unthinkable.

Gradually cricket became a religion, with a God, obviously a Yorkshireman, who expected his batsmen to score runs prolifically and without too much southern frivolity, his bowlers 'to get 'em out and give n'owt', and his fielders to hold all their catches. As a result their cricket over the years has been sound, serious and successful.

You may have noticed the large number of Yorkshiremen who believe they are never wrong and incapable of making a mistake. This slightly blinkered view means that there will always be altercations in their dressing-room. I still treasure the bemused look on Jack Bailey's face – he was up at Oxford at the time and playing for Essex in the vacation – when he came back from a Benefit 'do' at Scarborough, having talked individually to the four main Yorkshire bowlers. He simply could not believe the jealousy which existed between that distinguished quartet.

Although it is desirable to have a happy atmosphere in any team, it is not essential providing the team is doing very well. Harmony becomes really important when everything is going wrong. This is something which Yorkshire have found difficult to understand, because until recently it was a situation they had never experienced.

In 1968 Yorkshire, under Brian Close, won the County Championship, which they had almost come to regard as theirs by right, for the last time. That year the committee, under the chairmanship of Brian Sellers, a former captain and an autocratic ruler, made the obvious mistake of refusing to give Ray Illingworth a three-year contract. Three years later Brian Close, not a great diplomat but a splendid captain and infinitely better than the majority of county skippers, was sacked. Geoff Boycott took over and remained in charge for eight years.

From that moment the Yorkshire decline accelerated and the appointments of Hampshire, Old, Illingworth (at over fifty) and Bairstow, all in quick succession, and the highly publicized battles among the committee, have not helped. However, it would be entirely wrong to suppose that the decline was entirely the fault of Geoff, whom I first bowled against at Clacton in 1963 on one of those deliciously green pitches. I had him caught behind off the outside edge, but I did notice that he played very straight and close to his body, so I was not surprised that he became one of the game's outstanding accumulators of runs and records, if not of batting bonus points. In his 23 seasons with the club he has headed their averages on 20 occasions; in the other three he was second. His first year as captain ended with an annual report which was described as the worst in the club's history 'from a playing and a financial point of view' but Geoff made over 2000 runs and finished with an average of over 100. This produced two views, which has been splitting the county ever since. Some felt that here was a great batsman in the true Yorkshire tradition, who had been let down as captain by the rest of the players. Others felt that the team would have done better under a leader who scored fewer runs but gave more of himself to the team.

Whatever the truth, Boycott must accept some of the blame for breaking up what was still, potentially, an above average side. He quickly lost Don Wilson, Richard Hutton and Phil Sharpe, while it was noticeable that none of the newcomers ever maintained their early promise. It also seemed to me that Geoff believed that his team was worse than it really was, that he could never afford to lose his wicket or everything would fold, which made him even more cautious.

The Yorkshire supporter, who had been brought up with the conviction that Yorkshire were the best club in the country, watched sadly as they struggled unimpressively in all forms of the game until 1983, when under Ray Illingworth they carried off the John Player League. Something was clearly wrong. Unquestionably the committee made several mistakes, while Boycott had at least produced runs in the quantity one expected from a true Yorkshire batsman.

It also has appeared to me that nobody took sufficient notice of the fact that their admirable policy of playing only Yorkshire-born cricketers had a serious handicap, especially as during Geoff's reign the best possible use was not made of the talent available. I have no doubt that if Clive Rice and Richard Hadlee had joined Yorkshire, and all their home matches had taken place at Trent Bridge, Yorkshire would certainly have won the County Championship on at least one occasion.

Although I did have the considerable satisfaction of making my maiden first-class century against them at Fenner's, throughout my career Yorkshire were very much my county's bogey team. Indeed, it was 1960 before I had the satisfaction of participating in an Essex victory. The reason they rolled us over so regularly was that they normally batted better, bowled with more accuracy and penetration, and were superior in the field. They also had the knack of staging a recovery after an early breakthrough, frequently Illingworth inspired – I saw Ray make three of his first four hundreds.

The Yorkshire batting line-up in the 1940s, 1950s and 1960s consisted of five or six class players, two or three useful middle-of-the-table merchants, and some tailenders who hit the ball very far when they middled it. Their finest batsman was Sir Leonard Hutton, an artist, and the most accomplished bad-wicket player since the war. If he had a weakness, it would be a slight vulnerability against off-spin and inswing, probably because of a pronounced initial forward movement, which, post-war, meant that he was never in a position to hook very fast bowling.

How did Hutton compare with Boycott? Len was a joy to watch, even when he was scoring slowly, because his technique was not only very good but also elegant. Geoff is a magnificent run-machine, but he lacks the beauty and grace of Len, while he has always looked in some danger of being hit by the sharply lifting short ball because he has difficulty in swaying out of line. Both were expert counters, which helped when they wanted the strike, but Len was a much better runner between the wickets than Geoff because he knew instinctively what constituted a perfectly safe run for himself and also for his partner. It was a lack of judgement about the second aspect which has resulted in Geoff having acquired so many run out notches on his bat.

Len was a natural fieldsman because he moved so well, initially in the covers but eventually as a highly competent slip. In contrast, and much to his credit, Geoff had to work very hard to turn himself into a good fieldsman, as indeed he did as a batsman, and made himself into an accomplished and very reliable performer away from the wicket. Len was an occasional legbreak bowler, rather too occasional some opposing batsmen felt, while Geoff was a steady purveyor of medium pace inswing who could be useful in limited-overs cricket.

It always seemed to me that Yorkshire never fully appreciated the talent of Willie Watson. It still amazes me that, with two Yorkshiremen on the selection committee, Vic Wilson, who was never more than a good county player with a marvellous pair of hands, was taken to Australia in 1954–55 ahead of Willie who had scored a century in every island in the Caribbean during the previous winter. If Willie had batted regularly for his county at one to four rather than five and six, I am sure he would have scored more runs and gained more caps.

Frank Lowson was a quiet, compact, stylish opener, but lacked the spark which divides the fine county cricketer from the genuine international. The same might also be said to have applied to the more spectacular Ken Taylor, Phil Sharpe, Doug Padgett and John Hampshire.

When I was batting against Yorkshire the one absolute certainty was that there would be no easy runs, because their bowlers were mean as well as being good. Since the war they have produced three world class operators – Fred Trueman, Johnny Wardle and Bob Appleyard – in addition to a number of good Test and county bowlers.

I am certain that nobody has had the doubtful distinction of facing Fred Trueman in first-class cricket more often than myself. Quite apart from two decades of Essex v Yorkshire fixtures, I was on the receiving end in two Scarborough Festival matches, as well as a host of Gents v Players fixtures at Lord's. I even opened the batting against him in one of the more pointless Test trials when he was appearing for the Rest. In addition, I have played for England and toured with him on many occasions and have been his captain. I was even at the other end while he slogged a rare century. Also, I have worked with him for many years on Test Match Special. All of which means that I know the man, not just the legend.

My first memories of Fred are as a young, aggressive, volatile fast bowler with a magnificent body action. He routed the wretched Indians in 1952 by sheer pace and immediately became not just another fast bowler, but also a personality, who has been capturing wickets and headlines ever since. His peak as a bowler was between 1958 and 1964. He had lost a little of his pace, but had become the perfect attacking machine and, like good wine, he improved with age. On all pitches and in all conditions, it is doubtful whether there has ever been a more complete fast bowler. He had fire, control, the ability to move the ball, a glorious body action, limitless confidence in his own ability and a vivid imagination. He believed he was capable of bowling anybody out and that he was always doing something with the ball.

Throughout his Yorkshire career Fred was handicapped by seldom receiving adequate support at the other end. This inevitably resulted in his frequently being overbowled. Fortunately a powerful physique, combined with stamina, plus that glorious action enabled him to send down over 1000 overs each summer and pick up well over 100 wickets in the process.

I enjoyed batting against Fred. Quite apart from the numerous asides with which we invariably greeted each other, there was always the challenge of trying to make runs against a great bowler. Survival was my initial objective and I would spend most of the first few overs attempting to negotiate the sharply lifting ball from a half-cock position with my weight on my front foot and hoping that in his efforts to produce the yorker Fred would slightly overpitch and give me the opportunity to push him through the covers.

I used to reckon on picking most of Fred's bouncers before he released the ball, but this was not always sufficient as I discovered on a very fast pitch at Leyton. The selectors had decided that Fred was no longer the best fast bowler in England, a view with which Fred did not agree. He was determined to show everybody that he was still the quickest around, not that we needed any convincing. I arrived at the crease early with two of my batsmen back in the pavilion, while a third, Roger Wrightson – who had hooked Fred to the boundary on a slow pitch earlier in the season and had lost most of his teeth and his wicket trying to repeat the shot at Leyton – was on his way to hospital. It was distinctly lively out in the middle with Fred on the rampage and the odd tooth and a little blood still about, but it eventually passed. Just before lunch Fred was brought back for his second spell and soon produced a bouncer. I ducked, made the mistake of taking my eye off the ball before I knew how high it would rise, and was 'sweded'. Remembering that old piece of boxing advice 'always take a reasonably long count', which, incidentally, ensured that there could not possibly be another over before the interval, I stayed down. This allowed Fred to come up and say, 'Sorry, Trev, old son, there are many more I'd rather have hit than thee', leaving me wondering which particular selector he had in mind.

Some of my fondest memories of Fred have only a slight cricket connection, like a protracted pub crawl by speedboat in the Caribbean; listening to Fred holding forth on swing bowling with the aid of an orange to an American, who had the temerity to ask him if bowlers could swerve the ball; and pushing Fred into a swimming pool in Australia when he was fully clothed and causing a certain amount of havoc with the hose which was still in his hand when he reappeared above the water!

Johnny Wardle was the most complete spin bowler I have encountered. For Yorkshire he was employed in the traditional role of slow left-arm spinner, of whom they have produced so many great ones, a match winner on a 'turner' and a stock bowler on a plumb pitch. In Yorkshire they were inclined to compare him unfavourably with Verity and Rhodes. His bent arm behind his action was not beautiful and, to make matters worse, the England selectors usually chose Tony Lock, despite that question mark about the legitimacy of his bowling. Johnny was sensitive to any criticism and resented the fact that so many Yorkshire fans and former players did not appreciate his bowling as much as he believed they should, while he strongly objected to Tony being selected ahead of him.

What made Johnny special was that he gradually developed into a magnificent Chinaman and googly bowler, who, for about three years, was probably the best in the world. Not only did he spin the ball, but his background of tight cricket meant that he bowled far fewer loose deliveries than most wrist-spinners. He also had the ability to shut up an end, or at the very least to make it extremely difficult to score runs, by bowling orthodox left-arm spin into the rough from over the wicket.

Although an expert comedian on the field, with the timing which meant that he never overdid an act, Johnny was not a naturally funny man and his momentous row with the Yorkshire committee came as no surprise. Their relationship with their players over the years has not only been very poor, but has cost them dearly. The club may be more important than the most important player, but it was unwise to cast aside as many Yorkshire players as they have done since the war and still expect to maintain standards.

Bob Appleyard was an unusual bowler and for a few seasons a truly great one. He began his first-class career as a lively inswing bowler with a high action and developed into what I always considered to be more of an off-cutter than off-spinner. His height, action and pace meant that he was able to make the ball bounce. He was at his most effective from over the wicket and was very accurate.

On a wet pitch Bob could be utterly devastating. I have always thought that during his twelve for 43 (17–8–17–6 and 23·4–10–26–6) against Essex at Bradford in 1951 he came as close to being unplayable as anybody I have faced. He had only two men on the off side, and presumably would have been even more formidable these days, when a batsman cannot risk padding away outside the off stump.

What made Bob so unusual, and so difficult, was that though he was quick through the air and lacked flight in the normal sense, he did make the ball dip late. I batted against him on numerous occasions in the nets in Australia and was fascinated by the way he was able to send down so many deliveries which I was convinced were half-volleys, but never were.

Brian Sellers, captain from 1933 to 1947, was the most colourful of the Yorkshire captains that I encountered. He had a forceful personality even by his county's standards and possessed a ribald sense of humour, but never fully appreciated the extent of the social revolution in cricket after the war.

Essex met Yorkshire in the late 1940s, before their new brigade of players had really established themselves, and, aided by the Southend whelks, we were able to cause them several problems, not the least being that Don Brennan was confined to bed and unable to keep wicket. Brian nobly took over behind the stumps. The Yorkshire bowling was unusually wayward and, assisted by 57 byes, Essex headed for a more than presentable total. I was batting with Ray Smith during these proceedings, which were not altogether to Brian's taste. While standing back to Alex Coxon, the Yorkshire skipper suddenly rose from his rather majestic and somewhat uncomfortable crouch, raised one imperious gloved hand as Alex was about to bowl, walked up to Ray and asked him if he had ever scored a hundred. On being told no, the great man announced to the world in general that he would never have a better bloody chance and then allowed play to continue.

Norman Yardley, who took over from Brian, was an entirely different character, quieter and a far more accomplished cricketer. I thought him an outstanding tactician and an expert on wicket behaviour. He was unquestionably one of the best captains I have ever played with or against. It has been said that he was too nice to lead Yorkshire, but I cannot think of anybody I have preferred playing under.

My first memory of Brian Close was when, aged only 17, he twice smote leg-breaks from Peter Smith on top of the football stand at Headingley. I was immediately convinced that here was somebody who was destined to become a great cricketer, because he possessed so much power and natural talent. Somehow it never completely materialized. He had the ability to be an England regular but played in only 22 Tests, scoring 887 runs and taking 18 wickets. He will be best remembered as a very forthright, completely fearless, sometimes inspired, very confident – not always justified – demanding and ruthless captain of Yorkshire, Somerset and England.

As a result, the manner of his departure from Yorkshire was rather odd. I was covering a football international at Wembley and had read that Brian had been sacked in the *Evening Standard*. I bumped into Brian in the press box after the match, immediately gave him my sympathy and asked him when he had first known about the decision. I was more than surprised to learn that he had seen his chairman that morning and had been given two hours to decide whether he wanted to resign or be fired. It did seem an unhappy way to terminate the career of one of Yorkshire's major personalities.

How good an allrounder was Ray Illingworth? He was certainly good enough to have held a place in any county side as either a batsman or a bowler. At international level he was far superior against pace bowling than many who have been picked purely as batsmen; while as a bowler, although clearly not in the same class as Jim Laker or Lance Gibbs, and probably a form lower than Fred Titmus or David Allen, he was a highly professional off-spinner.

I never enjoyed batting against Ray because he was so frugal. I was not too keen to bowl at him either as he negotiated seam so well. He was a practical, thinking cricketer who seldom bubbled but could be relied upon to turn in the figures. An intelligent Yorkshire professional, Ray knew rather more about field placings, tactics and pitches than most England captains.

He proved himself to be an effective, unspectacular captain of England and he could have done likewise for Yorkshire if they had not made the blunder of allowing him to leave the county. He was still an allrounder of international calibre when he joined Leicestershire and was with them when he brought the Ashes home – the same year, incidentally, as the Boycott affair began. He was eventually appointed Yorkshire skipper when fifty, which was far too late, but the fact that under his command, with possibly the weakest team in their entire history, they still won the John Player League, does suggest that an earlier appointment might have been very profitable.

My most satisfying game against Yorkshire was at Headingley in 1960 on what could be best described as a slow green-top, the type of wicket on which the ball deviated off the seam throughout the entire game, but not quickly. Although runs could be acquired, they were liable to take time and effort, and batsmen were safer on the front foot. In other words, it was a pitch ideally suited to both my batting and bowling.

Doug Insole won the toss and we grafted our way to a laborious 180. It was a slow, painful exercise which was, understandably, not exactly appreciated by the spectators on that overcast Saturday, but I was well satisfied in the circumstances with my undefeated 60.

Yorkshire found batting even more difficult and were all out for 86. I opened our attack with Barry Knight, bowled throughout their innings and finished with seven for 40 in 28 overs, which included one that came back and found a way in between Brian Close's bat and pad, just when he was beginning to cause trouble.

We managed to muster 200 in our second innings, which included a lively 42 from Brian Taylor, a spectacular 42 from Roy Ralph, including four sixes, and a watchful 46 from myself. I cannot remember Brian Close bowling seam, as distinct from spin, more effectively.

The pitch had eased out a little by the Tuesday and Yorkshire reached a creditable 237, which left us the winners by 57 and I was well satisfied with my five for 61 in 33 overs. Looking back on 1960 I could claim to have had a highly satisfactory summer, with 1639 runs for an average of 39 and 117 wickets at 20, but never played in a Test. The allrounder spot in the England XI had gone to Peter Walker, who scored 900 runs with a top score of 68 and an average of 16, while his 57 wickets cost 29 each, which, despite his brilliant fielding, did cause a wry smile.

WON'T YOU COME HOME, BILL BAILEY

Frequently changed to 'Won't you go home, Trev Bailey' by spectators at home Tests.

HEADINGLEY

You never forget your first Test match because it marks a key stage in the career of any cricketer. Although you may never be chosen again, at least you have achieved the supreme goal of representing your country.

I was enjoying easily my best first-class season as for the first year I was a full-time cricketer, yet my selection in June 1949 for the First Test against New Zealand at Headingley came as something of a surprise. When I joined my England colleagues for the first time I felt rather like a new boy on his first day at school. Although I had played against them, I did not know them at all well and felt rather shy. In fact, I never felt fully at home in the England team until I had toured, despite the considerable efforts of my first captain, George Mann, to put me completely at my ease. It did not worry me, having always been reasonably self sufficient and knowing exactly what I wanted to achieve both at batting and bowling, but I did miss the easy camaraderie which was to come later.

The first thing to remember about my first Test was that it only lasted three days and 1949 was one of those summers when rain was rare. This meant we never had the opportunity to bowl the opposition out on a turning wicket. The Kiwis had a strong batting line-up and were determined to show what everybody, apart from MCC, already knew: that it was stupid to invite a team to come all that distance to take part in four consecutive and inevitable draws.

I was brought into the England team as an opening bowler to partner Alec Bedser and had every reason to be well pleased with

144

capturing six wickets in the Kiwis' first innings, including most of their frontline batsmen. However, what I remember most clearly was my somewhat unusual introduction to Harrogate, which explains why geography was never one of my stronger subjects.

As it was my first Test and might well be my last, Greta decided to come to the match, which turned out for both of us to be the commencement of a long and happy association with the headquarters of Yorkshire cricket. On the Sunday, Greta and I went out for a walk around Leeds, when I experienced a particularly vicious attack of hay fever by the side of a bus stop. At that moment up drew a bus marked Harrogate. My subconscious shouted seaside, less pollen and relief so we jumped onboard. When we arrived I turned to Greta who was less convinced that we had arrived at the seaside, and stated that all we needed to do was follow the children carrying buckets and spades to the beach. I am still looking for them.

Of my six Tests at Headingley, my most interesting was the Fourth against the Australians in 1953, in which we were outplayed, gave our worst performance of the summer and were distinctly fortunate to escape with a draw which enabled us to go into the final Test all square with the Ashes still at stake. In our defence, it is sometimes forgotten that we were handicapped by five injuries. Both teams were chosen with batting strength the main priority. We left out Brian Statham on a pitch which assisted pace, while Australia chose a four-man seam attack plus Richie Benaud, and had Lindwall coming in at 10 and Langley at 11.

The most dramatic moment was undoubtedly when Len Hutton, in front of his own crowd, was bowled second ball of the match by Ray Lindwall. It produced a gasp of incredulity louder than a clap of thunder. Later in our first innings I was not only run out but also, in my frantic dive for safety, landed so heavily on my left knee that it came up like a balloon. I was to become part of an unintentionally hilarious newsreel sequence showing Reg Simpson walking back to the pavilion with a damaged arm; Willie Watson limping off painfully, carrying his pad, having been lbw to a direct hit on his foot; and finally me hobbling back firmly convinced that I would be unable to bowl on the second day. This was rather serious as it was plainly a seamer's wicket and without me our attack consisted of Alec Bedser and two spinners.

As a result of intense treatment I found I could bowl off a short run. If we had held our catches we would have reduced their total by about a hundred runs, nonetheless I was well satisfied with my three wickets in 22 overs as I was still in some pain. During the day Bill Edrich was twice hit on his thumb in the slips and went to hospital, but fortunately discovered that it was only badly bruised, not broken. Our casualty list had now reached four and it was claimed that the only way to enter Headingley on the packed Saturday was to carry a case and report as one of the army of substitutes summoned to the aid of our walking wounded.

The fourth day was interrupted by rain, which made the pitch lively. I went to the crease to join Denis Compton, who had become our fifth casualty after being hit unpleasantly on the back of his hand, but at that stage I was more worried about lasting until the morrow than about Denis, who at that time did not seem especially inconvenienced.

I arrived at the ground for the final day reasonably confident that we would save the game, even though we were only 78 runs on and had five wickets down. It was then that I learned that Denis was unable to hold a bat and was having pain-killing injections in his injured hand. As a result I went to the wicket with Godfrey Evans, who did not last long, and I was even more concerned when, instead of Denis, Jim Laker joined me. I need not have worried because it was one of Jim's not-all-that-frequent good days with the bat, when he either hit the ball in the middle or missed it entirely. Having existed for some 15 minutes, Jim began to play some very handsome strokes while I, still uncertain about the Compton hand, simply dropped anchor. At 1.28 I used up the one appeal against the light allowed per session to make absolutely sure it was the last over before lunch, even though the sun has seldom shone more brightly over Leeds.

Soon after the interval, Jim departed for 48 off a ball which lifted sharply and I was at last joined by Denis who had had three pain-killing injections and managed to last for an important 25 minutes, during which we had two classic examples of how an umpiring decision can cause discontent. On the first occasion, Denis steered a ball down to Hole at slip and, not being certain whether the catch had been taken cleanly, stood his ground. As the non-striker, I was probably as well placed as the umpire, Frank Lee, to see what had happened and I certainly would not have liked to have given the decision. I thought Frank was entirely right to consult his colleague, Frank Chester, who ruled in favour of the batsman. The next ball,

Lindwall appealed for a leg-side catch by the keeper. I did not think that Denis had touched it, but by now the Australians were convinced they were playing the umpires as well as England. Oddly, this belief increased rather than decreased when Denis was adjudged lbw shortly after. The first question they asked me was whether I thought it was a conciliatory gesture.

In partnerships with Bedser and then Lock, our long-drawn-out innings continued until eventually I was caught and we came off for tea. By then we thought a draw was ours as we were convinced the Australians were never going to score 177 in just under two hours, about 34 overs, on a pitch which was certainly far from perfect. At least, that is what we thought at the time.

It was then that Len Hutton made one of his rare tactical mistakes. In the hope of causing another Australian collapse like the one at Old Trafford, and perhaps even a sensational victory, he forgot just how quickly runs can come when using an ultra-attacking field to bowling which is below standard. The outcome was that he never attempted to shut up the game until it was almost too late. Even more curious was that Australia certainly were not thinking in terms of victory, which they so nearly achieved, when they commenced their second innings. It was England's own fault that we so nearly allowed them to snatch a remarkable win and thus retain the Ashes.

Alec Bedser and Tony Lock opened our attack. Despite a good first over from Alec it cost six runs and then Tony, who was unable to find either his length or his line, went for 14. It is true that Hassett was bowled in Tony's second over, but by then 27 were on the board in under four overs. Arthur Morris and Graeme Hole continued the assault, then Jim Laker had the former stumped for a brilliant 38. The arrival of Neil Harvey only served to increase the tempo so that the hundred came up in the hour, which left 72 required in 50 minutes, which was very definitely on.

Another seven runs came off Alec's next over, but he had Harvey lbw with his last ball. This gave us a moment's respite to think how to stop, or at least slow down, their break-neck gallop. I suggested that we might possibly save the match if I took over from Tony and concentrated on denial by bowling on and outside the leg stump with six men on the leg-side and three on the off – a fine third man for the snick, a short square cover to block the single, and a wide mid-off. Not only did this make scoring difficult, but it also took me much longer to complete an over (the Law stipulating 20 overs in the last hour had not yet been introduced into the game or we would certainly have lost). As it was I sent down six overs for nine runs and took one wicket: when stumps were drawn, Australia were still 30 runs short with six wickets in hand.

For the second time that day I received warm applause from the Headingley crowd. It was the only time I have had plaudits from a crowd for steady stone-walling and purely defensive bowling.

Although in recent years the Headingley pitch has proved very helpful to seam bowlers, it can be ideal for batting and the outfield very fast. These were the conditions which prevailed against South Africa in 1951, when no play on the final day was a blessing to bowlers because there was no chance of a result. The game is best remembered because Eric Rowan scored 236, Hutton made a century with the style his home crowd expected and Peter May celebrated his debut for England with 138 runs of charm and composure. What is quite rightly forgotten is that I played what was probably my gayest innings for England. I had great fun during a most unlikely last-wicket partnership of 60 with Malcolm Hilton which ended with my trying to hit a six and holing out, somewhat uncharacteristically, at deep mid-wicket for 95.

LORD'S

Lord's has always been my favourite Test ground. First, it has usually been lucky for me, in that if I did not score runs I normally grabbed a few wickets, or vice versa. Second, a Lord's Test is not just another international match, it is the major cricketing occasion of the summer and an annual reunion for former players. Third, the Lord's Test is the best attended of all Tests in England and I have always thrived on a big audience – the bigger the better. Finally, Lord's is the headquarters of the game and over two centuries has gradually built up its own very special atmosphere.

My first of seven Lord's Tests was against New Zealand in 1949 and, in view of my later reputation, it is, perhaps, justifiable to quote what *Wisden* had to say about that particular innings. I went in at number seven with the score 112 for five to partner Denis Compton, when the pitch was starting to ease and Cowie had tired.

The change in England's fortunes came when Bailey joined

Compton. Fortunate to receive two loose balls down the legside which he turned for four apiece immediately he went in, Bailey showed complete confidence and for a long time he over-shadowed Compton. Bailey continued to punish anything loose, mainly by going down on one knee and sweeping the ball hard to the square-leg boundary. Ten 4's came in his first fifty made in sixty-seven minutes. With his side in danger, Compton concentrated on wearing down the attack, and not until England were out of trouble did he take the slightest risk. Then he brought into play his wide range of strokes and scored much faster than his partner. Bailey was unlucky to miss his first Test hundred, for which, with only seven wanted, he cut a ball on to the wicket-keeper's foot, whence it rebounded into the hands of second slip. His splendid innings lasted for two and a half hours and contained sixteen fours.

In contrast, my bowling was not only unsuccessful but also well below international standard. In 33 unimpressive overs I failed to take a wicket – indeed, seldom looked like taking one – and conceded 136 runs. Martin Donnelly, who made a brilliant double-century, displayed, not for the first nor the last time, an understandable partiality for my bowling as I had not yet acquired sufficient control.

My most worrying Lord's Test was against South Africa in 1955, in which Fred Titmus and Peter Heine made their international debuts. Peter May captained England at Lord's for the first time and we won by 71 runs, despite having been bowled out in our first innings for 133. Brian Statham did the damage, bowling unchanged for 29 consecutive overs and taking seven for 39. My personal worry had nothing to do with the cricket.

As usual I had driven up from my Westcliff home. We had won the toss, decided to bat, and found, as so often happens at Lord's, that the pitch was distinctively lively. We had lost a number of wickets and I was padded up when Billy Griffith, Secretary of MCC, came into our dressing-room at about one o'clock and asked me to take a phone call from my wife.

Greta would never have phoned me during a Test unless something was very wrong. My immediate reaction was that her mother had died, so I was totally unprepared when she informed me that Kim, my eldest son, had been knocked down outside our house when he had run across the road to his grandfather from behind a parked car. Greta had picked him up out of the gutter. The car driver, who had no chance to avoid him, happened to be a specialist and took him straight to the hospital where the injuries turned out not to be serious – indeed, he came home the following day.

The reason for the phone call was that Greta realized that somebody at the hospital would have tipped off the local paper, who in turn would have phoned the London Evenings. This meant that I would have heard about the accident in the worst possible way. Greta assured me that there was no point in my returning until close of play, as Kim was in no danger and there was nothing I could do.

Upset and shaken by the unexpected news, I had the added problem of informing my mother, who was at the match, before the placards shouting 'Son of Test Cricketer at Lord's Knocked Down by Car' appeared in the ground. It was, by now, the luncheon interval. When playing cricket I never drank anything but soft drinks at lunch when batting and either a half of bitter or a pint of ginger beer shandy when bowling. On this occasion I broke all the rules and swallowed four brandies. It was one of the few occasions I have gone to the crease unable to concentrate and I did not last long.

When I arrived home I immediately went with Greta to see Kim who was conscious, but drowsy, in the children's ward. What did surprise me was the request of a photographer outside the hospital when I was about to leave. He wanted to take a picture of my son with me inside the children's ward at 8.30 p.m.

My best remembered Lord's Test, but not my best Test, was against the Australians in 1953. It caught the imagination of the general public and because of the situation it gained a fame which was in excess of what it deserved and became something of a legend. It is interesting to note that the length of my stand with Willie Watson has also been greatly exaggerated. What really happened, and why all the fuss?

This Test was a delicately balanced affair throughout and illustrates the fascination the game at this level can provide. For five days, fortune continually swung from side to side – collapse and rally, fine batting, bowling and fielding. Australia's 346 and 368 and England's 372 meant that we required 343 for victory when we commenced our second innings on the fourth day with an hour to go.

It had been decided that if a wicket fell after six o'clock I should take on the role of nightwatchman. This turned out to be somewhat ironic in retrospect as I found myself padded up from six o'clock onwards in my normal position as number six. Our first three wickets fell for only 12 runs and I watched with apprehension as Compton and Watson negotiated an uncomfortable half hour, in which the latter might have been caught at leg slip off Ring. Len Hutton could not hide his disappointment as he unbuckled his pads in the dressing-room, knowing that with three of his best batsmen back in the pavilion our chances of saving, let alone winning the match, were remote, while the chances of our gaining two wins from the next three meetings against opponents who were certainly as good if not better than ourselves was fairly non-existent.

On the final day I travelled up to London with Greta by train and read various newspapers which had all written us off. This rather rankled. It was not that I anticipated the eventual outcome, but with Denis and Willie still at the crease I felt we ought to make them fight hard, even though the pitch was taking spin and Brown, Evans, Wardle and Statham were essentially attacking batsmen and unlikely to remain too long.

After a few anxious moments, Denis and Willie settled down and it came as something of a surprise when the former was lbw to what might be described as a genuine shooter.

When I joined Willie my sole objective was still to be there at lunch. My approach was to assume that every ball was potentially lethal and had to be stopped. Having survived for about half an hour, Willie and I had a short conference and decided that, without making it obvious, I would take as much of the leg-spin as possible, because the rough was making things very difficult outside his off stump for my left-handed partner. At lunch Willie had reached his half-century and I was in double figures, so we returned to the pavilion reasonably satisfied, though realizing that there was a very long way to go and that the most difficult time was likely to be mid-afternoon when Lindwall and Miller would take the new ball.

In the dressing-room I ate my normal hearty lunch which included some of my partner's, who did not believe in eating during an innings. Much to our surprise and delight, Johnston and Davidson shared the attack on the resumption of play, which gave us the opportunity to become reaccustomed to pace bowling before the all-out assault just before three o'clock. Benaud and Johnston bowled cutters for a few overs before the new ball was taken, but by this time we had had a dress rehearsal and had settled back into the groove.

It was noticeable that by three o'clock the crowd and the tension had increased. This was the crucial period and we were very happy when we returned to the pavilion for tea with the scoreboard reading 183 for four. For the first time I really believed that we could avoid defeat and I have seldom enjoyed a cup of tea quite so much. At no stage during that day did we ever consider going for the win and at no time was it necessary for Hassett to set run-saving fields. Both of us concentrated on defence, but like most batsmen gratefully accepted any runs which were available. Willie also happened to be a very fine runner between the wickets, a natural mover who never seemed to be hurrying but covered the ground far faster than most people, which meant we picked up plenty of singles.

In the final session, Hassett switched his bowlers around. Willie completed a splendid century and was eventually caught off Doug Ring, whom we considered the most dangerous bowler and probably should have been used more. The time was 5.50, the total 236 for five, when I was joined by Freddie Brown. We decided that if Ray Lindwall was brought back as we expected, I should take as much of him as possible. Instead Hassett decided on spin from both ends, possibly because the spinners bowled their overs more quickly and the days of 20 overs in the final hour had not yet been introduced. At six o'clock I attempted a cover slash off Benaud, in the circumstances a stupid shot, and was caught out for 71. With only half an hour to go we should, by this time, have saved the game without difficulty, but those last 30 minutes seemed to last for hours, especially as Freddie and Godfrey Evans had decided quite correctly that their best chance was to play their shots.

When Greta and I reached Westcliff, we found we had been sent some champagne and with the help of a couple of friends we celebrated quietly and effectively what had definitely been a day to remember.

In terms of allround value, my next Test at Lord's against Australia was far superior to my performance in 1953, but nobody remembers it, while my stand with Willie Watson caught the imagination and has gone down in cricket history. This was due to a number of reasons: Australia won by 185 runs because we failed with the bat on two occasions, subsequent performances by Laker, and to a lesser degree Lock, were to dwarf everything else in the series, and later the Australians were partially to disintegrate as a side. Nevertheless, at Lord's I achieved more than was normally expected of me as the allrounder in a team which contained five specialist batsmen, a wicketkeeper and four specialist bowlers. In the Australian first innings of 285 I took two wickets (McDonald, their top scorer, and Harvey) and held two catches off Laker in the leg trap. I was second highest scorer in our first innings of 171, then took four wickets in their second innings and had the satisfaction of catching Harvey at leg slip off Fred Trueman, which was certainly one of the five best catches I have ever taken. On the final day I joined Peter May with the total at 91 for four. Although there was neither the time nor the ability to make the 372 required to win, there was just a faint hope that we might hold out for another draw, but it was not to be and I was caught just before lunch for 18.

By the mid-1950s, Lord's had acquired a reputation for helping seam bowlers and it was noticeable that Middlesex finished most of their home matches. In these circumstances the selection of the West Indies side for the 1957 Lord's Test made no sense at the time, and still does not. They went into that match with only one pace bowler, Gilchrist, had Frank Worrell at just above medium sharing the new ball, and included four spinners – Ramadhin, Valentine, Smith and Sobers – plus Goddard at medium pace. In sharp contrast, England chose a strong batting line-up, three seamers plus Wardle, plus Close who never even bowled.

Selectors have often made mistakes, especially when they have plenty of players to choose from – it is never easy to compare the form displayed by different players in different teams. However, when selectors on tour blunder in this fashion it is much harder to understand, although it does happen. It puts me in mind of that classic England blunder in Australia in 1962–63 at Sydney, when England with three spinners available included only Fred Titmus, who took seven wickets, while Bob Simpson, not the most devastating slow bowler, took five wickets for Australia. As a result of this misreading of the pitch by the selectors, England lost a match they could have won.

Back at Lord's, we beat a strong West Indies batting side, which included the three Ws and had Smith coming in at seven, by an innings. They managed only 127 at their first attempt and I had the satisfaction of picking up seven wickets for 44. We amassed 424, of which my contribution was exactly one. Thanks largely to a magnificent 90 from Everton Weekes, who was hampered by a broken finger, the tourists did better in their second innings but I felt more than satisfied with four wickets, including those of Walcott, Weekes and Sobers. I have always liked Lord's, though never to quite the extent I did on that occasion.

OLD TRAFFORD

My most unforgettable Old Trafford Test has to be the one against Australia in 1956, not because I had a particularly good match (20 out of a total of 459 and match figures of 24–11–45–0) but because Jim Laker took 19 wickets, a feat which will, in my opinion, never be equalled, let alone surpassed. This is exactly what I said to Peter Richardson when we came off the field at the end of the game having won by an innings and 170 runs.

England won the toss on a pitch without pace, which turned appreciably on the first day. In fact, one might have said it had been especially designed for Tony Lock, whose pace through the air would compensate for the slowness of the wicket. The Australians realized before lunch on the opening morning that on a wicket of this nature they were in serious trouble. Keith Miller did not even bother to remove his sweater to bowl, while Johnson and Benaud, never a particularly effective bowler in England, sent down a total of 94 overs between them as we cruised comfortably to 459.

Apart from their opening pair, McDonald and Burke, who had the advantage of starting when the pitch had been temporarily calmed by the roller, Australia batted very indifferently on a difficult, but far from impossible, pitch. Essex would have expected to make at least 180 against the Surrey spinners and would have considered being all out for 84 after being 48 for nought as absurd. I would rate the 89 McDonald scored in their second innings as one of the best innings he ever played, again demonstrating that some of his colleagues surrendered rather tamely.

I have always maintained that the most remarkable feature of the whole affair was not so much that Jim should capture 19 wickets, but that Tony, in even more overs, should take only one. The answer was that Tony tried too hard and bowled too fast, while Jim just exploited the conditions superbly.

My most exciting of six Tests at Old Trafford was against South Africa in 1955. It took place in continual sunshine, contained centuries from Compton, May, Waite and McGlew, plus a highly improbable one from Winslow, some fine bowling, remarkable recoveries, and ended with South Africa just scrambling home by three wickets on the last day with only nine balls remaining. For sustained excitement and swiftly changing situations, it was probably the finest Test in which I took part.

We were disappointed to make only 284 in our first innings, despite 158 from Compton, but I was well content with a second-highest score of 44. South Africa started with a hundred partnership, but later McGlew was forced to retire with a damaged hand when 77. The tourists collapsed and then recovered as a result of a sound hundred from Waite, a spectacular one from Winslow, and an undefeated one from McGlew, who returned at 457 for seven. My one wicket cost me 102 runs in 37 overs.

Faced with a deficit of 237, we could hardly have had a worse start to our innings when our opening pair, Kenyon and Graveney, were back in the pavilion with only 2 on the board but May, Compton and Cowdrey all played well. Rather surprisingly, Lock was sent in at six and I went to the crease at the fall of the fifth wicket with 311 on the board. Things then began to go wrong as Titmus, Tyson and Bedser all departed too quickly. With nine wickets down I was joined by Godfrey Evans, who had fractured a little finger in his right hand. This did not prevent him hitting 36 runs in our last-wicket partnership of 48 which almost saved, and might have won, the match. As it was, South Africa, not without many alarms, just managed to reach the 145 they required for victory, which was in no small way due to a dashing 50 from Roy McLean.

My best Test at Old Trafford was the First Test against the West Indies in 1950. It was the only time England beat them that summer and took place on a 'beach', which turned square on the first morning. Perhaps the most perfect example of how this pitch, which the groundsman had not watered on the specific instructions of the Lancashire Committee, behaved occurred in the West Indies' first innings. Eric Hollies, a genuine slow bowler and never a big spinner, pitched a ball on off stump on a length to which the batsman played forward defensively. It easily beat the bat and Bill Edrich, though not the tallest of men, still had to take it high above his head at first slip.

Before the game commenced, it was obvious that the wicket would favour spin. John Goddard picked only Johnson of his three pace bowlers and England left out Bedser, which seemed to be peculiar at the time and even more peculiar in retrospect because Alec's cutter in those conditions would have been lethal. As it was, the respective opening attacks were the most amicable I have seen in any Test in which I played. The West Indies opened with Johnson and Gomez and England opened with Edrich, who by then was no more than an occasional slinger whose 16 wickets for Middlesex that summer cost over 42 apiece, and myself. For the only time in my career I was having serious problems with my run-up. It took me about two weeks to solve them and I doubt if I have ever bowled worse than in that match. Fortunately it did not matter, as Hollies, Laker and Berry did the necessary and we won, taking into account the vagaries of the wicket, by the considerable margin of 202 runs.

On winning the toss Norman Yardley decided to bat. I was number seven on the scorecard, but found myself walking out to bat on the first morning with the score 83 for four as Len Hutton had been hit on the hand at 22 and had retired hurt. Passing Frank Chester on my way to the crease, he wished me luck and I remarked that it was exactly the same as batting for Essex. Five runs later I was joined by Godfrey Evans for what was the most unlikely, and at the same time valuable, partnership in which I have ever been involved.

It was the first time that Godfrey and I had encountered 'Those two little pals of mine, Ramadhin and Valentine' who were to mesmerize England that summer on beautiful batting pitches. But they could hardly have asked for anything more helpful than this one at Manchester. Alf Valentine regularly pitched the ball around middle and it missed the off stump; while in addition to the 'Ram's' off-breaks biting and turning sharply, there was the added problem of not being able to pick with any certainty his finger-spun leg-break. In other words, nobody would have fancied our chances of putting on 50, let alone 161, a new record sixth-wicket partnership against the West Indies. I always relished batting on difficult pitches as I possessed a sound defence and a technique which allowed me to adjust, so I reckoned that I was better equipped to cope than many more accomplished players. But Godfrey was essentially an attacking batsman, whose favourite stroke was a shovel shot with plenty of right hand which sent the ball out in the midwicket area – certainly not the person one would expect to make a century (his maiden century in first-class cricket) in two hours 20 minutes against Valentine and Ramadhin on a dirt track.

When Godfrey eventually departed I was joined by Len, who demonstrated how to play on a very bad wicket with one hand, which fascinated me. However, after Len was out our tail failed to oblige and I was left without partners with 82 runs to my credit.

In our second innings I managed to exist for quite a long spell before being run out for 33, while we amassed a total which left our opponents the hopeless task of making 386. The real surprise was that Bob Berry and Eric Hollies proved infinitely more effective than Jim Laker, who was to be so devastating against Australia a few years later at the same venue, but on what was an easier pitch!

EDGBASTON

What do batsmen do in the dressing-room? There is no hard-and-fast rule and it varies from player to player and club to club. I would watch the cricket in the middle on four basic occasions. First, when I had not seen a bowler, or bowlers, before. Second, when an exhilarating strokemaker was in full cry. Third, when the game was in an exciting position. Finally, prior to when I went in to bat myself. I wanted to know exactly what was happening and to be geared up to go to the crease immediately a wicket fell, with my bat, a piece of chiropody felt with a hole cut in the middle which I stuck on my right hand between my first finger and thumb to reduce the jarring of the bat handle, and a piece of gum which I popped into my mouth before leaving the pavilion. I always hoped it would act as a magic potion, but it never did.

The only time this approach did not work was in the second innings of the First Test against the West Indies at Edgbaston in 1957. In the first innings we had allowed ourselves to be bowled out for 186 on a beautiful batting pitch by Sonny Ramadhin who took seven for 49 and they had replied with 474, which meant that we needed to bat well and for a very long time to save the match. I was not overoptimistic when I padded up with our score 113 for three. Doug Insole had been bowled for nought and Colin Cowdrey, our last recognized mainline batsman, joined Peter May. Everything suggested that I would not have to wait too long and I watched the first session with interest and a certain amount of trepidation. However, by the fourth I had begun to feel the strain. Eventually Peter (285 not out) and Colin (154) put on 411 runs, the 'little Ram' sent down 98 overs, which had an adverse effect on his bowling for the rest of the series, and Colin demonstrated how effective the front pad could be against an off-spinner bowling over the wicket and pitching just outside the off stump, though West Indies still swear that at least five of the eight hundred or so appeals made must have been out. By the end of their enormous partnership I was drained and when the wicket did eventually fall Godfrey Evans, correctly, went to the wicket. By that time not only had we saved the match, but we had also put ourselves in a position where we might even have snatched an impossible victory. As it is, the match was drawn with the West Indies 72 for seven.

In the 1950s Birmingham had not completely established itself as a permanent venue for international matches. The time had not yet come for them to be awarded the biggest attraction, Australia, so I played there on only two occasions.

Although over the years Edgbaston has had one of the better batting pitches, so that it has often been impossible to achieve a result in a three-day match without declarations, Tests have tended to finish well within the distance. This is typified by the First Test against New Zealand in 1958. It was a weak Kiwi team so my opportunities with the bat were few and I was not required to bowl very much, but at Edgbaston I was called upon to fill the role of the third seamer to Fred Trueman and Peter Loader. The tourists made 94 in their first innings and I picked up two for 17 in 20 overs, but Fred was the main destroyer with five wickets. They reached 137 at their second attempt and the game was over on Monday afternoon. Peter and Tony Lock captured three wickets apiece and I was more than happy with two for 23 in 20 overs.

TRENT BRIDGE

Trent Bridge has not been a lucky ground for me at international level. In my six Tests there, I never took many wickets, frequently sending down only a few overs, and my top score was 49. My first Test appearance there in 1951 against South Africa was all too typical. South Africa made 483 in their first innings and I took nought for 102 in 45 overs. We replied with 419 for nine. We declared on the Monday after rain over the weekend and I batted at number nine as we chased, not very successfully and rather stupidly, quick runs, my contribution being three.

I bowled two overs at the start of the South African second innings, then they were shot out for 121 by Bedser and Tattersall which appeared to have justified Freddie Brown's declaration and the sacrifice of wickets at the end of our innings. Unfortunately he had failed to appreciate that the pitch would remain awkward and we were bowled out for 114 by Rowan and Mann. I lasted for about

two hours for my 11. On my way back to Essex in my car, after what
had been an unhappy match which we had thrown away through a
tactical miscalculation, I heard on the radio that I had been dropped
for the next Test at Lord's.

The influence of weather on matches before the days of covered
pitches was considerable and this was especially true at Trent Bridge
in the First Test of the 1953 series. On paper, Australia looked the
stronger and better balanced side with five pure batsmen, three
allrounders, a wicketkeeper who could make runs and two bowlers;
while we had opted for six batsmen, Godfrey Evans who was capable
of scoring runs but not dependable, three bowlers and myself.

Australia won the toss, decided to bat on a perfect wicket and,
after the early departure of Graeme Hole, Arthur Morris and
Lindsay Hassett were soon firmly established. I have no doubt in my
mind that they would have put together a substantial first-innings
total and Len would have had difficulty in not overbowling Bedser
and myself if there had not been some interruptions for rain, which
made the pitch lively and enabled Alec to pick up two more wickets
with the second new ball just before the close of play. Australia
finished the day 157 for three.

Alec and I had to start the second day with a slippery ball against
Hassett and Miller who capitalized on our handicap, but then, from
the wealth of 237 for three, Australia collapsed to 249. Alec finished
with seven for 55 off 38.3 overs, the finest piece of bowling of that
type I have seen in a Test, and I was well satisfied with my two for 75
off 44 overs. I would rate Hassett's century as an innings of
exceptional quality.

By the time we began batting the pitch, despite the roller, was
difficult and we struggled to 92 for six and to an eventual deficit of
105 on the third day, when the pitch had become rather like a
pudding, a little too slow for Wardle but absolutely made for Alec.
The Australian total of 123 was mainly due to some brilliant bowling
by Alec (seven for 44) and Roy Tattersall (three for 22), but also
owed something to Don Tallon interpreting his captain's instructions to 'give it a go' as meaning an assault on the bowling instead of
an appeal against the light. The day ended with England 42 for one
needing 187.

Would we have made those runs? We shall never know, because it
rained throughout Monday and it was not possible to start until 4.30
on the Tuesday, by which time the game was dead. However, as

Hutton and Simpson experienced no problems taking the score to 120 for one, I think we probably would have won because Australian bowlers seldom exploited wet conditions in England as well as we do.

There was something more than a little unusual about my performance in the 1954 Test against Pakistan, which we won by an innings and 129 runs. My bowling was, I suppose, about par for my Tests on this ground. I came on second change and bowled three overs, which were ridiculously expensive as they cost 18 runs. Bedser and Statham had shared the new ball and Appleyard, who took five for 51, came on first change. Not surprisingly, I was not required in their second innings, when Statham, Bedser, Appleyard and Wardle divided the spoils.

The unusual feature of the match was that I was involved in a partnership of 192 in 105 minutes, but it was not quite as it sounds! My partner Denis Compton, who scored 278 in 290 minutes, did have just a little to do with that stand, my own contribution being a mammoth 27. On the other hand, it did allow me to confirm my belief that the runs can come faster if only one batsman is in full cry and the other gives him the strike at the commencement of every over because Denis and I scored more quickly than the Denis and Tom Graveney stand before us. I should also mention that the Pakistan attack was not very hostile, it was a very friendly pitch and Denis has seldom been in more devastating form.

THE OVAL

There can be few Test grounds with quite such an unattractive exterior and approach than the Oval. It reminds me of one of those Victorian pubs in the London suburbs, situated in streets of terraced houses which have declined from middle-class respectability into dingy, dirty flatlets and bedsits. Although nothing can possibly disguise its essential ugliness and basic vulgarity, the changes and the repairs undertaken over the years have given it the worn charm of an aged, yet essentially active grandmother. In the same way, once inside the Oval one quickly forgets the drab outside and the delights of driving through the Elephant and Castle, or Brixton.

My first of six Tests at the Oval in 1949 was unusual in that my position in the batting order was number five as our side contained only four frontline batsmen. We also used eight bowlers to dismiss New Zealand for 345, including four wrist-spinners and one

ABOVE The first and last supper. The 1953 Ashes-winning side, thirty years on. Left to right (standing) Don Kenyon, Willie Watson, Fred Trueman, Peter May, Roy Tattersall, Johnny Wardle, Tony Lock, Reg Simpson, Jim Laker, Tom Graveney, Brian Statham; (sitting) Godfrey Evans, Bill Edrich, Freddie Brown, Len Hutton, Denis Compton, Alec Bedser, T.E.B.

BELOW England v Australia, Old Trafford, Fourth Test, 1956. Laker's match, and the most remarkable Test in my career. Tony Lock catches Jim Burke in the second innings while the Rev D.S. Sheppard appeals to the Lord.

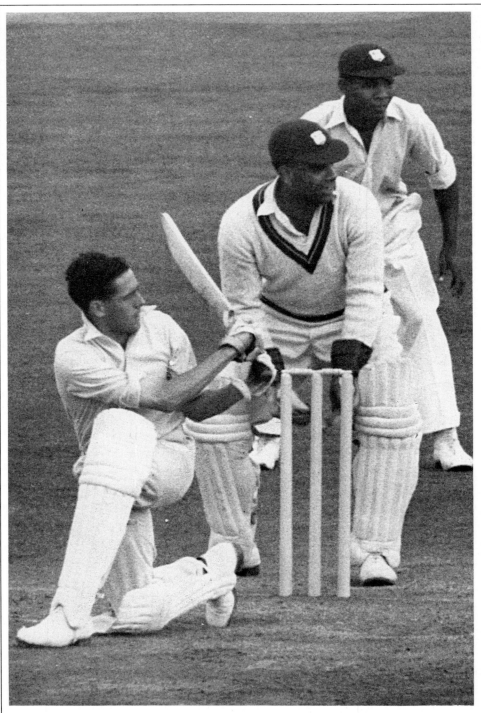

England v West Indies, First Test, 1950 . . . on the beach at Old Trafford. Clyde Walcott and Everton Weekes look on as I sweep to leg during my first-innings stand of 161 with Godfrey Evans. *Central Press*

ABOVE LEFT Batting on the mat against Bermuda on the 1953-54 MCC tour . . . and playing back for a change.
ABOVE RIGHT Another Roy Ullyett special, this time about the 1950-51 series against Australia.

BELOW England v South Africa, New Wanderers, Johannesburg, First Test, 1956-57. One of my most satisfying catches, that of van Ryneveld off Brian Statham's bowling. Colin Cowdrey is at second slip, Godfrey Evans behind the stumps. *Rand Daily Mail*

THE PLEASURES OF TOURING

OPPOSITE Waterskiing in Brisbane Harbour, 1950-51.
TOP LEFT Deck quoits with Brian Close on board the *Stratheden* bound for Australia, 1950-51.
TOP RIGHT Fishing in New Zealand with Roy Tattersall and Gilbert Parkhouse, 1950-51.
The New Zealand Herald
ABOVE LEFT Relaxing West Indies style at the Tower Isle hotel, Jamaica, 1953-54. *Pierre Chong*
ABOVE RIGHT Getting a close up of Cowdrey, Tyson and Compton on the way to Australia, 1954-55. *Topical Press Agency*

BELOW LEFT Teddy Boy Bailey and Teddy Girl Parks, South Africa, 1956-57.
BELOW RIGHT Beach cricket in Jamaica with Peter Richardson, Jim Laker and Barry Knight during a Rothman Cavaliers tour in the 1960s.

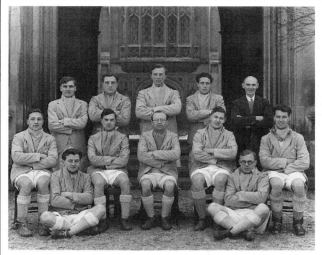

The Cambridge University soccer team of 1946-47. Left to right (standing) Guy Willatt, Doug Insole, Mike Bishop, T.E.B., Billy Manning (trainer); (sitting) Dennis Foxall, Guy Shuttleworth, Roy Perry, Harry Sunderland, Jim Gibson; (on ground) Malcolm Freeguard, Mike Crawford. Cambridge won that year's Varsity match 3-2. *Stearn & Sons*

Heading at goal during Leytonstone's Amateur Cup tie against Sutton at Leytonstone in 1948. *Express & Independent Newspapers Ltd, Leytonstone*

Derek Saunders, captain of Walthamstow, holds the cup aloft after our 2-1 victory over Leyton in the 1952 FA Amateur Cup final, played in front of a crowd of 100,000 at Wembley. *Topical Press Agency*

ABOVE Preparing for the big match, the third-round replay at Highbury against Manchester United of the 1953 FA Cup — we lost, but were not disgraced in front of the 55,000 crowd. *Evening Standard*

BELOW The side that never played, led by the England captain who never was — the Computer Test, 1971-72. Left to right (standing) Alan Knott, Jim Laker, Alec Bedser, Johnny Wardle, Geoff Boycott; (sitting) Colin Cowdrey, Len Hutton, T.E.B., Peter May, Denis Compton. Fred was unable to attend the photo-call due to business commitments. *BBC Hulton Picture Library*

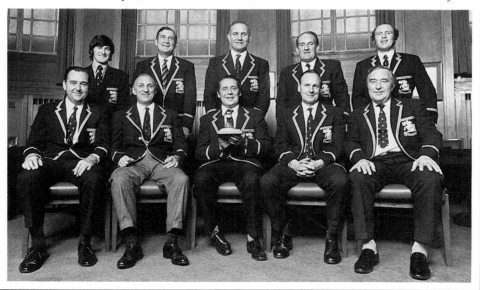

ABOVE The stalwarts of Test Match Special. Left to right (standing) Tony Lewis, Henry Blofeld, Ray Illingworth, Christopher Martin-Jenkins, Peter Baxter (Producer), Bill Frindall; (sitting) Don Mosey, T.E.B., Brian Johnston, Fred Trueman, Tony Cozier. *Patrick Eagar*

BELOW My first visit to Calcutta where there was the biggest crowd on any cricket ground in the world during 1985. *Graham Morris*

off-spinner! As Bedser and I shared seven wickets between us, there must be a suspicion that our selectors had erred. It is not easy to employ five bowlers in a three-day match, so eight would appear to be a slight miscalculation.

At the Oval against the West Indies in 1957, it could be justifiably claimed that my journey up from Westcliff for the three days required to win by an innings and 237 runs was entirely unnecessary. England won the toss on a pitch which was to prove a playground for Laker and Lock and scored 412, of which my contribution was run out nought. The West Indies replied with 89 in their first innings and 86 in the second innings when they followed on. I was not required to bowl in either rout, when 16 of the wickets fell to the Surrey twins. John Goddard, the West Indies captain, went down with influenza during the match and did not bat in either innings. I especially remember Frankie Worrell enquiring laconically how a batsman was supposed to cope with Tony Lock, who was pitching leg and missing off at above medium pace, unless he was no balled.

The Oval was the setting of my most important Test because it decided the fate of the 1953 Ashes, which had been in the possession of Australia for nearly twenty years. Both teams wanted a definite result and an extra day was added, though this turned out to be unnecessary. England included Trueman for the first time in the series, and May, who had class and was batting brilliantly; while the Australians brought back Johnston, who was fit once more, and left out Benaud, giving them an attack based around five seam bowlers, of whom Johnston was also a useful, though hardly a match-winning spinner. It was not only an unbalanced attack, but as the majority of the Oval pitches in 1952 and 1953 had also greatly encouraged spin, often as early as the first day, it seemed an unwise, not to say foolish choice. Nevertheless, we were disappointed, quite incorrectly, when Lindsay Hassett won the toss and elected to bat. Although it looked a good batting pitch, it contained unsuspected life and the atmosphere was ideal for swing, with the result that we bowled them out for 275. If Australia, who possessed both a stronger pace attack and greater batting depth, had bowled we would have been lucky to reach 175.

On the second day, rather strangely a Monday, the wicket had not only dried out but was also at its easiest, so it was disappointing that we managed to make only 235 for seven in reply, including a jolly partnership between Godfrey Evans and myself which ended when he ran himself out.

On the third day, I had useful short stands with Lock and Trueman and a longer one with Bedser, which took our total to 306. I was satisfied with my 64 as by this time the pitch was taking spin and Australia had no bowler able to exploit these conditions, while in Laker and Lock we had the ideal pair. After a few perfunctory overs from Bedser and Trueman, the Surrey pair moved into action and Australia were all out before the close of play for 162. We finished the day 38 for one, Hutton having, uncharacteristically, run himself out.

The 94 runs required for victory and the Ashes were knocked off on Tuesday without too much difficulty, though with great tension because it marked a renaissance for English cricket. At the end, the large crowd swarmed onto the ground, but not across the square. Such spontaneous enthusiasm was unknown because cricket spectators in England at that time were civilized and well behaved – one could sleep peacefully, especially if I was batting, without being woken by tuneless singing or, even worse, that mindless, soulless chanting which has now become so common at both demonstrations and cricket matches.

During the day I received two compliments. The first occurred as we came within reach of our target. Compton and Edrich were batting and Tom Graveney, who was next man in, suggested that if a wicket should fall it would be more fitting for me to go in next. Although it was never on, it was a nice gesture. The second consisted of a few words of praise from Ray Lindwall when the Australians joined us in our dressing-room for the start of the lengthy festivities, which broke up about six. I then departed to celebrate with my wife and friends in a couple of night clubs. The rest of the evening remains somewhat hazy, but I do distinctly recall the band playing 'Won't you come home, Bill Bailey', making a pleasant change from the version much loved by spectators, 'Won't you go home, Trev Bailey'.

I'VE GROWN ACCUSTOMED
TO HER FACE

I have visited Australia seven times and hope to increase my score. The first was as a member of the 1950–51 MCC tour when I imagined it to be, quite incorrectly, a cricketing Mecca. Equally false was my assumption that cricket was the favourite sport of Australians, which of course is gambling in any shape or form. My knowledge of this vast, new, sprawling country was, like most of my generation at that time, minimal – as I revealed within an hour of my arrival.

Our ship berthed at Fremantle where we were met by a number of local officials who were keen to take us for a drive and show us the sights. My host promised 'Kangaroo Paws' and I immediately became interested as wild animals have always fascinated me. I was somewhat disappointed therefore when these turned out to be flowers.

I soon noticed the number of Australians who seemed to favour a slate grey fedora hat, a wide vicious tie and invariably carried a well worn Gladstone bag. I assumed water must be a major problem and Australia had bred a nation of plumbers. It was at least a month before I discovered that those carefully carried leather bags did not contain a plumber's tools, but something infinitely more precious.

At that time there was an acute shortage of bottles and it was necessary to return the empties in order to purchase fresh supplies of beer. As the Australian is extremely fond of his beer, it was only natural that he would use a strong, sensible container for this vital task, while the shortage is explained by the need to have some beer always available at home because of the strange licensing laws.

It took me a little time to appreciate Australian beer, which was served very cold and was not dissimilar to our lagers. In the 1950s most of the beer in England came from wooden casks and lager sales were small, while few people ever considered using ice in any drink.

I never really became accustomed to the Australian licensing laws of that period, when most bars having been open all day closed at 6 p.m. I found a beer at 10.30 a.m., instead of a coffee, rather strange, but the real danger was to be caught in a bar between 5 p.m. and 6 p.m., known as 'national swill time'.

There was an understandable tendency for the worker to have a schooner of beer before returning home. This was fine, but it frequently developed into a fast drinking session, especially if one made the mistake of being in a school of six and all the glasses were empty some fifteen minutes before closing time. This was the signal for another six rounds to come up and go down very fast. Six schooners are enjoyable, but twelve in under an hour on an empty stomach are not the best preparation for a return to the 'little woman', even though Australian wives seemed to be considerably more tolerant of such excesses than their English counterparts.

To some extent the problem of the crash guzzle stemmed from a weakness, or maybe a strength, of the Australian male. He has a terror of failing to call his 'shout' whatever the time or the situation. It also was not helped by the Australian bars of that period, which were essentially utilitarian, rather reminiscent of a public urinal, with a large bar and a couple of ghastly, brightly coloured murals.

There can be few better ways of seeing Australia than as a cricketer, especially in my era when a tour lasted so much longer. We played two matches against the State teams, five Tests and a number of up-country matches in places like Toowoomba, Launceston, Renmark, Euroa and Northam. Nowadays the players are committed to a much briefer tour and tight schedule in order to accommodate six Tests and an ever-increasing number of one-day internationals, which the sponsors want because they make for good television.

We had sufficient time to enjoy the hospitality, which was never less than generous; the beaches, which were breathtaking, especially in New South Wales; and the climate, which for somebody like myself who worships the sun was ideal. Other features of Australia which left their mark during my first tour included the champagne in Western Australia, the Sydney rock oysters, and the enormous

164

helpings of meat. England was still on rationing and I sent food parcels home every week throughout the trip, as well as bringing back with me English bone china tea and dinner services which we could buy only in white at home.

In addition to the people and the country, there was the cricket. The Tests were a particular challenge as they were played in big stadiums, far larger than our international grounds, and in front of massive, volatile and distinctly partisan crowds. The reason for their big cricket grounds was that every town of reasonable size in Australia, where space has never been too serious a problem, has an oval. On the oval they play cricket in the summer and football in the winter – a certain amount of soccer, a certain amount of rugby, both Union and League, but mainly, especially in Victoria, a marvellous Aussie extravaganza called Australian Rules Football which takes up the whole of the cricket ground. The fact that the climate allows them to produce a good batting wicket in the summer after it has been pounded by scrums in heavy mud throughout the winter, makes a considerable difference and reduces upkeep. If only it were possible to use our cricket grounds throughout the winter months without having to keep the square sacrosanct.

It was on this tour that I first realized how much more emotionally involved one became playing for England abroad than at home. After four weeks on a liner everybody in the party really knew each other as people, not merely as cricketers. We became a small tight community of friends who shared together the triumphs and the failures. After a Test in England the players simply returned to their respective counties, so that victory or defeat never meant quite so much. This was illustrated on the last day of the Melbourne Test, when I walked round the outside of the stadium with John Warr, unable to watch what we knew would be the final rites, because we knew we had thrown away a match which we could have won.

What made that so depressing was that the objective of an Australian tour is to win the Ashes. Although we were not nearly as strong as our opponents, we realized we could have been two-nil up, instead of two-nil down. This meant that we had almost inevitably failed in our quest, because it seemed inconceivable that a team with our many deficiencies could come back from that situation. We had squandered a wonderful opportunity and it upset me, and I suspect the others, to a degree which it would never have done at home.

Another advantage of that sea trip out to Australia was that it assisted players and press to understand each other far better than is the case in the 1980s, when the relationship between the England players and the media might often be described as similar to that of the USA and Russia when the Cold War was below zero. During the four-week voyage we learned to communicate, because we talked, drank and played deck games and cards together. This enabled us to avoid those incidents which do so much harm to the game.

Incidentally, as there were far more national newspapers then than today, the numbers of pressmen and the pressure on them for that exclusive story from the editor was even greater, although of course there was no television. I can still recall my amazement at the fifty-odd journalists who arrived at Bunberry to see a match of no importance in a little country town. There were more journalists there than if there had been an international war in progress.

The players expected to be criticized, but we also knew that the English press were keen to see us do well. They wanted to write us up, rather than down, but this would inevitably depend very much on our own performances. If we played badly, they would seek reasons, some of which would have nothing to do with events on the field. Although they were sent to write about the cricket, the more able journalists would naturally file any good news story which arose, especially if writing for the popular press. But they were not the scavengers of Fleet Street, the hard newsmen whom in the main they disliked and even despised, rather in the same way as a soldier will act on the information of a spy but does not want to entertain him in his mess.

Although not infrequently the subject of press criticism, I found journalists easy to mix with and I cannot remember ever having a row with any of them. The fact that my brother was one probably helped, plus the fact that I have written all my life, preferring to horridly split my own infinitives than to allow a 'ghost' to do it for me.

Nobody enjoys reading harsh and sometimes unfair criticism about himself. Appreciating this point at the outset, I made a point of never reading an account of any game unless I had done very well. I knew better than anybody when my own performance was below standard so there was no point in reading what somebody else had to say about it, particularly as his knowledge of first-class cricket was almost certainly less than my own.

The degree of emotional involvement of cricketers on tour

explains why they are far more sensitive when it comes to bad umpiring. An England player who has hit the ball but is adjudged lbw at Lord's will be aggrieved, but can expect little sympathy from his county colleagues when he returns home. In all likelihood they will suggest that the umpire was correct, knowing that he has never admitted to being out. In contrast, a bad decision received by a member of a touring party is a subject for discussion and commiseration long after the next Test.

Personally, I have the utmost difficulty remembering most of the Tests I played in England, or even who was in the side, so bad decisions have long since been forgotten. However, I can still recall in detail some poor ones which occurred on tour, and not only those in which I was personally involved.

On the 1953–54 tour of the West Indies I was bowling in the Fourth Test to Everton Weekes on the mat at Trinidad, unquestionably one of the finest batting pitches it has been my misfortune to bowl on. It was so easy-paced that although requiring over 450 to save the follow-on we achieved it. On the first morning I brought Dick Spooner up to the stumps because I had decided to use a short run and try to move the ball off the seam. Everton was in his thirties when he went for a cut, snicked it and Dick took the catch. What made the incident memorable, apart from wanting the wicket and Everton going on to a double hundred, was that the umpire made the fatal mistake of trying to justify a mistake to the suffering bowler by explaining that he had heard a noise, but had not seen any deviation. Deviation with a keeper standing up to a fast-medium bowler? In the last over of the same morning, at the other end, Denis Compton had another batsman caught by Tom Graveney waist high at first slip, but he was given not out.

At Adelaide, on the 1958–59 tour, I attempted to push Ray Lindwall to leg and was given out, never an easy decision for an umpire, caught down the leg side by Wally Grout when my bat was nowhere near the ball. It would not have made any difference to the outcome as we lost the match by 10 wickets, but I was unhappy at the time because Ray had not even bothered to shout and Australians are not allergic to appealing.

It was my good fortune to make three tours to Australia. Although the record books may seem to indicate that my initial visit was a disaster (we lost four out of the five Tests), we did in fact perform rather better than had been expected and, with a little luck, could even have won the series, though the Australians were a much stronger team. We were beaten in the First and Second Tests by narrow margins.

I always think of it as the 'if only' tour. If only Denis Compton had averaged thirty instead of a near unbelievable seven in the series . . . If only Bill Edrich had not been left behind, but had been brought in place of Dewes, or Sheppard or Parkhouse . . . If only the good wicket on which we had done well to dismiss Australia for a mere 228 in the First Test at Brisbane had not been turned into a 'sticky' before we had a chance to bat. Even then we might have made it if only Arthur McIntyre, included in the side almost incredibly as a possible fifth bowler on the evidence of his bowling in the nets, had not been run out going for the fourth run in the final innings . . . If only we had not lost two bowlers in the Third Test, when I made the mistake of using my thumb instead of my bat to drop a Ray Lindwall bouncer at my feet, and Doug Wright pulled a muscle being run out . . .

An X-ray showed my thumb was broken and I had one of my first encounters with what might be termed the 'anything for a picture' photographer. At the hospital I was given an injection in the vain hope that I would be able to continue batting. On emerging I encountered a photographer who asked me of all people – merely to look at a needle is enough to make me faint – if he could have a picture of the injection. I explained that it had already been done and my thumb was bandaged. He explained that that did not matter. All he needed was a nurse, a needle and my other hand and he would reverse the negative!

The 1950–51 tour began badly for me as I had severe fibrositis in the shoulder and was unable to bowl properly during a game played in Colombo on our way out, or in the Perth nets. It was even suggested by our press that I, along with Bob Berry, John Warr and Brian Close, should be sent home. The outlook was grim, as the message I had received on my way over had done no good. Fortunately I was sent to a first-class physiotherapist in Perth, who to my relief cured me with deep massage. As a result I picked up some wickets in Brisbane and then Melbourne and clinched my place as Alec Bedser's new-ball partner.

I did much better than had been expected because the fallacy that only wrist-spinners, slow leftarmers and very fast bowlers took wickets in Australia was still in vogue. My batting disappointed me because I felt I should have made more runs, but we did have the satisfaction of registering in the Fifth Test that victory which had eluded us for so long.

On my second tour to Australia in 1954–55 we achieved our objective, the retention of the Ashes, with a powerful side, despite such obvious selectorial blunders like the inclusion of Vic Wilson instead of Willie Watson, who was in an entirely different class as a batsman, and Jim McConnon instead of Jim Laker. However, we came closer to losing than an eventual scoreline of three–one might suggest.

We could hardly have had a worse start as we lost the first battle by the not-inconsiderable margin of an innings and 154 runs. This was largely due to one of those classic selectorial blunders, the decision to play four pace bowlers (now standard West Indian practice) – Frank Tyson, Brian Statham, Alec Bedser and myself – although we had spinners like Johnny Wardle and Bob Appleyard available. This mistake, which I could not believe when Godfrey Evans told me the team in the lift at our hotel, was responsible for Len inserting the opposition after winning the toss and Australia amassed a little matter of 601 for eight declared.

We won the next three Tests by small margins, mainly due to the sheer speed of Frank Tyson and the support provided by an above average, well balanced attack – especially Brian Statham – plus two memorable innings from Peter May and one from Colin Cowdrey. It has often seemed to me that if Len had included Alec Bedser in the Second Test at Sydney, which he probably should have done because in conditions favouring swing Alec would have been more effective than anybody, we would have won that game more easily but then would probably have lost the series.

We were, quite correctly, put into bat by Arthur Morris and shot out for 154. I then opened the bowling with Brian Statham because it was ideal for swerve and neither Brian nor Frank were swing bowlers. It was, in fact, one of the few Tests in which I relied on swing rather than seam for my wickets, picking up four in the first innings including numbers one, two and three. Now Alec Bedser was not only a far better seam bowler than myself. When it came to swing, he was in an altogether different class. In those conditions at Sydney I believe he would have taken at least six wickets for very few. This would have kept him in the side for the next Test, depriving us of the variety of Johnny Wardle and Frank Appleyard who played such an important role in dismissing Australia in their first innings before the Tyson typhoon swept in to wash the opposition away in the second.

From the playing angle this was my best tour as an allround fieldsman, third seamer and a dependable middle-order batsman who averaged a respectable 37 in the Tests. There was also the delight of winning the series in Adelaide which was unquestionably one of the most satisfying moments in my cricketing career.

My wife joined me for a month which at the time was comparatively rare, unlike now when the unfortunate manager has to cope not only with his players, but also with perhaps a dozen wives, several girlfriends, a gaggle of kids, a few well-meaning parents, and even the occasional minder, agent and lawyer. In my day the players could not afford the expense, even though the tours were about twice as long. It was also not encouraged, though at least MCC were not quite as stupid as the Australian Board of Control, who used to insist on players' wives staying in different hotels.

When Greta arrived, Dorothy Hutton and Jean Evans were already there and she quickly found herself engulfed by a number of luncheon parties, where everybody seemed to wear enormous hats and were more formal than the Women's Institute in this country, which has in fact never really been Greta's scene. She loved Melbourne and Adelaide, but has never really quite come to terms with Sydney, perhaps because it is so Americanized. On the other hand, I now consider Sydney my favourite city in Australia, though they all have much to offer. I have also acquired a special affection for Hobart, which seems to me closer in many respects to New Zealand than to the mainland.

I played in three Tests at the Gabba in Brisbane and though England lost on each occasion I have always done reasonably well as an individual. I managed to spend quite a few hours occupying the crease, which on one occasion brought forth the suggestion that I should climb out of the iron lung as I moved from the teens into the prosperous twenties after some three hours. The Australian barracker is not famed for his sensitivity and in retrospect it is somewhat ironic that it should be at the Gabba of all places that I should strike what was then the most profitable shot played in cricket.

A local businessman announced that he would give £100 to the first player to hit a six in the Test, which would be worth well over

£1000 today. Although his offer had appeared in the local press, I had not seen it because I made a point of never reading newspapers unless I had had a good day – and the first two of that Test, when Australia amassed 601 runs after being put in, and I had also put down an easy catch, hardly fell into that category. Rumours floated around the dressing-room without really interesting me, as sixes were hardly my forte, but the offer obviously registered in my subconscious because during a somewhat lengthy sojourn a little voice told me to loft Ian Johnson into the crowd. On returning to the pavilion during the interval one of my colleagues said that he thought he had read about it, but what made me feel that there might be some substance to the story had been the reaction of the Australians on the field. They had appeared rather more aggrieved than usual when the umpire had put his arms aloft and I thought I caught something close to 'lucky lugger'. Yet I was still not sure as nobody had a local paper. At close of play I have seldom changed faster. I sped back to my hotel and found the vital passage informing me I had won a hundred quid. Minutes later the phone rang and a gentleman, sadly I have forgotten his name, asked if he could come up and present me with a cheque.

This kind gentleman's generosity enabled me to throw a little party at the Lennons Hotel, which not only coincided with my birthday but also helped us to forget a heavy defeat. We used three rooms with each bath full of ice and drinks. It was a good night, but I sometimes wonder what the other residents thought, especially at around 5 a.m., when one of my colleagues – it had to be Peter Loader – decided to knock over one of the bottles which stretched in what appeared to be an unending chain down the whole corridor and they all toppled over.

The following day most of the team made their way to Rockhampton, but five of us, Evans, Statham, Compton, Tyson and myself, returned by air to Melbourne. We arrived at the Windsor Hotel at about 12.30 and as most of us had not been to bed and we had had to catch an early plane we looked decidedly rough. In the foyer we encountered Sir Robert Menzies, who had an apartment at the hotel, was an outstanding politician, had a passion for sport, especially cricket, and was probably the best after-dinner speaker his country has ever produced. He was also essentially a nice person, who took one look at our dishevelled quintet and said, 'You boys look as if you could do with a grog.' Immediately he led us to his suite

171

where we stayed for the next hour. What a host, what a politician, what a man!

In every respect my final tour to Australia in 1958–59 was the worst and the most disappointing. On paper we looked a powerful and balanced side with plenty of confidence and experience. We arrived expecting to return with the Ashes, instead we were soundly thrashed. The sad feature was not so much that we lost, but that we failed to play to our potential and, even worse, surrendered without a reasonable fight. What went wrong? There was no single reason, rather a combination of different factors.

It has often seemed to me that England teams are fairly poor tourists, tending to be blasé, often aloof, rather too ready to complain and, on this occasion, probably too arrogant. Even before things started to go very wrong on the field cliques had formed, resulting in less team spirit than on any other of my tours. It was not a question of punch-ups or bitter arguments, just continual niggling and players drifting down separate streams, so that the togetherness was missing when most needed. Eventually we were sunk without trace by a good, but not exceptional Australian side. In addition we had a convenient alibi for our failure, the 'throw-draggers', and it is handy to have ready made excuses when things are going wrong.

Over the years Australia have worried even less about the bowler with a suspect action than in England. I had encountered a number whom I thought should have been no-balled, but never were, as umpires disliked becoming embroiled in unpleasant incidents. In addition, they had to rely on their eyesight without the aid of a slow-motion camera. However, on this tour the situation was plainly out of control because every state, with the exception of Queensland, included at least one bowler with a dubious action.

The majority of the Australian offenders were what I term 'throw-draggers', bowlers who opened up in their delivery stride so that their front foot pointed towards the slips (in the case of a rightarmer) and then released the ball not unlike a javelin thrower. This method enabled the bowler to be considerably faster than his run-up suggested. It also enabled him to camouflage a faster or slower ball without any discernible change in his action. It takes a fast bowler with a full arm action years to perfect a slow delivery which the batsman has difficulty in picking, but Ian Meckiff possessed a beauty from the outset of his first-class career.

I once discussed the throwing problem with Alan Davidson, who as a bowler with a classical body action was not a supporter of the bent-arm brigade. The Australian opening batsman, Jim Burke, who was also an occasional 'dart-throwing' off-spinner, was mentioned. Alan told me about a cricket contemporary who had injured his back and could not bowl quickly. However, when his team in grade cricket had been thrown out cheaply by Jim his friend's reaction was to take up chucking off-breaks – which he did with considerable success and without ever being called.

Another problem that some of the 'throw-draggers' had was a very extensive drag, especially Rorke who was one of the fastest bowlers I have even seen or faced. This was helped by the fact that he broke the batting crease with his right toe before releasing the ball off his front foot from way in front of it. At times it seemed to me there was a danger of his landing on my left foot as I pushed forward!

Although the number of 'chuckers' in Australia was something of a joke, it was difficult for us to complain because two of our own party, Tony Lock and Peter Loader, were highly suspect. Having seen the success Tony was permitted to enjoy in English county cricket, I deliberately went searching on behalf of Essex for a finger-spinner with a bent arm. I always had misgivings about Peter's bouncer and his admirably disguised slower ball which was a well spun off-break. His bouncer was difficult to negotiate because it was always so much quicker than anything else he bowled and I could never pick his slower ball, even when I was standing in the slips. However, there were so many throwers around that the Australian authorities realized that they would have to do something drastic, because all their young quickies were starting to imitate the throwers, instead of the genuine bowlers.

Ian Meckiff, one of the most pleasant of all Australian cricketers, sincerely believed there was nothing wrong with his action. My belief is that he should never have been allowed to progress so far without being stopped by club officials, but on the other hand the same could also be said to apply to Tony Lock. Why on earth did Surrey and the English umpires allow him to bowl in his second style?

The Australian authorities quickly and efficiently purged their cricket of throwers, but in the process it seemed to me they became hypersensitive about anything that had even the slightest resemblance to a throw.

The reason I had such an indifferent tour as a player was due to a bad back, which by the end of the tour was hurting every time I put my left foot on the ground. I found it feasible to bat in discomfort, but I could never do this when bowling. The outcome was that I failed to bowl effectively. Fortunately a manipulative operation under an anaesthetic completely cured me, and I achieved the 'double' in the following summer. In retrospect I should have either had an operation in Australia or gone home after the Second Test, instead of trying to carry on under a handicap. It resulted in my Test career ending perhaps somewhat prematurely.

I learned to water-ski in Australia, or to be more accurate I learned to perform without distinction on two skis. I always intended to progress further and have repeatedly reached the stage of dropping one ski, but then the tour or holiday would end so that I never made that vital step. But I did find it satisfying being pulled along, jumping the odd trough and thinking about the past, the present and the future without any distraction. It was more fun than swimming and I never mastered the art of body surfing, though I became quite expert at being dumped by both big and little waves.

I first rose on skis one sunny Sunday on the Hawksbury River, when the water was warm, the beer cold and the barbecue delicious. My host was Sid Barnes who had retired from the game and was producing a fairly abrasive column in an Australian paper. Behind his rough exterior, a dislike for the Establishment which was close to paranoic, and a sharp business acumen which would have positively revelled in the commercially marketed cricket world of the 1970s and 1980s, Sid was a kind and, in some respects, rather lonely man.

The management were never too enthusiastic about my water-skiing and they certainly would not have approved of a marvellous day close to Brisbane Harbour, when in my efforts to do some of the more difficult things I frequently fell off and swam around collecting skis before remounting without a care in the world. That evening as we ate the barbecued chops – why is it a burnt chop or steak tastes so good out of doors, when you would send it back in a restaurant? – somebody mentioned the number of sharks which also swam around the Harbour. It almost put me off my food, because when sharks are in the vicinity I do not believe in being on the beach, let alone in the water.

Of all the many occasions on which I have skied in Australia, the one I treasure most was about six o'clock at night off an absolutely deserted beach some ten miles out from Glenelg in South Australia.

The sea was calm and dyed red by the setting sun. The only noise was the purr of the engine, ahead was the prospect of beer and food in what might be most aptly described as a beach bungalow. I was at peace with the world even though this was on my last tour and the cricket was going badly.

In many respects New Zealand reminds me of rural Great Britain without a large population, an industrial revolution and big cities. Although it is further away than Australia, it tends to be closer to us in tradition, climate and outlook. It is not dissimilar to Tasmania, which lacks the frantic Australian hustle and bustle, so that one can afford to sit back and relax, not for the odd two minutes but for a full week. It has always seemed to me that New Zealand is a good place to live, especially for anyone with outdoor interests but, unlike Australia, the chance of making a vast fortune is improbable.

My own two tours to New Zealand were inevitably too hurried and something of an anti-climax, following as they did our Australian adventures. Our main interest after some five months away was to return home, so we never had the opportunity to sit back and relish the many attractions of the land of the Kiwis. Even the cricket in my era came as something of a disappointment after the battles in Australia, because their standard was much lower and we were usually too strong, even though by then we had unconsciously tended to relax. The Auckland Test in 1954–55, for example, finished early on the third day after we had bowled them out for 26 in their second innings, which enabled Reg Simpson and I to catch a plane for Honolulu and America three days ahead of schedule.

It was in New Zealand, in 1950–51, that I scored my one and only Test century. It was very much a two-part affair, a first fifty of solid graft taking about four hours while the rest of my 134 runs coming in a comparatively frivolous two hours, including a distinctively unlikely ninth-wicket partnership of 117 with Doug Wright. On this occasion the pitch was lifeless, which was unusual as most of their wickets tended to be rather slow and green, allowing movement off the seam, far closer to our own than those in Australia. As a result of the conditions, over the years New Zealand have produced many good fast-medium seamers, frequently tall gangling men, and steady run-accumulators, but very few high-calibre strokemakers or slow bowlers.

Although time was limited, I still have some marvellous memories

175

of the delights I encountered in New Zealand. Mount Cook on South Island was superb, the Maori culture was fascinating, and the hospitality everywhere was overwhelming, but what I remember best were my introductions to two sports in which I had no practical experience and little interest, fishing and hunting.

Fishing had never appealed to me as I lacked the necessary patience, as well as the ability to remove a hook from a fish. It was too reminiscent of one of my innings – a long wait while nothing much happened – but it was very different when I went out on a boat in New Zealand. All I had to do was to throw over a baited hook and haul in an edible fish, which somebody else then unhooked. I even cast an unbaited line and still managed to catch one.

After one fishing trip we were met by a photographer and I demonstrated to two of my colleagues the size of 'the one that got away'. This appeared in the local newspaper. A couple of days later I received a parcel and was very intrigued by the contents, a rectangular piece of wood about 18 inches long and about four inches wide. There were two holes about 8 inches apart and string at either end. I was completely mystified until I read the instructions. 'This is a "Whopper-Stopper". Hang round neck, insert thumbs in the two holes and then tell that fishy story.'

Apart from a little very unsuccessful rabbit shooting in my teens, I had never gone hunting as I was a poor shot and had always been rather squeamish about blood. But having never grown up, guns always retained their fascination, so when I was invited to join a wild pig and deer hunting expedition and was entrusted once more with a .303 rifle, plus loads of ammunition, I could not resist. It provided an unforgettable experience as Johnny Wardle, Reg Simpson, Vic Wilson and I walked and climbed miles through the rugged wilderness. On one occasion after hearing a fusillade of shots which suggested a major engagement, I frantically scrambled to the top of the hill to find Johnny and Vic lying prone. I asked the score. Although the noise suggested at least eight down, they had not claimed a single victim, but Johnny reckoned he had been close. It seemed to me that the hunters were in considerably more danger than the enemy, but that was not enough to stop me going on another expedition.

This time we were accompanied by a deer ranger and his dog, whose job was to control the number of deer in the forests. It turned out to be another wonderful, exhausting day, although I reckon that ranger's dog was lucky to have come back as he came closer to being shot than any of the deer we were hunting!

The MCC used to fly to New Zealand from Sydney Harbour in a flying boat, the perfect way to travel – safe, smooth and luxurious. Many years later I took a party on a tour of the Sydney suburbs. Our guide pointed out the flying boat anchored in the harbour with the same reverence as we would treat a listed building. For the first time I began to think of myself as an ancient monument.

FANAGALO

The magic word from Zulu land.

My best social tour by a long way was my only tour of South Africa in 1956–57. Their cricket supporters provided hospitality on a scale that none of the other countries could even approach. It was summed up when we arrived in Johannesburg and discovered on our first day that we had been allocated an efficient unofficial social manager, Joe Pamensky. Years later he became one of their leading cricket administrators, but when we were out there his job, which he tackled with skill and enormous enthusiasm, was to provide the English team with whatever entertainment they required and to lay on the requisite transport. Nothing was too much trouble for our hosts. When I took my wife for a few days to the Kruger National Park, Wilf Isaacs, who had flown with the RAF against Germany, not only loaned me his shooting-brake but also made certain it contained a wide variety of luxurious food and refreshment.

What struck me as somewhat ironic was that, whereas in the West Indies the whites had supported the MCC, in South Africa it was the blacks – or, to be more accurate, the Indians and the Coloureds because the blacks have never followed cricket in any great number. This brings me to apartheid. It will be appreciated that my tour took place before the invasion of England by coloured immigrants, so at home we had no ethnic problem, while crusades had not yet become a popular pastime, possibly because we were too busy recovering from a war we had won and struggling in a peace which we definitely lost.

Travelling out on our ship was Professor Tomlinson, who had

completed an extensive report on apartheid in South Africa. His intelligent, carefully researched, reasoned and considered resumé of the situation made a pleasant change from the uninformed, prejudiced and hysterical outbursts to which I have usually been subjected. Although, as cricketers, we were non-political, we could not shut our eyes to a situation in which there was no satisfactory solution for the different groups involved, who not only disliked but also were frightened of each other. There are many black tribes and the differences, apart from language, are considerable. The Indians do not meld easily with native Africans, nor do Hindu with Moslem. The Cape Coloureds are understandably suspicious of everybody. The English speaking South Africans tend to dislike the Afrikaaners, many of whom were still thinking in terms of the Boer War when I was there. In other words it was not the clear-cut, black-versus-white situation so misunderstood by those who have never been to South Africa.

Three aspects of the deplorable system made a particular impression on me at the time. First, on the boat coming out I was reading *The Tribe that Lost its Head* and was amazed to find on arriving in South Africa that it had been banned. Second, the opening of the treason trials came close to black farce, though not for those concerned.

Third, there was the bus strike. Fares from the black townships had, after some 20 years, been put up by a penny for those travelling to work in Johannesburg. The black community decided to boycott the buses in protest, which meant about an eight mile hike in to the city and back every day. A friend of mine had always paid the fares of a charming, elderly lady, who came to do her ironing twice a week. When I saw her arrive exhausted I naively enquired why she had not taken the bus. Her reply simply stressed the violence which existed, and still does: 'If I had come by bus, they would have burned down my home the first time and, if I had done it again, they would have killed me.'

The tour did not begin too well for me. I was driven from home by a friend and encountered exceptional commuter traffic. I missed my boat train, but managed to catch the ship before it left Southampton. As usual I enjoyed the cruise out. It had the added bonus of allowing us to witness Table Mountain at dawn covered by its tablecloth of mist, unquestionably one of the most beautiful sights I have seen and a perfect introduction to a fascinating country.

It was Peter May's first tour as captain and Doug Insole, our vice-captain, demonstrated that he could make runs at Test level by heading our averages. His four other appearances for England occurred in different series. It does make a difference if one is given more than one match in a series, and to suffer this four times merely underlines that selectors do make mistakes.

I enjoyed my most successful trip as an allrounder, heading our Test bowling averages with 19 wickets at 12.21 apiece and coming fourth in the batting. Because of our strong attack, I did not have to do as much bowling as usual in the other games, but I did have the satisfaction of scoring over 700 runs, including a couple of centuries.

The tour itself turned out to be that contradiction in terms – dull in terms of the cricket played but exciting in terms of the situations it produced, so inevitably large crowds turned up to see South Africa come back from two-nil down to square a series we ought to have won. The weakness of both sides was lack of quality batting, plus the fact that most of the runs were accumulated laboriously and often painfully, so that there were occasions when even I was among the quicker scorers, though not too often. In sharp contrast the bowling was of a high standard, which helps to explain why the Springboks gathered their runs at under 30 per hour and we were only fractionally faster. It would have been different if Peter May, who was at his peak, had not experienced an inexplicable inability to make runs in the Tests, finishing with 153 in 10 innings, including a top score of 61. In the other matches he simply could not stop scoring them, including six centuries!

In terms of form at the time I would rate our attack as the strongest with which I toured, is reflected by the tour bowling averages in which the most expensive, Jim Laker, captured his wickets at under 18 apiece. We had three quick bowlers, Tyson, Statham and Loader, plus myself at fast-medium and three spinners, Laker, Lock and Wardle. On this tour I would rate Wardle as the best wrist-spinner in the world.

Our batting problems were underlined in the First Test when, shortly before the commencement, Peter asked me to open the innings with Peter Richardson, although I was never an international number one. I enjoyed going in first with Peter because we both had a fondness for the ludicrous. I immediately reminded my new partner that we had been selected for a job which in the past had been entrusted to some far more accomplished batsmen, including that immortal pair, Sir Jack Hobbs and Herbert Sutcliffe. This appealed to Peter, leading to exchanges out in the middle which included comments like 'Come one, Herbert' from me (I naturally took the knighthood), and 'Well played, Sir Jack' from Peter after I had managed an involuntary edge for one.

The South Africans, not famous for their sense of the absurd, appeared slightly baffled. However, apart from being good company Peter was a splendid runner between the wickets – along with Willie Watson and Colin Cowdrey the best I have batted with. Not being exactly overburdened with shots, I was always grateful for somebody at the other end who was on the lookout for sharp, but safe singles. It also tended to disconcert and annoy the opposition.

I was never more than a stop-gap opener, but nobody was Peter's Test partner more frequently than myself, which shows that there is nothing new about a shortage of opening batsmen. Our first opening stand ended at 28, when I was caught behind off Heine for 16. Peter went on, and on, and on to register what was then the slowest century in Test cricket, but the important thing from our angle was that we won the match by 131 runs. I had the satisfaction of taking three for 33 in their first innings and five for 20 off 15.4 overs in their second, when we dismissed them for 72. Although these figures delighted me, the only wicket I can still remember was diving forward in the slips to catch, two handed, van Ryneveld off Statham, probably the best slip catch I ever made.

The Second Test was won as a result of some quite exquisite wrist-spin from Johnny Wardle. At the same time, our extremely limited opening pair could afford to be more than satisfied with stands of 76 and 74 against Heine and Adcock, a distinctly hostile pair.

When Peter and I came in at lunchtime on the first day of the next encounter, at Durban, our score was 103 for nought. It did not make much sense, but what followed made rather less as I watched, becalmed but comfortable, all our main batsmen depart. Tayfield bowled a remarkable 14 consecutive maidens; not so remarkable was that nine were to me. At an early close we were still in the reasonable position of 184 for five, but we collapsed badly on the following day. I added only nine to my overnight 71 and we were all out for 218. In retrospect I should have had a hundred on that first day, but it is always so much easier in retrospect while the end result, a draw, would have been the same.

Our fourth meeting was the most exciting of the series and we lost by 17 runs. Tayfield bowled beautifully to take nine wickets in our second innings, but we were not helped by the umpiring. As we used to say at the time: 'Don't malign Malan, he's doing the best he can.' Unfortunately, his best was way below the expected standard. At the start of the last over of the fourth day, requiring 222 to win with all our wickets in hand, I pushed forward to Tayfield, very carefully took my bat away, allowed the ball to hit my front pad, told the keeper not to be a fool when he shouted 'catch it', and was given out caught at forward short-leg. It has been said that I was still standing there in disbelief and anger when the entire South African team had left the field, showered and departed home. That was a slight exaggeration, but I was unhappy, especially as we went so close on the final day.

We lost the final Test on what can only be described as the worst type of bad wicket, a win-the-toss, win-the-match pitch and Peter May made his worst mistake of the tour by calling incorrectly. We were also without the services, through injury, of our two best bowlers, Brian Statham and Johnny Wardle. On the first day we bowled accurately, but South Africa managed to recover from 78 for five to 138 for five.

The wicket was difficult, but not nearly as unpleasant as it was to become. It had no pace and no substance, so that the shooters did not just keep low but shot straight along the ground and with increasing frequency. To play back was to invite disaster, which was one thing I had in my favour when I opened with Peter against a match-winning total of only 164. I think I would rate my 41 as my best innings in Test cricket. Apart from playing off my front foot, I often batted well down the pitch to the two fast bowlers in an attempt to upset their length. It was a question of time before the unplayable ball arrived, so it was vital to score off anything slightly overpitched. After two hours I received a Heine shooter, and despite a fine 24 from May we were all out for 110.

We restricted South Africa to 134 in their second innings, but the 189 that we then required was never on, even for an outstanding batting side which we were not. I thought we had an outside chance during my second partnership with Peter May, but it was not to be. Because it was so difficult to score runs off their seamers, I reckoned we had to try and hit Tayfield whenever possible, even though by now the ball was liable to turn sharply. It was one of the comparatively few occasions in my international career that I eventually perished in the outfield hitting with the tide, but not far enough.

The greatest fascination of the tour was provided by the country which contained so many beautiful things like the Victoria Falls, the view from the top of Table Mountain, a native kraal, the veldt at dawn, hippopotamuses taking a bath in the Zambesi, and the majesty of the landscape where they buried Cecil Rhodes. In those days Rhodesia was part of the tour.

Not for the first, nor the last, time I usually found the animals more interesting than the people and my most delightful moments were spent in the game reserves. My day in the Wanki Reserve was unquestionably the most hilarious. Although the Wanki was officially closed because the rains had started, we persuaded a warden to allow us to enter. We left our hotel at 3 a.m. in a taxi driven by an essentially urban, coloured driver with suspect wheel ability, which was confirmed even before we reached the national park. We were forced to cross a flooded river in the dark and our man at the wheel decided to go through in top gear. Inevitably he stalled in the middle, with the result that Doug Insole, Godfrey Evans, Johnny Woodcock of *The Times* and myself found ourselves pushing hard for dry land with visions of snakes and crocodiles very much in mind.

We drove from 6 a.m. to 4 p.m. without encountering another human, just a large and varied collection of wild animals, including three superb cheetahs. Although nobody was meant to get out, we frequently had to leave the safety of our car in order to shift it from the mud. The climax of a marvellous day occurred when we encountered an elephant. We had been complaining that we had not seen any when Godfrey emitted an excited sqeak and there it was, a gigantic creature only 15 yards away and moving fast. I filmed it with my cine-cinema through a window, but Doug wanted a close-up, which was too much for our terrified and hysterical driver who promptly went into a ditch. We decided to replace him, though I am not sure that Doug at the wheel was not a greater hazard.

My wife joined me during the tour. Greta flew out from Southend airport to Johannesburg by Trek Airways with Colin Cowdrey's wife, Penny. The journey took them three days and nights. This included one stop in the desert to refuel when they had to turn back because some Arabs had raided that particular stopover. It was the type of flight which Biggles would have undertaken if he had gone into commercial aviation, but it was all we could afford and both wives arrived eventually, none the worse for their experience.

For most of the visit we stayed with friends – a former Essex cricketer, Reg Taylor, a former Cambridge undergraduate, and an ex Royal Marine. In addition to being much more comfortable than a hotel, it provided us with a more accurate view of life in South Africa and it was also much cheaper, which was essential. We were also able to spend several days in the Kruger National Park. Although more commercialized than the Wanki Reserve, it was my idea of an absolutely perfect holiday, a prolonged picnic in the sun, garnished with the jungle, vast numbers of wild animals and with all the amenities of civilization, like comfortable beds, food and champagne, close at hand. Our daughter Sharon is a continual reminder of that holiday, and I have always followed the career of Penny's son, Christopher, who was born a day before my daughter, with more than usual interest.

BROWN SKIN GAL

All de world knows our skipper Len,
Plays and misses only now an den.
A batsman of de very highest class,
But down rite Yorkshire when it comes to brass.
Chorus of MCC version on 1953–54 tour

I have lost count of the number of times I have been to the West Indies during the past two decades. I must have been out there at least once a year, so I am inclined to think of Barbados as my second home. How very different it was when I made my first visit in 1954–55 as vice-captain of Len Hutton's team for what was to be the hardest, most unpleasant and controversial of my tours, with the unofficial championship of the world at stake. When I left Jamaica to sail home on a very ancient banana boat, I would not have worried if I was never to see the Caribbean again.

Looking back now it is easy to understand why so many things went wrong, starting with the composition of the side's management which consisted of a captain who had never led a team abroad, a vice-captain who lacked experience and a player manager who had never even been to the West Indies. It was naive of the MCC to select such an inexperienced trio for a tour which was bound to be exceptionally demanding for a number of reasons, some of which had nothing to do with cricket.

First, the West Indies had a strong side, which was then but not now even more formidable on their own pitches.

Second, the rubber was for what could have been termed the unofficial world cricket championship. This added to the pressure on the umpiring which was bound to suffer from inexperience.

Third, for the first time we had chosen a genuine England XI, so that a West Indian victory meant so much more.

Fourth, the West Indies were becoming independent and quite apart from the pleasure of beating England for the supreme title,

185

victory would demonstrate the supremacy of black over white, even though their team did contain several white West Indians.

Fifth, we had a battery of fast bowlers, who believed in making life physically unpleasant for opposing batsmen, which was undoubtedly resented by the opposition and their supporters.

Sixth, like so many England teams we were slightly arrogant and distinctly intolerant of the accommodation provided and some of the arrangements. These were then the responsibility of the West Indian Board of Control who, as they were paying for it, tried to cut the costs to a minimum. The situation was not helped by the West Indian side itself being rather divided by both colour and island differences. In those days it was inconceivable to stage a Test at any of the four major grounds – Sabina Park, Kensington Oval, Bourda and Queen's Park Oval – without including at least two locals in the XI, so that politics, not cricket, governed the selection of the West Indies team. As a result there was little fraternization between the two teams. When we returned home I hardly knew Weekes, Worrell and Walcott, with whom I was to become so friendly later.

Finally, there were the Caribbean colour problems which were so complex that they took me years to unravel and I am still not sure that I have analysed them correctly. I had been brought up to believe that colour was immaterial: what mattered and counted was the character and the cricketing ability of the player concerned. I soon discovered that this outlook was far too naive for the West Indies, where degrees of colour were considered so vital.

I became somewhat irritated with white West Indians but far more with Englishmen who were in residence out there and believed, somewhat illogically, that they were a major asset, who came up to me saying that England simply had to win. Their reason was that their life would not be worth living if the West Indies were victorious because it would disturb the balance of power, or, as a Victorian would have put it, 'make the natives uppity'. I wanted to beat the West Indies and was prepared to devote myself to that objective, but I was not remotely interested in how five Tests affected the white population who, in the main, seemed to be doing reasonably well, certainly considerably better than most of their darker-skinned brothers.

In Guyana I discovered one of the many variations on skin texture, when a charming little Indian came up to me at a reception for the MCC after we had thrashed the local XI. He told me the decline of their team was the result of colour prejudice. It was at least twenty minutes before I realized that he was not complaining about whites being unfair to blacks, but blacks being unfair to Indians. Later, much later, I learned to distinguish between the subtle variations of shades, which meant there were separate cricket clubs in Barbados for the whites, the blacks and the coloureds. I also gradually began to appreciate the marked difference in character between the various territories which once made up the British West Indies and realized that the glorious dream of a united West Indies would never occur because there were too many dishonest and greedy politicians and not sufficient wealth and employment. The days when one said 'rich as a Carib' had long gone.

On the field black, white and coloured had always played against and alongside each other in the West Indies for club, island and national eleven, so it can be said that cricket had done much to break down the barriers. It is therefore rather sad to see some nameless politicians, who desperately seek to be known outside their own unimportant little island, exploiting West Indian cricket and using it as a lever to stir up further racial trouble.

There is no doubt that in the past it was easier for white players to gain initial selection than black, but eventually it was the runs made or the wickets taken which counted, though it was a long time before there was a black captain – though not quite so long as it took England to appoint a professional. Now there must be more than a suggestion that it is harder for a white player to gain selection than a black. The wheel has turned.

For the benefit of spreading the gospel, but certainly not for the benefit of a team tackling the West Indies, our tour started before Christmas in Bermuda. The three things I remember most about my short visit were my introduction to the stylized version of the Calypso by the Talbot brothers; the astonishing sight of Errol Flynn consuming, of all things, iced cherry brandy out of a pint silver tankard; and a dreadful Christmas Day dinner at Government House, which should never have been inflicted on anybody. The meal was mundane, the company austere, and the drink in short supply. For two hours after dinner we played charades, never my favourite game, without any further refreshments. Just before we made our escape one of our party was reprimanded by our hostess, a dragon straight out of Oscar Wilde, for putting his feet on the settee in a desperate attempt to introduce some realism into a scene.

When we arrived in the West Indies we saw Jamaica crumple against our pace bowlers in our first meeting. Although they batted better on the second occasion, we still fancied our chances of winning the First Test with pace. Accordingly, we chose four quickies plus Lock and forgot balance. It did not work. We finished by losing a game we could have won, even though we were not invited to follow on after insipid batting in our first innings. Our use of four fast bowlers evoked a fair amount of criticism, Jim Swanton writing as follows: '16 overs an hour we had – or four short of the normal average. In the course of a day the loss of 20 overs naturally means a great deal.' Although at the end of the first day the West Indies were only 168 for two, the time when West Indian bowlers would perpetrate an unacceptable over-rate of 12 per hour was light years away.

There were several other odd features about this game. In their second innings I bowled genuine leg theory, sending down ten overs for 11 runs, while Everton Weekes of all people was an hour scoring six. In our second innings Kentish employed it against England to make sure we did not reach our target and took five wickets. The inability of the class batsmen on both sides to cope adequately with this form of attack resulted in it not being used again on the tour. The players themselves realized that it could kill the game as a spectacle and it was stopped without any legislation.

For the only time in my Test career, I was undefeated in both innings . . . and opened my account with a six. The latter was not quite so dramatic as it may sound. I had gone in at 282 for four, which represented unusual prosperity. At that juncture, with Kentish firing well wide of the leg stump, we might not have been able to guarantee a win but we certainly had no reason to fear defeat, yet with no addition to the total Graveney was caught at leg slip and Evans, who had been upset by his captain on the previous evening, was bowled 'cowing' at a straight ball. Lock showed that he intended to stay but after ten minutes he managed to pad a ball from way outside his leg stump on to his wicket – 282 for seven. The collapse continued as I watched, with something approaching apoplexy from the other end, Statham and then Trueman departing for one apiece.

At 285 for nine I saw Alan Moss emerge from the pavilion. Though I have always been fond of Alan, his batting did not inspire much confidence, especially after witnessing five wickets fall for three runs and for no particular reason. I have never objected to being not out, but nought not out, having gone in at number six, was unacceptable. The time had come for desperate measures and mine took the shape of a six off Ramadhin, followed by some aggressive strokes from both of us in a stand of 31 which ended all too soon with Alan running himself out.

If the First Test was a disappointment, the Second in Barbados was a disaster. In their first innings Clyde Walcott played one of the most majestic innings I have seen, scoring 220 out of a total of 383. His driving off both front and back foot was exceptionally powerful and in stopping a very hard hit off my bowling the third finger of my right hand was chipped, although I was able to continue bowling. It is still out of shape – why was I born with such stupid little hands?

In the course of Clyde's innings I sent down what was, I believe, the most remarkable maiden over of my career. My first ball pitched just outside the off stump, would have hit middle and off, and was fractionally short. Only a superb piece of fielding in the covers prevented Clyde hitting it for four off his back foot. My next ball was identical, except a shade fuller in length. That also would have reached the boundary if not for an athletic interception in the covers, but the stroke was off his front foot. This sequence was repeated throughout the over. Although it ended as a maiden, it could have cost 24 runs!

The third day of the Test, 9 February 1954, will go down as one of the bad days of English cricket. It started at 53 for two with Hutton and Compton at the wicket on a beautiful pitch with a fast outfield, yet we scored only 128 runs off 114 overs in a full day's cricket, which lasted five hours as the Test was played over six days. To put everything into perspective, the second new ball became available when there were only 77 runs on the board; Ramadhin sent down 51 overs for 50 runs and four wickets; while Valentine was rather more expensive as his three wickets in 51.5 overs cost 61 runs; and, to emphasize our run-rate, I scored more quickly than any of my colleagues. We lost the match by 181 runs.

Two-nil down with three matches to go against the strongest batting line-up in the world was not the most encouraging position. In these circumstances it was hardly surprising that we had been written off by the popular press because our performances on the field had not been good enough, and also by Jim Swanton and most of the so-called serious press because we had also failed to lose with the apologetic grace and false smile of a civil servant from a minor public school. The outlook was bleak and, to make it bleaker, the next stop was Guiana, which, unlike most of the West Indies, has little to recommend it apart from the airport when you are about to depart. However, it was here that our comeback began.

Although we thrashed the Guiana team by an innings and 98 runs, we were unhappy about the standard of the umpiring which was worse than that experienced in Jamaica and Barbados. We therefore requested another pair for the Test, and suggested Burke from Jamaica and Walcott from Barbados. Considering we had lost when they had officiated we could hardly have been fairer, but the local Board felt it to be a reflection on their own umpires, which it was not – merely a condemnation. In the end we settled for the local groundsman, Menzies, and Gillette, who had said he would never umpire a Test again after the Indians had been rude to him in the previous year. This oddly chosen pair proved to be efficient, while we started our recovery as a result of producing our best allround performance.

The Third Test provided my first experience of a 'bottle party' during a cricket match. It began after McWatt, a local hero, foolishly decided to take two to Peter May at third man and was run out by a yard. If McWatt had made his ground it would have brought up the hundred partnership with Holt. Ramadhin came in next and before he received a ball the bottles started to arrive until the ground was littered. We all took refuge in the middle of the pitch, where we were safe from the flying bottles, but inevitably play was held up for some time.

There is a delightful story that Len Hutton said, 'We want another wicket tonight.' We certainly did, as that would have meant that they would have had nine down with Valentine to come and Holt hobbling on one leg, but Len, like all of us, was bemused by this totally unexpected barrage. Wardle did a drunk act with one of the bottles which helped to restore normality to the scene. The bottles were gradually collected and play was eventually resumed. We dispensed with third man and fine leg at both ends in the interests of discretion, which allowed Tom Graveney to make the best remark of the tour when he went up to the 'little Ram' and said: 'If you hit the ball down there, Sonny, you can bloody well get it yourself.'

Why did it happen? I always maintained it stemmed from three factors: a disappointing performance by the home team, a series of lost bets and drink. Not unnaturally a number of the spectators had bet on Everton Weekes scoring a century, and they were on to a very good thing until he was bowled by Lock for 94. Unfortunately Everton stayed at the crease, possibly mystified by how he had missed a straight ball which just took the bail. The little Indian umpire gave him out and some of the unlucky speculators decided the ball had bounced back off the pads of Godfrey Evans.

The second popular bet was on Christiani making runs. Quite apart from being local, he had scored a seventy and eighty for Guiana against us in the previous match. He was caught out by Willie Watson off Jim Laker in a diving catch, stayed there and was given out by the same little Indian umpire. On this occasion some of the disappointed punters decided that Willie had not made a clean catch.

In an effort to recoup their losses, and depressed by the failure of their heroes to show their expected form, some spectators decided to have a flutter on McWatt, another local. When he and Holt began to rescue their side with a highly improbable partnership, they bet on a stand of a hundred, which, until the fatal run out, looked a certainty. Again, the same little Indian umpire gave him out – and suddenly it was raining bottles.

At stumps the little umpire Menzies did not run off the field, but he wisely moved very quickly. Sadly, a police guard had to be stationed at his home over the weekend.

Having won the previous Test by nine wickets, our next Test against the West Indies was on the most perfect batting pitch it has been my misfortune to encounter as a bowler, the mat at Queen's Park Oval, Trinidad. It was so true that a draw was always favourite, but before that I had the pleasure of captaining MCC to the first victory over Trinidad on the mat since 1930. The highlight for me occurred when batting with Denis Compton after tea when, with wickets in hand, I had decided the time had come to launch our assault. The first over Denis rightly played as a maiden, which provided me with an irresistible opportunity.

Before the next over commenced, I summoned Denis to the middle and gave my instructions with a straight face: 'You stay there Denis, and I'll play the shots.' While my words were very gradually sinking in, I had retreated to the safety of my crease, slogged about 20 and returned to the pavilion, content that with Denis in command we would be home and dry.

The Test was less satisfactory as the West Indies made 681 for eight declared, which meant that when I went out to open the innings with Len Hutton for the first time on that tour, we needed a little matter of 532 runs to save the follow-on. Play was delayed at the start of the fourth day because the ground under the mat, which had been repaired, was still wet, rather suggesting sharp practice. England were 130 for one and, with 46 to my credit, I was hoping for a hundred with the bat to compensate for the 104 already obtained with the ball. It was not to be, but we did save the follow-on.

The moment I remember most was when, with the umpteenth new ball, King hit Laker over the eye with a bouncer. I dashed for my movie camera to film him coming off the field. Unfortunately, he retreated to the pavilion, with his handkerchief being used to stem the blood, in a swerving, swooning run pursued by members of the West Indian team anxious to help, which meant my eventual film was too jerky.

We arrived back in Jamaica several days before the final encounter with the depressing knowledge that our best fast bowler on the tour, Brian Statham, was unable to perform. We examined the glistening grey pitch at Sabina Park with considerable care. We had to win, what was our best chance?

We decided, quite wrongly as it turned out, that we must win the toss, score heavily and rely on our spinners to bowl out the opposition twice, assuming that the wicket would prove receptive to spin in the latter stages. The result was that we went into the final Test with three spinners, Laker, Lock and Wardle, plus only two seamers, Trueman and myself, and simply prayed that Len would call correctly.

I still treasure the despairing look on Len's face when he returned to the pavilion having called incorrectly. He thought, and so did we all, that the best result we could attain was a draw: there was no way that we would dismiss the West Indies twice on what was a beautiful batting pitch. Their batting line-up had in fact been strengthened by the inclusion of a young slow leftarm spinner, called Gary Sobers, for the injured Alf Valentine, and you do not bat at number five for Barbados, ahead of Denis Atkinson, unless you can make runs. In this, Gary's Test debut, he came in at number nine!

If anybody had asked me before we went out to field what I would have settled for as a bowler, I would have said three for 100 in 35 overs. Even then, I reckoned I would need to bowl well for these figures.

Having been given the new ball and choice of ends by Len, I chose to bowl into a breeze which was also blowing across the ground and might have helped an inswinger. The reason was obvious as Fred Trueman was not only yards faster, but, like me, relied very largely on the outswinger. Fred had to come down wind and I thought that after his initial burst I would replace him at that end.

I said a little prayer and opened with my usual new-ball field: mid-off, cover, two slips, gulley and third man on the off side and short mid-on and two leg slips on the leg. My target was the off stump, my length full and the short legs were there not so much for inswing but for the ball that did occasionally nip back. Once I had taken a wicket and was occasionally beating the outside edge, third man joined the slips. But I was never happy without a mid-off – I was a fast-medium seamer who sometimes swung the ball and a mid-off allowed me to maintain a full length without being pushed through the covers when a delivery failed to move, which occurred frequently.

What happened on 30 March 1954 was totally unexpected, very exciting and still makes no sense. I simply experienced one of those dream days when everything went right. The ball moved more than I expected, though not to a great extent, and the bounce remained even, but every time a shot was played in the air it went to hands which accepted the chance gratefully.

The outcome of a quite extraordinary day was that at stumps the West Indies were all out for 139 and England were 17 for nought with Hutton on 8 and myself on 9. My figures, easily my best in Test cricket, were 16–7–34–7. For once I was unable to sleep and spent part of the night wandering about my hotel, a case of mental, rather than physical, exhaustion.

On the following day I went out to bat with Len against King, who was bouncer-happy, and Gomez. Len took a single in King's first over and I spent the next six weaving and ducking as King proceeded to average between three and four per over. It was rather a waste of effort because I did not hook and it came as no surprise when later in the match he pulled a muscle. While King was hurling them down at me, I watched the maestro take two and four off the medium-paced Gomez.

Len went on to score a masterful 205. Although his innings did not contain a single chance there occurred during it an incident which typified the problems of that particular tour. By teatime on the third day, Len was both mentally and physically drained. As he fought his way through the crowded pavilion steps on his way to the sanctuary of the dressing-room, he gently pushed aside a swaying figure whom he did not really notice. Once inside, we provided Len with tea, a cigarette, a light, removed his pads and emphasized that we needed more runs from him.

Having made sure he was back in the right mood to continue the battle, he was just about to strap on his pads when there was a knock at the door. I opened it to reveal a political lackey demanding to see our captain. He claimed that Len had insulted his prime minister, the swaying figure whom Len had unwittingly pushed as he had made his way into the pavilion. I still chuckle to think of this happening at teatime at Lord's.

We eventually won the match comfortably to square the series. It was to be a very long time before I set foot in the Caribbean again, though I suppose I could claim to have been a shade unlucky not to have been selected for the next England tour out there in 1959–60. I had enjoyed a reasonable summer in 1959 as well as having fully recovered from my injured back. For the only time in my career I scored just over 2000 runs and captured 100 wickets, which would normally have been sufficient to gain a place in an England touring party, especially as my personal record in the West Indies with bat and ball had been very respectable.

As it was, I had to wait until 1963 before I returned to the West Indies with the Rothman Cavaliers for a short tour of Jamaica with Denis Compton as captain. It was enormous fun so I went again, this time as captain, in the following year, when we also visited Barbados. Having been largely responsible for choosing the young players we took for the experience, I was delighted to note how well the majority did subsequently. Keith Fletcher, Alan Knott, John Hampshire and Robin Hobbs went on to play for England, while Ron Headley was capped for the West Indies.

On my second trip, the Cavaliers played Barbados twice. In the first meeting we were fairly fortunate to obtain a draw against their full side, but our second match coincided with a Test match against Australia in Jamaica for which as usual about half the Barbados XI were required. As a result, their Board decided to pick, under an experienced captain, what was virtually their Second XI. This gave me the opportunity to see the depth of talent in this remarkable little island and provided me with my first look at two youngsters who were to do so well in English county cricket and for the West Indies in the years that followed, Keith Boyce and John Shepherd.

I have already mentioned how I took Keith Boyce on to the Essex staff. Les Ames, who was the tour manager, decided to take on the less spectacular John Shepherd. John gave his adopted county quite outstanding value for a very long time, so I feel Kent might have displayed more consideration when they eventually decided to dispense with his services.

While with the Rothman Cavaliers I had dinner with Frank Worrell and his wife in Jamaica and Everton Weekes and his wife in Barbados. I put to both wives the same question and received an identical reply. I asked them where they would most like to live if money was not a consideration. To my considerable surprise, without hesitation they both chose Manchester. Of course, they did not mean the city but the surrounding districts and, most of all, the people who had made them so welcome and at home.

After those two immensely enjoyable trips, my visits to the Caribbean became increasingly frequent. I hosted parties out there during the last three MCC tours. In the first I saw Tony Greig have easily his finest Test; and in the second I witnessed Michael Holding bowling two of the fastest overs I have ever seen, one to Geoff Boycott and one to Ian Botham.

I have been to Barbados with the English Press Cricketers Association which, somewhat ironically, consisted largely of football writers. Our party was unquestionably the most smartly turned out, especially on arrival, but it contained the thirstiest, most garrulous and most inept cricketers it has been my great pleasure to tour with.

I also went to Barbados to acquire the necessary background for my biography on Sir Gary Sobers. At the same time, I was able to research his story for the television programme 'This is Your Life'. Gary and his wife, Sue, were the most generous of hosts, and driving round the island with Gary was tantamount to accompanying Prince Charles through London in an open car. At one point in my visit I suggested to Garnett Ashby, who had introduced Gary to adult cricket in their country league, that he must be a proud man. His reply was simply, 'Oh no, mun, I just lit de candle.'

In some respects the most fascinating excursion to the Caribbean took place when I visited a number of islands – including Trinidad, St Lucia, Antigua, Tobago, Barbados, and Jamaica – looking for suitable hotels to be used for a Far Horizon tour to coincide with the next MCC visit. When I had first gone to Barbados there were only about five hotels and we stayed at the Marine in the middle of Bridgetown, now government offices, while tourism, which has become their main industry, was comparatively unknown. Although Jamaica catered for a large influx of tourists, all the other islands, with the exception of Trinidad, which was the most prosperous, were essentially dependent upon agriculture.

The growth of the tourist industry, especially in Barbados, has been spectacular and perhaps too fast for the island's own good. However, the moment I remember most clearly about my tour of the hotels had nothing to do with accommodation. It occurred when I decided to have a nostalgic look at the Queen's Park Oval. Here I found the most important personage in Trinidadian cricket, Sir Errol de Santos, busily counting out the money that had been taken at the ground from a 'Saturday Night Jump Up'. Imagine the equivalent of 'Gubby' Allen personally totting up the cash from a dance held in the Long Room at Lord's!

For the past eight years I have been associated with the annual Fred Rumsey Pro-Am Cricket Tour, originally as one of the more senior captains. I played my final match on the minute Empire ground and decided that Barbados was a suitable place to retire from the game. Since then I have acted as the disorganized organizer. The number of club cricketers who have repeated this trip is proof enough of the enjoyment this cricket holiday has provided. It was especially designed to accommodate cricketers of all standards from Minor County to village, down to that extra, extra, extra B, where nobody is ever run out because nobody is capable of moving into top gear.

FOOTBALL CRAZY

When I came down from Cambridge in the summer of 1948, my appointment as assistant secretary meant that I would play for Essex the following cricket season, but I still had to find a club for my other sporting love, football, which had first begun as a very small boy. At Alleyn Court I took part in at least two organized matches every week throughout the two winter terms. In addition, we spent every morning break kicking a ball about, and on most afternoons when there was not a match we would have a pick-up game immediately after school until it was too dark to see.

I was also taken along by my father to watch Southend United, who were in the Third Division South and normally attracted crowds of around 10,000, while it was not unusual to have around 7000 for a London Combination reserve game against one of the big London clubs. One match remains particularly vivid. The 'Blues' had very surprisingly achieved a draw at White Hart Lane in the FA Cup and I went on my own to the replay on Wednesday afternoon at the stadium. There was a record crowd, but no hint of violence so that a child was perfectly safe. The fact that I was much too small to see was no problem, because someone simply lifted me on to the top of a small tea bar on the terraces from where I had a perfect view of the proceedings.

At school I was taught the rudiments of the game, even though these stemmed tactically back to the days of the Corinthians. At throw-ins, the half back took the throw. His opposite number marked the winger, with the attacking inside forward being marked by his opposite number, and the defending full back providing additional cover. In the five-boy forward line, the centre forward led the line and was expected to score most of the goals. The wingers went down the wing and centred. The two inside forwards were expected to make and take goals, and also spent some time in pleasing triangular movements involving wing half and winger. The full backs were usually large lads who could tackle and kick the ball a long way, and, from time to time, the opposing winger. The centre half was the best player with a roving commission to attack and defend. The goalkeeper was usually a problem, because few boys were prepared to risk spending most of the game doing nothing, especially when it was cold and raining. In pick-up games, or when shooting at goal, everybody was keen to go between the posts, but it was different for matches.

I started my school football career as a diminutive, rather apprehensive winger. I then progressed to an inside forward with some imagination and an insipid tackle in which I almost invariably finished on the ground, sometimes but not always accompanied by a member of the opposition. Finally I became the centre half and at 13 I think I could claim to have the potential to have developed into a class footballer, because I was a natural ball player, fast and had acquired the basic skills. More important, I knew what to do with the ball when in possession and had the instinct to take up a good position in the context of the play, whether I was in attack or defence.

I did not play soccer again until I was 17 when I used to run a scratch XI in the school holidays. We used to enjoy ourselves playing against the teams from the local fire service. I gained further experience during my three years in the Royal Marines, when on occasions the standard was quite high because there were a few professionals around, but the matches lacked the continuity which I required, and which I did not have until I went up to Cambridge after the war. This culminated in our winning what *The Times* described as 'the Best University Match for Years', saying that 'Trevor Bailey played the game of his life'.

My experience of playing soccer in the Royal Marines, two years in the Cambridge University XI and a number of matches for Southend United, enabled me to assess my ability with some accuracy. As a child I had dreamed of becoming a star player, but this could never occur because I had spent those vital formative years between 14 and 21 playing rugby, or in the forces. As a result, I usually knew exactly what was required, but lacked the technical skill to achieve it.

I never mastered the double shuffle; my left foot was no more than a reasonable swinger; I never sold a convincing dummy; I could not climb high and head crosses down with the centre of my forehead; I found crosses from the left more difficult than from the right, as I could head reasonably well with the left hand side of my forehead, but not with the right; and my tackling was weak. Those were the basic skills which I would have acquired and then constantly practised during those important missed years. If I had mastered them – and I did possess the ball sense, dedication and patience required – I might have become more than a reasonable performer. What had I to offer a football team? Pace off the mark, and over a distance; a dependable right foot; stamina; an accurate pass; enthusiasm; a natural instinct, perhaps most vital of all, for being in the right place at the right time and where to move off the ball; an ability to take corners precisely; and a love for the big occasion.

The obvious choice was Southend United, not the first team but the Reserves who played in the London Combination. The club was on my doorstep and I could train with the players, making sure that it would be on the two occasions each week when practice games were staged, as I had no wish to spend my time lapping round the stadium. In addition, I had played several times for the club, my father-in-law was a director, and I knew the manager, Harry Warren, very well. To make matters more attractive, I was not seeking money. All I wanted was a game of football once a week.

How times have changed, as that is exactly what Harry could not provide, because at that time he had 32 full-time professionals on his books. As a result I entered senior amateur football with the Essex club, Leytonstone.

These were the great days of amateur football when over 100,000 turned up at Wembley for the Amateur Cup final. I cannot remember playing a Saturday home match at either of my two clubs, Leytonstone and Walthamstow Avenue, before less than 5000. For Amateur Cup games gates would be about 9000 and more for FA Cup matches.

One season Walthamstow enjoyed a highly successful run in the FA Cup, beating both Stockport County and Reading before managing a one-all draw against Manchester United at Old Trafford. We obviously could not have accommodated all those who wanted to see the replay on our own ground, with a capacity of about 12,000, so it was switched to Highbury. It was before floodlights were permitted in the competition, but 55,000 turned up on Wednesday afternoon for a 2.15 kick off!

With money like that around, it was inevitable that most successful amateur clubs were 'shamateur' in practice, though the amount paid to players varied considerably. My own view of the situation was realistic. I enjoyed football so much that I would have played for nothing, but certainly had no objection to receiving extra pocket money.

At that time there was a maximum and minimum wage for professional footballers, which was one of the reasons why the standard among the top amateur clubs was so high. Many accomplished players who possessed the ability to play First Division football decided that they were better off financially with a secure job and the extra money they picked up in their boots than turning professional. There were also a number of talented youngsters, usually with an acquisitive father, who settled for a job and amateur football rather than taking the pittance offered to them on becoming a professional. Then, if the young footballer did exceptionally well in amateur games, and especially if he was capped, he would sign on for a professional club which might be prepared to pay £1000 or more under the table. In those days that represented a considerable amount of money.

I played my first game for Leytonstone as inside left with the very accomplished Leon Joseph on the wing, but within a month I had become an established member of the team in an entirely new role, centre forward. I played there for two very happy and enjoyable seasons, after which I departed on a winter tour with the MCC.

I was never a genuine centre forward because I was neither strong enough nor good enough in the air, while my shooting was no more than adequate, but I was a useful decoy for our main goalscorer, Alf Noble, which is why I held my place. Alf was an outstanding amateur player who could have made a top class professional. I used to move out to the right or left, take the centre half with me, thereby leaving that little gap which was all that Alf required.

Football on Saturday was the highlight of my week. It provided me with more enjoyment than playing for Essex, because it lasted for only 90 minutes, whereas cricket went on for six hours per day, six days per week. Apart from the cup matches with their added incentive of sudden death, my favourite games were the local derbies between Leytonstone and Walthamstow, which took place on Christmas morning and Boxing Day. I have never enjoyed my Christmas dinner more than in the afternoon following a hard morning game, while the Boxing Day meeting provided a somewhat masochistic way of removing the excesses of the festive season.

Although the Leytonstone I played for was highly successful, always near the top of the Isthmian League and doing very well in a seemingly endless number of cup competitions – the Essex Cup, the Thameside Cup, the FA Cup and the London Senior Cup – we never won while I was there the one that really mattered, the Amateur Cup. We did come close with a replayed semi-final against Bromley, when I experienced two horribly ineffective games which haunted me for weeks. Nobody ever needed to tell me after I had played badly, I knew it better than anyone.

When I returned from the 1950–51 tour of Australia, I had not only become an England regular but also put on over a stone in weight. This did not worry me until the end of the summer at Scarborough, where I began my pre-season football training, usually accompanied by Willie Watson. I cannot say that I enjoyed our sessions at the Scarborough football ground because the Festival and fitness did not blend naturally, but they helped.

I reported back to Leytonstone only to find that in my absence they had found an infinitely more capable centre forward than myself, Vic Groves, who later was to play with distinction for the Arsenal. This neither surprised nor disturbed me because I had never rated myself as a centre forward. I immediately began an extensive training programme and for a month was content to play in Leytonstone Reserves.

Although I was still heavier than I had been, this was in many respects an asset because I was stronger and therefore more difficult to knock off the ball, while my 5 ft 10 in was quite tall by football standards. After those four weeks I decided that if Leytonstone were unable to find me a first team place, I would reluctantly go elsewhere.

I resigned from the club on the Monday, informed the press and went out to play Canasta with my wife at the house of two close friends. We failed to complete one game, because the phone never stopped ringing with requests for me to join a whole series of clubs in the Third Division, the Southern League, and in various other leagues, both professional and amateur. It was all very flattering and was due mainly to my having become well known as a cricketer, in rather the same way that plenty of football clubs would want Ian Botham thirty years later.

Although some of the offers received were very tempting financially, my objective was to find a club which was likely to do well and had a ground which I could reach in an hour by car. This narrowed my choice to virtually three clubs, because I had no intention of joining a Southern League side.

On the Wednesday evening I saw the Barking and Walthamstow Avenue committees. I chose the latter because they had an immediate vacancy in their forward line and, having played against them so often, I knew they were an above-average ambitious club. It proved to be an inspired choice as we went on to capture the Amateur Cup that season. Although Walthamstow had a very distinguished record, that was something which had never happened to them before. In the following season they experienced their best-ever run in the FA Cup. I could not have chosen a better time to join the Avenue and I had two highly enjoyable and successful seasons with them.

For my first season my position was inside right, which I enjoyed. On the wing I had a 16-year-old with enormous potential, Donald Rossiter, who signed on with Arsenal at 17 but sadly never made it to the top. Our line was led by Jim Lewis, who was by a very long way the best centre forward I encountered in amateur football. His secret was that he expected to score goals and he had the confidence to shoot in situations which I would never even consider.

Our progress to Wembley, apart from two stutters against Wimbledon whom we eventually beat 3–0 in the third encounter at Highbury, was impressive, including a 3–0 win over Walton and Mersham at Craven Cottage in the semi-final. In my first season with my new club we achieved the main ambition of every amateur club in the country. I have always thrived on the big occasion and they do not come much bigger than running out in front of 100,000 spectators, winning the cup and collecting a winner's medal. The match itself was not as good as we had hoped. We had played far better in most of our other games and we eventually had to settle for victory in extra time. It was the only occasion I ever had cramp, which was due to the long grass and the 'give' of the Wembley turf, definitely a surface where it pays to let the ball do the work.

The following season Walthamstow had an even stronger team, the best side in which I played. Rossiter had departed, so I was moved to the right wing which had been my position for Cambridge. It was probably my most effective place as I was able to cross accurately and also score goals. Although people tend to remember our draw in the FA Cup at Old Trafford against First Division Manchester United before losing the replay at Highbury, we did beat Stockport County without too much trouble at home, while in many respects our finest performance was to defeat Watford 2–1 away in the replay on the heaviest pitch I ever encountered. In these conditions it was felt that the fully trained professionals would be too fit, but we managed to win at a canter in extra time.

As things turned out, our FA Cup run was to cost us dear. After the exertions of our replay at Highbury against Manchester United, we played away in the Amateur Cup on the Saturday. We lost our full back in the first few minutes and went down and out of the Cup, which, at full strength, I fancied we would have retained. After that, although we won various trophies, the rest of the season was rather an anti-climax and it saw the break up of our team. Five turned professional, Jim Lewis played for Chelsea as an amateur, and I went on two successive tours with the MCC and never played serious football again.

People were always critical of my playing soccer, just as they have been with Ian Botham, because of the danger of injury which could have upset, interrupted, or even terminated my cricket career. I enjoyed the game so much that I was prepared to take the risk, but after missing two successive winters logic advised retirement. It had been hard for me returning to football after missing one full season, so it would have been even more demanding after two. In addition, I was bound to have lost some of my pace on which I was so dependent. Although my heart favoured one more season, I had sampled the delights of top class amateur soccer and I was not prepared to settle for anything less. I therefore decided to retire from the game.

To my utter amazement, I did not miss football and very quickly completely readjusted to living without the stimulation that it had provided. It made me realize that I could be happy without participating in sport, which had contributed so much to my life. I knew then that when the time came for me to stop playing cricket, it would not leave another void.

Like so many participators, I have never been a good spectator. I enjoy watching all sport providing the standard is high, but not on a regular basis, or for too long. I could never have become one of those football supporters who goes week after week and, though I love tennis, one day at Wimbledon is quite enough. I have always needed the stimulation of personal involvement and found this through covering sport for a newspaper, radio or television. It was then entirely different, because I had to concentrate in order to do the job correctly. After retiring as a player I began writing on football, initially for the Sunday *Observer*. Later, in the mid-1960s, I was invited to contribute some articles on an Australian Test series to the *Financial Times*, and I eventually became their cricket and football correspondent, a very happy association stretching over some 25 years.

I also spent several years on the board of Southend United, which initially were most enjoyable. We met once a fortnight, but not for too long, and never spent any time discussing tactics which were left to the manager. I began to lose interest when our meetings started to drag on into the night and some of the new directors started to believe that they really did know something about the game. I eventually resigned when we were relegated to the Fourth Division, despite a reasonably talented team. This, in my opinion, was largely due to our manager, who clearly had failed to make the best use of the players at his disposal.

Unlike my fellow directors, I never became emotionally involved in either the club's successes or failures, of which there were rather more. I remember travelling to see Southend United play Gillingham away in the FA Cup and, with us leading 1–0 with three minutes to go, feeling well satisfied. It was then that our opponents equalized with five United players in their penalty area. I was not amused by this tactical naivety but that was nothing compared with my feelings when our centre half, a good player, was galloping back towards his own goal hotly pursued by the opposition's centre forward and decided to concede a corner from outside the penalty area . . . but managed to fire the ball into the top left-hand corner of our goal! There was not even time to kick off again, but my frustration departed at the sight of my literally speechless chairman who had put his rather natty headgear on the ground and was jumping up and down on it. It was at least five minutes before I stopped laughing.

The only time I took an active part in the team's tactics was when we were between managers and were losing 2–0 at half-time away from home. I suggested that we left our two inside forwards up front with our big fearless centre forward. Both inside forwards were small and nippy, one brave and lucky, the other clever and somewhat apprehensive. We also played our two wingers deep and wide, the one on the left a dasher who was unable to centre with his left foot and the one on the right a casual, clever and rather erratic performer. It was a ghastly system, but it worked. We won the match, and did not lose again that season, simply because the opposition failed to appreciate what was happening, with two full backs marking two non-existent wingers and the centre half and defensive wing half having problems marking three attackers.

I have had the good fortune to see all the outstanding League teams, commencing with the 'Busby Babes' and including Nicholson's Spurs, whom I think gave me more pleasure than any other side; Revie's Leeds; Clough's Derby County and Nottingham Forest; and the decade which belonged to Liverpool. I have watched England under Sir Walter Winterbottom, Sir Alf Ramsey, Don Revie, Joe Mercer, Ron Greenwood and Bobby Robson, and most of the finest international and continental teams.

I have noted numerous changes to the basic formations of my era, all of which are perfectly acceptable as long as the manager fits a system to his players rather than fitting his players to a system. However, the big difference between the football of my vintage and that of the present has nothing to do with systems; indeed, the object of the game, to score more goals than the opposition, has remained exactly the same. It lies in the equipment.

We used a leather ball, which on a wet and muddy pitch became increasingly heavy. I possessed a fairly strong deadball kick and reckoned to achieve my objective when taking a corner, which was to provide a heading chance at the far post. There was no problem when the ball was new, irrespective of the width of the pitch. On the other hand, in the second half on a heavy ground there were many occasions when I had difficulty in reaching the near post at head height, because of the weight of the ball; while a top class goalkeeper was pleased to reach the halfway line from a goal kick. Some teams deliberately immersed a new football in a bucket of water before the kick off on a dry ground in order to reduce bounce and make control easier.

The new-style ball was the outcome of floodlights. The manufacturers designed a protective white coat which kept out the wet and stopped flaking, and eventually all leather balls were treated in this fashion. The difference was considerable, something which I discovered in my first floodlit game at Highbury. This happened during a cup competition between the reserve teams of the London League clubs and senior amateur sides. I took my first corner of the match and aimed for the far post, but was amazed to see it sail over everybody's head, even that of my opposite number who was lurking just beyond the penalty area, for a throw-in on the far side. The new ball, which we termed plastic although it was not, could be kicked much further and was far easier to swerve. It also removed the element of fear when trying to head a very high punt upfield by the keeper. If you misjudged heading the old style ball and it landed on the back of your head instead of the front, it was extremely painful and could cause concussion.

In addition to the new-style ball travelling further and faster, it inevitably caused a revolution in footwear. In my era we wore boots which encased the ankles, had hard toecaps and studs of leather. I bought my boots a shade too small and the look of utter amazement on my wife's face on seeing me sitting in a bath reading a book and wearing a brand new pair of football boots was unforgettable.

It is not only the weight and design of the boots which have changed, but also, apart from the feet, the contents. Preparing for a match used to take me some time. I first put vaseline on my toes and enveloped them with a thick cover of cotton wool. I then put on my first pair of socks. My next task was to strap both my ankles with crêpe bandages at least a yard long, which was followed by my second pair of socks and shin guards – some people used two pairs. I would finally lace up the boots with long, strong laces before collecting a pair of cotton tie-ups from the trainer. The most important part of me was now ready for battle.

Today, the players wear light slippers with built-in studs, which means that they can run much faster. Their boots are more suitable for caressing a ball, but would have been no good for dealing with the cannonballs of yesteryear. As both the ball and the players travel more quickly, the tempo of football has increased and there are occasions when it becomes positively frenetic. An over-emphasis on speed, especially when combined with man-to-man marking, can reduce the game as a spectacle. I sometimes feel that there are too many runners and not enough footballers about . . . then Dalglish or Barnes or Hoddle will conjure up a piece of pure footballing magic to sweep away my temporary despondency and leave me purring with pleasure.

QUE SERA, SERA

When I resigned as secretary of Essex, I felt it would be unfair to my successor to become a member of the county committee, and that a clean break from club administration for about ten years was desirable. After that I might return, as it seemed to me that I could have had a little to contribute, but because I was never approached by the committee it never occurred. It has not mattered, as Essex, I am delighted to say, have done exceptionally well, while I have more than enough to do in my spare time.

Where I have been fortunate is to have enjoyed my post first-class cricket career so much that I can truthfully say that I never missed not playing. Some of my activities ended in failure, which was to some extent due to my not having been able to devote sufficient time to them, but they all provided enjoyment, satisfaction and excitement, even when they failed to produce any money. To make matters even better, I have been able to arrange working winter holidays in the sun for my wife and myself.

One mistake I made was not taking sufficient exercise after a fairly active life. Although I continued playing cricket for several years with Westcliff, that was not really enough, especially as I missed at least half the matches because of my commitments with Test Match Special. On the other hand, I certainly enjoyed returning to the club scene, which was made all the more pleasant by having my eldest son, Kim, in the team. What I thought just a shade disappointing, particularly before the introduction of a league system, was the number of dull draws which were predictable much too early in the contest. However, I found club games were infinitely more satisfactory than charity matches as I have always enjoyed my cricket far more when the result means something to everybody in a side, so that even if defeat is not considered a major disaster, it is at least a minor one. I also played for the Old Alleynians in the Cricketer Cup. Although we never won it, we did at least have the satisfaction of reaching the final. What was so delightful about these contests was that they gave me the opportunity to visit for the first time a number of school grounds in delightful settings, as well as to recall some former schoolboy battles. It also seemed that these matches were played in exactly the right spirit – fiercely competitive, but with humour and without incidents.

I began writing for the *Financial Times* in the early 1960s, when still playing first-class cricket. Later I became their cricket and football correspondent, which means that I have covered a large number of the main events in both sports. Although there were occasions when these clashed I was able to combine the two reasonably well, even though it sometimes necessitated complicated journeys. I was certainly the only person in the world who saw Poland beat England at Katovici on the Wednesday and England play New Zealand at Trent Bridge on the following day!

During my stay in Poland I visited a couple of Polish soccer clubs with Billy Wright, the former England football captain and a keen cricket lover. Although both teams were ostensibly labelled amateur, their morning training routine was not dissimilar to that of a professional First Division side in England, except for a greater emphasis on the importance of the ball. I asked our helpful interpreter if spectators ever showed their displeasure when one of the home side was playing badly, and if so what they did. He told me they simply shouted at him to get back to the mines, where most of the crowd were employed and life was less rewarding.

In the press bus, on the way to the World Cup match at about four o'clock, Billy remarked that at the same time the following day I would be having tea in the commentary box at the Test. Although he was right, I nearly failed to make it as I was unable to leave the football stadium until long after my coach had departed. I had to rely on a hire car and a driver who did not speak any English to take me to a military aerodrome many miles from the city. I prayed that my scheduled flight had not taken off, because with no money left, no knowledge of the language and no other flights, a Polish military zone was not the ideal place to be stranded if one was to describe the first ball bowled at Nottingham in the morning. I was even more worried when we arrived, because not only had we failed to encounter any coach and hardly any traffic on our long drive through the night, but the airport lounge was empty. Fortunately, all was well as my driver, who would not accept a tip, had arrived ahead of the rest of my party. My relief was considerable.

My most interesting experience of covering both sports occurred in the summer of 1974 when I commuted between West Germany, where the World Cup was being played, and England where the Test series was against India. On one occasion I was phoning a cricket article from the German press centre and extolling the virtues of Andy Roberts who was causing much havoc among Hampshire's opponents. This was overheard by a footballing colleague who, fearful that he might have missed a story, wanted to know Roberts's club and what position he played.

The World Cup was won by West Germany after a splendid match against Holland in Munich and took place on the Sunday of the Edgbaston Test against India. This entailed my catching a plane to Hamburg on the Saturday evening and another flight on the following morning to Munich, where I met up with the rest of the British press contingent and had lunch. They looked at me rather strangely when I said I wanted to be at the stadium nearly three hours before the kick-off, and even more strangely when I mentioned that my first task on arrival would be to phone through my cricket article from the press centre in the ground.

I caught the first plane back to England on the Monday morning and was distinctly weary by the time I had driven from Heathrow to Edgbaston. Mercifully the Test ended early on the Monday, but I still had to stop my car three times on my way home to prevent myself falling asleep.

My most demanding, educational and fascinating assignment for the *Financial Times* was unquestionably covering the Munich Olympics. In two weeks I wrote on football, hockey, boxing, judo, swimming, diving, dressage, eventing, show jumping, field athletics, fencing, track athletics – and a massacre. It was my first Olympics and when I arrived at the vast press village I did not fully appreciate the size of the undertaking or the amount of work involved. It began to register when I saw the sports editors of several national newspapers having a meeting with their journalists immediately after breakfast and allocating the numerous morning, afternoon and evening events. I now understood what Jim Manning had meant when he advised me to go to Munich because an Olympics was the supreme test for any sports writer. Sadly it was to be Jim's last Olympics. One of the finest controversial sporting journalists I have encountered, I am especially proud that he was my proposer when I joined the NUJ.

Appreciating that there are problems in being in a number of different places at the same time, I held a solo meeting and decided to play my personal hunches by going to see as many events as possible in which I fancied British competitors to do well. To my delight it worked, and I was especially pleased by our success in the equestrian events which took place a long way from the main arenas and could easily have wasted time I could ill afford. I was also greatly helped by the cooperation of equestrian writers.

The two moments of sporting magic which I treasure most occurred in a hockey match between West Germany and Holland and when I was being shown sabre fighting by David Acfield, who was in the Essex XI and a member of the England fencing team. In the first the German inside forward picked up the ball on the halfway line, swerved past two defenders as if they did not exist, sent the goalkeeper the wrong way and scored. The masked keeper led the applause to provide an example of both sporting perfection and sportsmanship.

I must confess I was not too impressed by the sabre duels which seemed to me, as a non-expert, fast, noisy and rather brash. Then I saw one contest in which even I could appreciate the grace, elegance and style. On asking David who he was, he nearly bowed and said that he was the Polish master. He did not stand out, he shone.

On the morning of the massacre my Editor phoned about breakfast time and asked for a news story as quickly as possible on the reaction of the athletes. As I expected, the competitors were too concerned about their own special events for which they had been training for several years to be very affected, or to realize the extent or the implications of the crime. So I described the scene as it appeared to me and recommended that the games should continue. I probably over dramatized and it was not what my Editor wanted. But he stopped me when I started to apologize, saying that I was there to write sport not news. It was not until several years later that I learned that he had been in favour of the games being cancelled immediately.

Until comparatively recently when sport in the *Financial Times* was moved to the Saturday edition, I wrote every Sunday for the Monday edition, winter and summer, plus a daily account of all Tests and midweek international football matches. I have enjoyed it enormously, especially the freedom which I discovered the moment I joined the paper. I asked John Higgins, who then looked after both art and sport, how technical I could be. He told me as technical as I liked, because if the readers could not understand it they should not be buying the paper.

Occasionally, very occasionally, a minor problem has arisen because there is not a sports section. A classic example occurred in my account of the match at the Baseball Ground between Leeds United and Derby County, who had just gained promotion. I went along to do a piece on how the newcomers compared with Leeds when they had just come up to the First Division. In my report I wrote, 'Up front, Hector, brave and sharp caught the eye.' I thought nothing more about it until I received a delicious letter from an Epsom stockbroker who had been a Derby County supporter for 30 years. He was excited by a forward line of Hector, Brave and Sharp. Add Achilles to that trio and they would surely have been unstoppable.

Apart from writing, my main business interests have included broadcasting on radio and television, especially with Test Match Special; administering a couple of sports shops; toy wholesaling; helping to run the Ilford Indoor Cricket School; and public relations and consultancy. The financial returns from these ventures have varied from reasonable to token, through non-existent to actual loss, but they have all been interesting and provided me with enjoyment, at least until they began costing too much money.

What I liked most about a retail shop was being busy selling to a continual stream of customers. Unfortunately this seldom occurred, except over the Christmas period, but there are few more satisfactory sounds than ringing up sales on a till in the knowledge that some of that money, though never in the quantity I would have liked, is coming your way.

Having never fully grown up, toys have always exerted a powerful fascination. What I enjoyed most about the wholesale toy trade was the challenge of choosing the right toys to buy at the right price. As a result the toy fairs at Harrogate and Brighton were not only decidedly tiring but also fun. To make things difficult was the enormous variety on display and the certainty that what I was convinced was a winner would not please some customers.

My supreme test was provided by the three weeks I spent purchasing toys in Hong Kong, a place which has never ceased to delight me. It was different going to the office by ferry, while my visits to a seemingly endless number of small, back-street toy factories, accompanied by my interpreter with a quite unpronounceable name whom I called John, proved an enchanting experience. One of the many items I was seeking was a range of four plastic cars to retail at 2s11d. In about the twentieth factory I found exactly what I wanted, but the price was too high. I explained the problem to John who arranged to have the cost reduced by having the chrome around the wheels removed, but they were still too expensive.

The scene was now set for two hours of intensive bargaining of which I could not understand a single word, but at the end I had my range of cars in the quantity and at the price I could afford, though in addition to the chrome off the wheels, the windows and most of the paint had gone as well. I was quite elated until I returned to my hotel and examined my four purchases in detail and realized that they had been stripped down to such an extent that they no longer resembled cars. We had to start all over again next day.

Earlier that year I had seen the MCC under Ray Illingworth playing in Australia and New Zealand. On my arrival home from my trip I had to go straight from Heathrow to the League Cup final at Wembley, where I encountered a brother journalist whom I did not see often. He remarked that I looked very brown and well and I said that I had flown in from the United States that morning. My return from Hong Kong happened to coincide with the Wembley FA Cup final and again I went from the airport to the ground. There I ran into the same journalist in almost the same spot and he made almost the same comment. It provided me with a classic piece of one-upmanship: 'Oh, I've just flown in from Hong Kong this morning.' Game set and match!

Although I am proud to have been one of the founder members of the Ilford Indoor Cricket School and to have been its chairman since it was started in 1955, I was not the driving force behind the enterprise, more of a figurehead, though not, I hope, entirely a decoration. In the early days when we struggled to survive, and today when we are firmly established, the key figure has been Harold Faragher, a former captain of Ilford CC who also made some appearances for the county. The period I enjoyed most were the early years, when after having spent an evening coaching we had to lift the nets and then roll down a vast carpet for indoor bowls on the following morning. It may have been hard work, but the laughter was long and loud.

The school has never been a major financial success, but it has done, and is still doing, an enormous amount of good for Essex cricket at all levels, which, after all, was our original intention. It sometimes seems to me that the Essex CCC have never fully appreciated the assistance the club received from the Ilford School back in those days when the county existed on membership, gates and Test match receipts and, with no commercial sponsorships, were fighting a continual survival battle. The county players were allowed to use, without charge, the Ilford facilities throughout the winter and for immediate pre-season training. In addition, it is where quite a number of the present side had their first experience of coaching.

The objective of public relations is to publicize, promote, enhance and, most important of all, influence. How this is achieved will greatly vary, but when handled well it certainly can produce results for people, businesses and products. No politician, business, union, institution, or personality can afford not to use this form of indirect advertising. I found the strange world of public relations amusing, enchanting and, because it means different things to different people, sometimes baffling, especially as many clients never appeared to understand what it was all about, or even what we were trying to achieve.

There is more than a touch of Disneyland about PR and it is populated by even odder characters, including kings and queens, black and white knights, princesses who certainly do not need rescuing and princes who do, magicians and clowns, witches and bitches, humans and animals. It has vitality, ideas, life and has even acquired its own special cliché-riddled language.

I learned that 'obtaining a slice of the action' was making money from a particular project. 'Positive thinking' could mean almost anything, while one of my favourites was and still is maximising 'optimum client visibility'. I was fascinated by the number of times 'viability' appeared in proposals which usually looked and sounded very impressive, but if one carefully analyzed the beautifully presented thirty-page document, one discovered that the fundamentals could have been adequately covered in two. Today, I am fully 'orientated'.

Every relations company has to issue press releases, the objective being to gain a mention in the press or on radio and television, in other words a form of advertising which is cheaper than buying space. However, I am certain that the industry does produce far too many press releases and the majority finish up in wastepaper baskets, unwanted and unread. This is all too understandable when one receives the following classic:

Statement from the Vice-Chairman

The Blank Blank Corporation, in announcing the re-alignment of brands between advertising agency A and advertising agency B, is in line with the rest of the international system set-up in regard to the two international agencies.

A great deal of the development work on brand Blank Blank is done throughout the A agency's international system and the re-alignment makes for easier co-ordination for the client. The allied brands and the development work is in many cases local and requires high quality creative expertise, which is available from the B agency, as they have new management with a highly creative team led by Mr Bloggs, Creative Director, London, also Mr Biggs, who recently moved into the agency with long experience overseas on the Blank Blank allied brands.

Although I have been involved in a wide variety of PR accounts, the majority have tended to have a sporting connection covering cricket, football, hockey, athletics, rowing, tennis, bowls and golf. Some of these have brought me into contact with multinational companies, which have provided some intriguing experiences largely because the efficiency and expertise I had expected from these financial giants was conspicuous by its absence.

It seemed to me that everybody was frightened ('terrified' would be a more accurate word) to make a decision when it involved money for which they would eventually be accountable. As a result, the budget for a PR account was often too small, mainly because the value could not be justified by sales, as is usually the case with straightforward advertising. In complete contrast, they were only too happy to spend lavishly on junkets and entertaining, especially when they would be present themselves and the whole exercise could be written off as expenses.

One of my first encounters with a multinational was when I was appointed consultant for the Ford Motor Company to devise and set up a first-class cricket promotion for which their internal PR were to provide the back-up. Commercial sports sponsorship was in its infancy and this particular project was attractive, simple and very popular with the county clubs who gave it their blessing, but it never received even adequate internal PR support. At the time Ford were engaged in a number of sporting sponsorships including their Fair Play League for soccer, which was a born loser. I was always fascinated by their unintentionally funny advertisement showing a diabolical tackle and carrying the marvellous caption, 'We'll cut out all that malarky'.

In their cricket promotion Ford supplied each of the 17 counties with a new car. The clubs could use these in any way they wanted, providing they were parked in a reasonably prominent place during every home fixture. A small scoreboard was attached to the roof of the car which carried the details of the three players leading in the race for the three fastest hundreds, and the bowler who was closest to the target of a hundred wickets. At the end of the season the four winners were to receive a Ford car at a suitable lunch or dinner and a new car was a most attractive award.

My part in the exercise was to work out the details of the competition; to acquire the permission of the TCCB and the counties which, not surprisingly, was immediately forthcoming; to make sure that the clubs were fulfilling their obligations to the sponsor; and to organize a presentation lunch or dinner after the season had finished. Throughout May, June and July I tried every other week to obtain a date for the latter, but with no success. I was also a little surprised to be phoned up by the largest Ford dealer in Birmingham during the Edgbaston Test. He was unaware of the cricket promotion even though it was to be publicized in every Ford garage. He wanted some publicity during the Test and the thoughtful Warwickshire CCC immediately cooperated, while I began to realize why I was having problems acquiring a date.

After further failures in August and September I began to lose some of my enthusiasm, though I did phone again late in September to warn them that one of the winners would have flown to Australia with the MCC if they did not act soon. On a Monday morning in early October I was summoned to the Ford headquarters at Brentwood and asked if I could arrange the presentation lunch for Wednesday week. As we were inviting all the national press, the rest of the media and suitable representatives from the MCC to make awards and the chairmen and secretaries of the 17 counties, this was, to put it mildly, rather short notice.

I drove straight to Lord's and managed to set everything up thanks to the cooperation of the MCC and TCCB, who were not unmindful of Ford's contribution to cricket that summer. I returned home distinctly pleased with myself until I heard that Ford wanted me to call the following morning as there was a problem.

I was met with apologies, but the lunch could not be held on the Wednesday and it would have to be moved to the Thursday. They had managed to overlook one minor incidental: the Wednesday coincided with probably the most important date in their year, the opening of the Motor Show.

I had a problem restraining my near hysterics, returned to Lord's, organized a late start for the TCCB meeting which allowed some important members of the cricket hierarchy to be at the presentation in nine days' time, and supplied Ford with the names and addresses of all to be invited so that they could send out the invitations.

There were still two more little hiccups to come. First, having decided to issue the invitations themselves in order to save money, they found that their typing pool was unfriendly and ended up sending invitations by telegram – which might be termed verbose. Second my consultancy fee arrived about six months late, probably about par for the course. But what intrigued me was that it was sent twice. I would love to have paid in both cheques, just to test the efficiency in that never-never world of corporate finance. How many years would it have taken them to realize their error?

In complete contrast, the Wrigley Softball Cricket Tournament with which I have been closely associated since the outset has proved to be a big success. I believe it has already done a considerable amount to assist cricket, and will do even more in the future. Yet it all began with a casual remark from Gary Sobers.

We were talking cricket and Gary said to me that if we wanted to improve the standard in England we ought to start playing softball. I nodded sagely, but unintelligently, because to me softball was simply a form of junior baseball, and promptly forgot all about it.

This was stupid on my part, as any suggestion about cricket by Gary deserves the most careful study.

It must have been at least eight years later when the penny started to drop. I was on one of my annual pilgrimages to Barbados for the fun, sun and the rum, when I chanced upon an adult softball cricket match. What had long worried me about English cricket was not the lack of coaching, which is more available than ever before, but the number of children who never had the opportunity to play the game at primary school level, which caters for at least 95 per cent of the population. Softball cricket provided an obvious answer. It had to be a reasonably good game for adult softball cricket leagues to flourish in Barbados. It was very inexpensive, far cheaper than football. There was virtually no danger for players, spectators or children in the vicinity. It could be played on almost any surface in a comparatively small area. It was much faster than normal cricket, while no time was lost through ten-year-olds donning pads and gloves. It encouraged a young batsman to play straight and move into line for the simple reason it paid him to do so.

It is one thing to believe one has a good idea, but it is an entirely different matter to be able to implement it. First, it was necessary to obtain the approval and the assistance of the NCA and ESCA. This was forthcoming and I received much assistance from Brian Aspital, secretary of the NCA and Keith Andrew, the chief coach, with whom I had once toured Australia. ESCA have done much to raise the standard of school cricket and is run by a dedicated group of cricket loving schoolmasters. Their secretary, Cyril Cooper, quickly appreciated the possibilities, and without his advice and help with the schools the whole scheme would never have escalated to the degree it has now done.

In order to publicize the project a commercial sponsor was vital. I initially approached Barclays Bank, who showed considerable interest. Unfortunately their budget for the coming year had been allocated and they eventually decided not to promote, much to the disappointment of myself and supporters at Barclays.

Just as my original concept was the result of a chance remark, the Wrigley Softball Tournament provides the perfect example of how being in exactly the right place at the right time can make all the difference. I had accepted an invitation to attend a press lunch which was given each year by the Wrigley Company, who for a decade had been supporting grass-roots cricket. It so happened that I found myself sitting opposite Les Palmer, who had just taken on the responsibility of supervising his company's involvement in cricket. In the course of the meal Les asked me if I had any suggestions for a new cricket sponsorship. The Wrigley Softball Tournament for Primary Schools, now in its sixth year and going from strength to strength, was born.

My first intention had been simply to introduce into primary schools organized cricket using an old tennis ball. However, after discussions with Keith Andrew and several teachers I opted for an amended version of the game, which had several advantages. First, it was fast moving and involved every child, not merely the star performers. Second, it could be completed in an hour's recreational period. Third, it could be easily supervized by one teacher. Finally, most important of all, it was fun to play. It has always been my belief that a game which fails to provide fun and enjoyment for the participants is a waste of time.

SEND IN THE CLOWNS

The Test Match Special team I joined in 1966 contained two summarizers, Freddie Brown and Norman Yardley; three principal commentators, John Arlott, Alan Gibson, Brian Johnston; an overseas representative; Bill Frindall as scorer; Jim Swanton, who delivered a daily close-of-play sermon; and Michael Tuke Hastings, who produced the programme from his headquarters at Broadcasting House.

John Arlott will, correctly, go down in history as the voice of cricket. Although his Hampshire burr made him instantly recognizable, what made him so very special was his choice of words and phrases. He was easily the best painter of verbal pictures I have encountered. His eloquent descriptions brought to life what was happening out in the middle, and it did not have to be cricket. Probably his most brilliant commentary was a memorable and hilarious twenty minutes he devoted to putting on the covers at Lord's during a drizzle.

I had the honour of being summarizer during John's final two cricket commentaries. The first was during the Centenary Test against Australia, at the conclusion of which he received from the crowd the type of ovation never before given to a broadcaster. The second was during the Gillette Cup final when John came out with: 'This is Van der Bijl coming in to bowl looking like a younger, taller, stronger version of Lord Longford . . .' a deliciously accurate description to which John then added the master stroke, '. . . but not nearly so tolerant'.

John's knowledge of cricket history and players was extensive but he was less expert on the game's technicalities which, as a limited player himself, had to be second hand.

I had a special affection for my sessions with Alan Gibson. He brought to our box an erudite, whimsical, classical sense of humour, which appealed.

Everybody's favourite uncle, Brian Johnston, was combining television with radio at that time and had not yet become the centrepiece and resident comic of our team, though his love for excruciating puns, which I share, was very much in evidence. His initial advice to me was simple and true.

'Boilers,' he said (every name to Johnston ends in ERS, like Woodders for Woodcock, Swanners for Swanton and McGillers for McGilvray), 'remember you are talking to the blind. You have to supply the eyes for the listener.'

Although I have always tried to observe this principle, I still manage to forget it from time to time. There was one occasion when John Arlott asked me how one played a bouncer off the front foot. I stood up and gave a perfect demonstration, but despite my accuracy and enthusiasm it could not have meant much to the listeners.

One might say that Bill Frindall has turned scoring into a minor art form. He has developed his own system and become a human computer able to produce any relevant, or irrelevant, statistic at a moment's notice. He has an insatiable appetite for figures, which are much appreciated by the many followers of the game who really are interested in records, even if so many have relatively little significance.

Jim Swanton invariably prefaced his daily summary, which was in essence his essay for the *Daily Telegraph*, with the words 'But, first the scorecard'. The pace with which this was delivered would, to some extent, depend upon what had taken place during the day.

The format and composition of Test Match Special have of course changed. At the close of one summer John Arlott summed it up perfectly when he said: 'We are not a sporting programme, we have become pure folk.' This is true when one takes into account the number of letters we receive from people who tell us that they prefer our broadcast when it is raining. My wife has rather rudely described our efforts as a 'Goon Show' with a cricketing theme. However, there can be no doubting its appeal.

Inevitably there have been a few complaints, mainly from failed broadcasters, that Test Match Special has become too frivolous.

This may be true for the minority who want their cricket broadcasts purely factual, but I am sure we would lose many more listeners, especially among the ladies who enjoy our particular brand of chit-chat.

Our objective is to describe the game and also to try to entertain. Sometimes we fail, but the fact that there is now a small army who watch on the television with the sound off and the radio turned on does indicate that we have acquired a few followers.

The regulars who have joined Test Match Special since I began back in 1966 include commentators Christopher Martin-Jenkins, Don Mosey and Henry Blofeld, the dual-purpose Tony Lewis, summarizer Fred Trueman and Peter Baxter who produces the show.

Christopher was a good club cricketer, has an above average knowledge of the game and is a highly accomplished broadcaster. However, I feel that he has yet to reach his peak. He is a very talented and amusing after-dinner speaker, with a keen sense of humour which does not come across on the radio to the extent it could and, I believe, will.

Don is a forthright northerner with decisive views on many subjects. Inclined to be intolerant, he has never been prepared to suffer fools or incompetence and can be prickly. I have found my sessions with Don particularly rewarding, probably because we complement each other, north and south; have a mutual respect for each other; detest what is false, whether it be people or the way cricket is played; and possess a not dissimilar, somewhat sardonic sense of humour.

Henry talks far more quickly than any of my colleagues, which enables him to impart information on a whole range of subjects not connected with the game such as buses, helicopters, ice-cream salesmen, birds (both armed and winged), trains and butterflies. His Etonian background, accent and delightfully eccentric personality has enabled him to become a much loved cult figure in Australia. Invariably courteous, generous and considerate, you can be sure he will commence a reply to any question with 'My dear old thing'.

Tony is equally efficient as a commentator or a summarizer. He possesses a lovely Welsh lilt, a varied vocabulary and a wealth of knowledge on cricket, of which he sees a considerable amount – something which his native county, which he captained, appeared to forget when he was removed from their committee.

222

I do not hear very much of Fred except on my car radio when he has agreed to do the last stint to enable me to make a quick get away. I suppose he is inclined to fall into the same trap as myself, which is to be ever-critical of the modern game. It is so easy to do, but unfortunately in recent years much of the cricket produced by England has been substandard. A great thinking bowler, he finds it hard to understand bowlers who are unable to maintain a reasonable line and length and waste the new ball.

Fred has a seemingly endless store of cricket anecdotes and is forever producing some question to test the commentator, especially Brian Johnston. One Saturday he asked Brian to name the only Yorkshire cricketer who had also won the Grand National. He refused to supply the answer until after the weekend. On the Monday, Brian not only supplied the answer, Wilson, but also produced the additional information that he had also shot down a zeppelin – not a bad hat-trick for Wilson, and an obvious victory for Brian!

When I first joined Test Match Special, Peter Baxter was one of Michael Tuke Hastings's many minions. He now has the responsibility for producing the programme and controlling a group of raving extroverts. In addition, and to my way of thinking far, far more important, he makes sure we have coffee before the start of play and tea at the interval. He is perhaps the most proficient and highest paid tea caddy in the business.

What is the difference between the commentator and the summarizer? The commentator's job is to describe the action while the summarizer, who should be an expert on the technicalities of cricket, will come in at the end of the over, after the fall of a wicket, during a break in play, and when fast bowlers are using very long run-ups and nothing much is happening. The big dread of the summarizer is for the commentator to come out with a judgement which is wrong, like saying that the batsman has been dismissed by a googly when the bowler's repertoire does not contain one; or the batsman has missed an awayswinging yorker when it was a straight half-volley; or a run down through the slips with an angled straight bat is described as a delicate late cut.

I always considered Norman Yardley to be an ideal summarizer: accurate, informative and very sensible, and able to explain not only what happened but also the reasons why. His knowledge about pitches, tactics and the technicalities of the game was exceptional, which was hardly surprising as he was brought up in the pre-war atmosphere of the Yorkshire dressing-room, where every aspect of the game was analyzed in considerable depth with professional realism, and had captained both his county and England. Articulate, expert and possessing considerable charge, I thought his interpretation of events on the field and his post-session summaries were sound, balanced and never less than fair.

I believe it is the summarizer's job to assist and support the commentator, but occasionally this can be difficult as some of them can be hypersensitive, resenting even the most delicate suggestion that they might have erred slightly, let alone got it entirely wrong.

I have always believed a summarizer should try to be honest. He should praise the good, make excuses for the players when circumstances like the pitch have made batting very difficult, and not forget that it is far easier in the commentary box than out in the middle where, with the pressure on, the obvious is often far from obvious. However, when the cricket is below the expected standard, I believe that he should say so – he cannot ignore bad cricket.

What do I mean by bad cricket? Here are just a few examples: a bowler who cannot bowl straight; an opening bowler who wastes the new ball; a spinner who lacks control; a batsman who is a bad hooker holing out on the boundary hooking; a batsman who plays half-cock to a spinner on a turning wicket; a bowler who cannot bowl to his field; the captain who cannot set a field, or is constantly changing it to 'chase' where the ball last travelled.

A classic example of poor captaincy occurred in Johannesburg when South Africa were playing a West Indian XI. In the last over before tea in the South African second innings, Graeme Pollock was bowled after providing an enchanting forty-odd, a reminder of just how very good he had been. This brought to the wicket the South African captain, Clive Rice. He drove the first ball he received, a half-volley, through the covers for four, a splendid stroke and a splendid start. The next ball was good length and straight. Clive attempted to cow the ball over mid-on and got an outside edge, which went over the slips to the boundary. This was the last over before tea, he had just lost his best batsman and the game was in a crucial phase. If anyone had attempted to play such an irresponsible shot in that situation in my team, I would have wanted to shoot him. What I could not understand was how it could have been done by the captain, especially somebody who had led Notts so efficiently.

Commentators and summarizers from overseas come in many different shapes and sizes ranging from Alan McGilvray, with his precise, almost whispered, ascetic delivery and completely unbiased and factually accurate account of events on the field, to the Pakistan summarizer whose sole contribution to the proceedings was a rather unintelligible and most enlightening 'And that was another very good over'!

Alan, now retired, was the only comentator who often used field glasses balanced on top of his microphone throughout his commentary. A highly professional broadcaster and a former first-class cricketer, he was invariably a pleasure to work with because he had a deep knowledge of the game itself. He was inclined to be intolerant of the mediocre, whether it be in play or in standards of behaviour. He always reminded me of my Latin master who accomplished, against all odds, the feat of enabling me to acquire a credit in the subject. Over the years he not only became acclimatized to the levity of Test Match Special, but enjoyed it.

Tony Cozier is probably the best known cricket commentator in the world these days, as he has seldom missed a West Indian tour in the last decade and a half. Also a journalist and a complete professional, he has the ability to adapt his style to that of the broadcasting team with which he is working, whether it be the rather serious approach of Australian radio and television, the ebullience of the West Indian commentaries, or Test Match Special, where humour and the inconsequential combine with the game to give it its own very special flavour. Like most West Indians, Tony likes to laugh and one of the things which particularly amuses him is when he receives a racialist letter condemning blackmen. What the sender fails to appreciate is that Tony is a white Bajaan.

Although Tony has not yet come round to my way of thinking that 70 overs in a six-hour day from four fast bowlers constitutes poor spectator entertainment, unless wickets are falling, he has a point because the West Indies batting is usually entertaining and fast bowling is exciting, providing there is not too much of it. However, cricket without a reasonable over-rate and slow bowlers is, in my opinion, rather like toast without butter and marmalade.

The longevity of Test Match Special stems from the rapport built up over many years with our listeners. This is reflected by the very heavy mail we receive, not just from Great Britain but from all over the world, as well as numerous phone calls, telegrams and overseas cables. In addition to the mail we receive a large assortment of gifts and goodies. We do our utmost to eat the latter, with Brian Johnston's capacity especially impressive, but are seldom able to deal with everything. These are then passed on to more deserving recipients.

John Arlott, unlike Brian, was not a lover of such delicacies as chocolate gâteau, fudge and jujubes, but he did fully approve of the occasional crate of Laurent Perrier Champagne which I obtained for the team. He believed, quite correctly, that a glass before lunch was the medicine any civilized doctor would have prescribed.

There is not the time, nor do I possess the memory, to recall all the things and communications which have found their way into our box over the years, but here are a few I treasure. I was very impressed by a beautifully written letter saying how much the writer enjoyed the programme, asking three pertinent questions and making one astute comment. He also mentioned that he was, literally, a member of a captive audience as he was writing from a prison in the Midlands.

During Dennis Lillee's first tour to England in 1972, I happened to mention in passing that though I was very impressed by his speed, action and control, I was concerned by his ultra-lengthy run up. Children tend to imitate their heroes and my worry was that in their efforts to copy Dennis we could be in danger of breeding, both in Australia and England, more marathon runners than fast bowlers. A few days later I received a postcard, signed 'worried grandma', which read as follows: 'You are absolutely right. My grandson, Shaun, aged three, now runs from 17 yards before releasing the ball from three paces at me.'

I was about to leave the pavilion at Lord's one year at the start of a luncheon interval during one of the all too many bomb scares when a young lady wearing a colourful boater handed me a heavy tin and said that it was a cake for the commentary team. Not wanting to take it with me to the grandstand box where I was dining, because it was very heavy, I went back into the pavilion where a policeman relieved me of the tin. Although the young lady had looked rather more like a Sloane Ranger than a terrorist, one cannot be too careful these days. It turned out that it contained no bomb, but a cake which was certainly heavy enough to have sunk the entire commentary team, though I must add that this was an exception as at least 95 per cent, like the letters we receive, are delightful.

One lady listener rang up during the Headingley Test in 1975 to ask me what the Australian, Gary Gilmour, had on his finger, and was it permissible? Her enquiry was passed on and I was able to inform her over the air that he was wearing a ring, which was allowed, providing it did not assist the bowler. Incidentally, I would never advocate wearing one while playing cricket as it is an invitation to be hit on that finger, which will swell and necessitate the ring having to be cut off.

The most intriguing cable came from a close friend in Tasmania during the final Test at the Oval in 1981. It told me that Australian television would be using our ball-by-ball commentary along with the pictures from the television. Apparently the television channel had noticed how many viewers watched television with the sound turned off and listened to the Test Match Special broadcasts. When they had asked the Australian viewers why, they had received a torrent of answers with the reasons. Obviously Test Match Special is neither intended nor designed for television, but it was rather pleasant to find this practice was almost as popular in Australia as it is at home.

Although the vast majority of my cricket broadcasts have been as a member of Test Match Special for the Tests and the limited-overs finals in England, I have done some radio in South Africa, where that grand old man of cricket radio, Charles Fortune, lives. Out there his voice is probably even more imitated than John Arlott's. I have also joined up with truncated Test Match Special teams in Australia and India.

My Indian adventure, which had me going to Calcutta in 1984–85 for a somewhat unlikely mixture of Christmas, cricket and carols, was started by Tony Lewis, who has a love for India and casually suggested that we and our respective wives have Christmas together in Bombay. For various reasons, not the least being the itinerary, it proved impossible, but I was convinced that the attraction which India clearly held for Tony meant that it had to have something for me, even though Don Mosey reckoned that taking a wife to Calcutta was grounds for divorce.

What did surprise both my wife and I was the extent of the fascination, which meant that our five weeks was over far too soon. We both want to return. Although Christmas Day in Calcutta was somewhat unusual, it was certainly fun, beginning with a press cocktail party for the England touring team, which had been organized largely by Chris Lander from the *Daily Mirror* and

Graham Morris, a freelance photographer. The media male voice choir rendered, in no uncertain fashion, the Christmas carols, which had been made topical by Michael Carey and Peter Baxter and were much appreciated by the players. Our party continued, while the players went away, donned their various fancy dress costumes, many of which were remarkably good, and returned before eventually departing for their own fairly late Christmas lunch, while we then sat down to our celebration.

In order to have a look at India before the Test, I flew down to Cuttack with the England party and the media on Boxing Day for the one-day international, which started on the following day and which England won to go two-up in the series. This gave me my first opportunity to sample one aspect of Indian cricket which I never really enjoyed, their uncivilized hours of play. It was particularly bad at Cuttack, because our hotel was a long way from the ground, which meant breakfast just before 7 a.m.

The match itself began when one should be eating bacon and eggs, reading a newspaper and drinking tea. The luncheon interval coincided with a morning coffee break and stumps were drawn at teatime. I never really became accustomed to these hours, which became even more confusing when I started just after the luncheon interval to speak to listeners in England, who were reluctantly rising from their beds.

My luncheon box at Cuttack also came as a slight surprise. It contained plenty of rice, some vegetables, I think, a dubious hard boiled egg, a well spiced chunk of chicken, and no eating irons. My fingers experienced a certain amount of difficulty coping with the rice, and with no washroom available my copy for the *Financial Times* was even more grubby than usual.

The Calcutta Test will go down as one of the most boring draws ever, but it still attracted more spectators than any other five-day cricket match in 1985, which is an indication of the astonishing enthusiasm for the game in India, and Calcutta in particular. The failure of the England seam bowlers to exploit fully the very helpful conditions on the morning of the first day allowed India to rally. Rain for most of the second made a draw the most probable result. The sluggish pace of the Indian batting on the third day, after they had made absolutely sure that they could not lose, made the draw almost inevitable. The unwillingness of Sunil Gavaskar to declare until after lunch on the fourth day finally killed it, and I have doubts whether he would have done so even then if the crowd had not become so understandably hostile. Sunil's incomprehensible captaincy turned the game on the fourth day into a farce.

The final stages were enlivened by some attractive batting by England and the bowling of Sivaramakrishnan, the one Indian bowler of international calibre in their side. Why Sunil allowed the English batsmen to have such a long look at him in a dead game did not make much sense, though it delighted David Gower.

In complete contrast, the Madras Test was a splendid match with a wealth of strokes in which England obtained a two-one lead, outplaying India in every department. It also underlined still further, despite the recall of Kapil Dev, that the Indian attack was well below international standard, and why, until they beat England in Bombay, they had gone 30 Tests without a win.

My colleagues in the Indian version of Test Match Special were Michael Carey, with the dry succinct sense of humour one associates with the *Daily Telegraph*; Jack Bannister, a mechanical expert after my own heart who was concerned when his new camera refused to function and eventually learned it did require a film; Ashish Ray, with his precise classical English; Ralph Dellor, playing his first innings for us; and Peter Baxter, who combined the roles of producer, summarizer, news reporter and general liaison with England with that of providing ice-cream and refreshments for his motley crew. In addition, we had the Indian version of Bill Frindall, Kiran Mavani, decidedly quieter and less involved in bizarre statistics.

Test Match Special held its first dinner in India – and, with the logic which one automatically associates with the programme, held it at a Chinese restaurant, even though we did not have a left-hand wrist-spinner in our party. However, Ashish, resplendent in formal Indian attire, added tone to the gathering.

For five weeks I was living in the same hotels as the England team and watched them win the one-day series and take a commanding lead in the Tests. What was especially pleasing was that they showed considerably more character than many of our recent touring sides, which enabled them to raise their game and to play above their potential. It was also very noticeable that there was a big improvement in their relationship with the media.

As a result of seeing so much of them individually and collectively, both on and off the field, I was able to compare them with the overseas teams of my time. Some aspects have changed, but others have remained exactly the same.

The biggest difference is obviously financial. An England regular playing in all five Tests against the West Indies, the one-day internationals and the Sri Lankan Test during the summer of 1984, and then chosen for the four-month tour to India and a brief limited-overs tournament in Australia, would earn about £20,000, plus all expenses. In addition, he would be paid about £9000 by his county club. Even taking into account inflation, and ignoring the numerous perks and very profitable rewards that are now available as a result of commercial cricket sponsorship, this does compare rather favourably with my £450 per annum salary as secretary of Essex and the £200 to cover my six-month tour of Australia.

Increased rewards combined with increased tours makes the players financially independent much earlier than in my day. This process was accelerated by Kerry Packer's World Series Cricket and has inevitably increased player power and reduced the power of the game's administrators, though thankfully not to the same extent as in tennis. In Australia, this is reflected by an unhealthy lack of discipline, with the result that the party they sent to England for the 1983 Prudential World Cup were closer to a rabble than a team. However, this did not apply to the England team in India, though their behaviour, as well as their cricket, in New Zealand during the previous winter had left much to be desired.

Because cricketers are able to earn so much more these days, though nothing compared with the huge sums available in individual sports, they can easily afford to take their wives and girlfriends with them for part of a tour. In my time this was discouraged by the MCC, while economics made it comparatively rare. A gaggle of wives, especially if accompanied by kids, does make a manager's life more difficult. I remember Alec Bedser complaining about the arrival of one of his fast bowlers in Sydney. Alec felt he should have been breathing fire and destruction, but as he was carrying a baby and toy Koala bear, this was hardly feasible.

On an Indian tour, where both the culture and the way of life is so different from our civilization, there is less social life. As a result it seems to me there is even more to be said in favour of wives joining the party, which is certainly borne out by the results.

Another big difference these days is the popularity and the increasing importance of one-day internationals, though I have a horrid suspicion that Australia may have promoted such a surfeit that they will ultimately lose their appeal as well as reducing attendances at Tests to an alarming degree. Although the high class performer will do well in both Test and limited-overs cricket, there is a definite place in the latter for the negative bowler, the useful bits-and-pieces bowler, and the happy hitter whose bright 40 can sometimes win a one-day game. As a result, England have sometimes included a player in their touring party because of his one-day expertise, even though he may not be of Test calibre.

Modern ground fielding has definitely improved and the diving, sometimes unnecessary though invariably spectacular, adds to the atmosphere. On the other hand, based on the number of catches put down by both teams in India, there must be some doubt as to whether the same can be said to apply to the catching.

The official entourage accompanying a touring party has grown considerably. In India there was a manager, assistant manager, physiotherapist cum general factotum, scorer and an Indian baggage manager, while out there they were joined for a time by the secretary of the TCCB, the chairman of the selectors, the president of the MCC. It was rather different from when I went to the West Indies, for what was a tough tour, under a player manager, Charlie Palmer, who had never managed a side before and had never been to the Caribbean!

Among the things which have not altered are the joy and elation experienced by every player, even if he is not in the team, when England wins abroad. It means so much more than at home and is especially exhilarating after a bad start and when the chosen side has been, not always without cause, largely written off before the trip has even begun.

There is an intense satisfaction in proving the critics wrong. On my first tour to Australia the selectors were castigated for making such an obviously bad choice of team which, according to the press, should never have been sent and, on the evidence of two weeks, should even have been sent home. I can therefore appreciate the feelings of Fowler, Robinson, Gatting and Foster in particular, who demonstrated that they were far better than many people had believed.

With the return of the South African rebels, especially Graham Gooch, England regained the Ashes in the summer of 1985 in considerable style. David Gower not only continued his winning ways as captain, but he also found his true form with the bat, while Robinson and Gatting displayed an understandable partiality for a very insipid Australian attack.

INDEX

Acfield, David 67, 211
Adcock, Neil 181
Alexander, Earl 64
Allen, Basil 81
Allen, David 80, 142
Allen, 'Gubby' 64, 84, 85, 196
Alley, Bill 113, 115
Alleyn Court 15–21, 35, 36, 38, 197
Alleynians, Old 209
Ames, Les 90, 195
Andrew, Keith 107, 218, 219
Appleyard, Bob 138, 140, 141, 160, 169
Appleyard, Frank 34
Arlott, John 220, 221, 226, 227
Arnold, John 82
Ashby, Garnett 195
Ashton, Sir Hubert 63
Aspital, Brian 218
Atkinson, Denis 192
Australia 44–6, 61, 71, 102–4, 107, 109, 124, 137, 139, 145–8, 150–4, 159–77, 220, 222, 226, 230
Australian Board of Control 170
Avery, 'Sonny' 34, 51, 109

Bailey, Jack 60, 135
Bailey, Jim 82
Bairstow, David 135
Bannister, Jack 229
Barber, Bob 91
Barclay, John 125
Barclays Bank 218
Barker, Gordon 58, 70, 75, 79, 96, 107, 111, 130
Barnes, Sid 45, 174
Barnes, Sydney 119
Barnett, Charlie 80
Barrington, Ken 118
Bartlett, Hugh 122, 123
Bates, Ted 125
Baxter, Peter 222, 223, 228, 229
Bedford, Ian 102
Bedser, Alec 53, 92, 116, 117, 119, 144, 145, 147, 155, 158–62, 168, 169, 230
Benaud, Richie 145, 151, 152, 154, 161
Bennett, A. C. L. 34
Berry, Bob 156, 157, 168
Berry, Les 97, 98
Blofeld, Henry 222
Border, Allan 112

Botham, Ian 74, 111–4, 195, 202, 203
Boyce, Keith 66, 67, 195
Boycott, Geoff 108, 134–7, 142, 195
Bradman, Don 15, 44–6, 102
Brearley, Mike 102, 103
Brennan, Don 141
British Empire XI 33, 34, 53
Brown, Freddie 105, 106, 151, 152, 158, 220
Brown, Sid 99
Burke, Jim 154, 173
Burke, P. 190
Buse, Bertie 115
Buss, Mike 122
Buss, Tony 122, 125, 126
Butler, Harold 108

Cambridge University 15, 36, 39–45, 56, 57, 59, 92, 122, 123, 197, 198
Cannings, V. H. D. 86
Carey, Michael 228, 229
Carr, Ronnie 64
Cartwright, Tom 129
Catt, Tony 91
Chandrasekhar, Bhagwat 87
Chapman, Percy 102
Chester, Frank 146, 156
Christiani, R. J. 191
Clark, E. W. 105
Clark, Horace 60, 71
Clark, Len 53
Clarke, Bertie 34
Clarke, E. W. 107
Clay, Johnny 78
Close, Brian 115, 135, 141–3, 153, 168
Clough, Brian 205
Coldwell, Len 132
Compton, Denis 47, 69, 92, 99, 100, 102, 103, 109, 146, 148,

149, 151, 154, 155, 160, 162, 167, 168, 171, 189, 191, 194
Cooper, Cyril 218
Corrall, 'Paddy' 95
Cowdrey, Christopher 184
Cowdrey, Colin 89, 92, 155, 157, 169, 181
Cowie, J. 148
Cox, George 122, 124
Coxon, Alex 114
Cozier, Tony 225
Crabtree, Harry 18, 34, 38, 51, 66, 95
Crapp, Jack 80
Cricketers Club 88
Curran, K. M. 82

Daniel, Wayne 104
Daniels, David 67
Datta, P. B. 41
Davidson, Alan 151, 172, 173
Davison, Brian 98
Deakins, Leslie 127
Dellor, Ralph 229
Derby County F.C. 205, 212
Derbyshire CCC 47, 52, 62–4, 72, 74–6, 123
de Santos, Sir Errol 196
Dewes, John 44, 56, 168
Dexter, Ted 122, 124, 125
Dilley, Graham 89
Dodds, Dickie 89, 107
Doggart, Hubert 44, 56, 122, 124
Dollery, Tom 128
Donnelly, Martin 42, 43, 149
Dooland, Bruce 108, 109
Dors, Diana 133
Douglas, J. W. H. T. 58, 70
Downton, Paul 91
Drybrough, Colin 102
Dulwich College 20–6, 40
Durley, Tony 75, 76

Eagar, Desmond 83
Edmonds, Phil 101, 104
Edrich, Bill 99, 100, 102–4, 109, 146, 155, 156, 162, 168
Edrich, John 118, 119
Elgood, Brian 44
Emburey, John 104
Emmett, George 80
ESCA 218
Essex CCC 14, 15, 34, 38, 39, 42, 45, 47–143, 154, 173, 197, 200, 208, 211, 214, 230
Evans, Godfrey 90, 91, 146, 151, 152, 155, 156, 158, 159, 161, 169, 171, 183, 188, 191

Fagg, Arthur 89, 90
Faragher, Harold 213
Farnes, Ken 51
Financial Times 204, 209–12
Fishlock, Laurie 116
Flavell, Jack 132
Fletcher, Keith 49, 66, 111, 130, 194
Flynn, Errol 187
Ford Motor Company 216, 217
Fortune, Charles 227
Foster, Neil 231
Fowler, Graeme 231
Free Foresters 24
Freeman, 'Tich' 51, 130
Frindall, Bill 220, 221

Garlick, Gordon 105
Garner, Joel 111, 113, 114
Gatting, Mike 100, 111, 231, 232
Gavaskar, Sunil 229
Gentlemen v Players 69, 95, 99, 138
Gibb, Paul 73, 78
Gibbs, Lance 142
Gibson, Alan 220, 221
Gilchrist, R. 153

Gillette, E. S. 190
Gilligan, A. E. R. 122
Gilligan, A. H. H. 122
Gilmour, Gary 227
Gimblett, Harold 114
Gladwin, Cliff 75, 76
Glamorgan CCC 68, 76–9
Gloucestershire CCC 63, 79–82
Goddard, John 153, 155, 161
Goddard, Tom 79
Gomez, G. E. 156, 193
Gooch, Graham 112, 231
Gower, David 98, 118, 229, 232
Graveney, Tom 79–81, 92, 119, 155, 160, 162, 167, 188, 190
Gray, Jimmy 82, 84
Gray, 'Chick' 97, 126
Greenhough, Tommy 9
Greenwood, Ron 205
Greig, Ian 122
Greig, Tony 122, 195
Griffith, Mike 122, 125
Griffith, S. C. 'Billy' 22, 122, 123, 126, 149
Griffiths, Colin 89
Griffiths, Hugh 42
Grimmett, Clarrie 15
Grout, Wally 167
Grove, Charlie 128
Groves, Vic 201

Hadlee, Richard 108, 109, 136
Hall, Wes 125
Hallam, Maurice 97, 98
Halliday, Harry 34
Hammond, Wally 51, 80
Hampshire CCC 59, 82–6
Hampshire, John 135, 138, 194
Hardstaff, Joe 108, 109
Harris, Charlie 110
Harvey, Neil 147, 153
Hassett, Lindsay 147, 152, 159, 161

Hayes, Frank 91
Hazell, Horace 115
Headley, Ron 194
Heine, Peter 149, 181, 182
Hendren, Patsy 51
Hendrick, Mike 74
Hever, N. G. 79
Higgins, John 212
Higgs, Ken 92
Hilton, Malcolm 91, 148
Hobbs, Sir Jack 15, 180, 181
Hobbs, Robin 118, 133, 194
Holding, Michael 125, 195
Hole, Graeme 146, 147, 159
Hollies, Eric 128, 155–7
Holt, J. K. 190, 191
Horrex, Graham 75
Horsfall, Dick 52
Horton, Henry 82, 84
Horton, Martin 133
Howard, Geoffrey 61
Howard, Nigel 92, 93
Howorth, Dick 130, 131
Hurd, Alan 71
Hutton, Len 19, 92, 109, 134,
    137, 145, 147, 148, 151, 156,
    159, 160, 162, 169, 185, 189,
    190, 192–4
Hutton, Richard 136

I Zingari 24
Ilford Indoor Cricket School
    212–4
Illingworth, Ray 58, 94, 112,
    135–7, 142
Imran Khan 125
India 8, 100, 138, 210, 227–31
Ingleby-Mackenzie, Colin 82–5
Inman, Clive 98
Insole, Doug 40, 41, 44, 48–50,
    52, 56–61, 68, 69, 72, 74, 78,
    104, 111, 142, 157, 179, 180,
    183

Jackson, Capt G. R. 64
Jackson, Les 75, 76
Jackson, Percy 130, 131
Jackson, Vic 95
Jardine, D. R. 15
Jenkins, 'Roly' 130–2
Jepson, Arthur 110, 111
Jerman, 'Gerry' 121
Johnson, H. H. H. 155, 156
Johnson, Ian 154, 171
Johnston, Bill 45, 151, 161
Johnston, Brian 220, 221, 223,
    226
Joseph, Leon 200

Kallicharran, Alvin 128
Kanhai, Rohan 128
Kapil Dev 229
Keeton, Walter 110
Kelleher, H. R. A. 107
Kent CCC 24, 86–91
Kentish, E. S. M. 188
Kenyon, Don 132, 155
Kiddle, Horace 8, 24, 25
King, F. M. 192, 193
King, Ian 86
Knight, Barry 60, 63, 66, 75, 78,
    84, 85, 118, 133, 142
Knight, David 21
Knight, Roger 21
Knott, Alan 88, 90, 91, 194
Knott, Charlie 82

Laker, Jim 70, 72, 116, 117, 120,
    121, 142, 146, 147, 152, 154,
    156, 157, 161, 162, 169, 180,
    191, 192
Lancashire CCC 55, 56, 61, 62,
    91–4, 155
Lander, Chris 228
Langford, Brian 116
Langridge, James 122, 123, 125
Langridge, John 122, 123

Larwood, Harold 51, 108
Lawrence, D. V. 82
Lawrence, Johnny 115
Lee, Frank 146
Leeds United FC 205, 212
Leicestershire CCC 58, 63, 77, 94–8, 112, 142
Lenham, L. J. 122
Lenham, N. J. 122
le Roux, Garth 125
Lever, Peter 92
Levett, 'Hopper' 91
Lewis, Jim 202, 203
Lewis, Tony 222, 227
Leytonstone FC 199, 200, 201
Lillee, Dennis 125, 226
Lindwall, Ray 45, 54, 99, 100, 102, 145, 147, 151, 152, 162, 167, 168
Liverpool FC 205
Livingston, Jock 106
Lloyd, David 91
Loader, Peter 117, 119, 120, 158, 171, 173, 180
Lock, Tony 94, 117, 118, 120, 140, 147, 152, 154, 158, 161, 162, 173, 180, 188, 191, 192
Lomax, Geoff 113
Long, Arnold 125
Longford, Lord 220
Lowson, Frank 138

MCC 21, 24, 38, 63, 64, 87, 101, 102, 104, 134, 144, 170, 177, 178, 185, 191, 200, 203, 217, 230, 231
McCarthy, Cuan 99
McConnon, Jim 78, 169
McCool, Colin 113, 115
McDonald, C. C. 153, 154
McGilvray, Alan 221, 225
McGlew, D. J. 154, 155
McIntyre, Arthur 168

McLean, Roy 155
McWatt, C. A. 190, 191
Malan, B. V. 182
Malvern College 39
Mallett, Tony 23–5, 40, 105
Manchester United FC 199, 203
Mann, George 102, 144
Mann, N. B. F. 158
Manning, Jack 106
Manning, Jim 211
Marks, Vic 111, 116
Marlar, Robin 69, 124, 125
Marner, Peter 90
Marriott, C. S. 21–4
Marshall, Roy 82, 84, 86
Martin-Jenkins, Christopher 222
Mavani, Kiran 229
May, Peter 116–8, 134, 148, 149, 153–5, 157, 161, 169, 179, 180, 182, 190
Meckiff, Ian 172, 173
Menzies, B. 190, 191
Menzies, Sir Robert 171
Mercer, Joe 205
Middlesex CCC 21, 98–104, 111, 153
Miller, Keith 45, 54, 151, 154, 159
Milner, Joe 84
Milton, Arthur 81, 82
Morgan, Derek 76
Morris, Arthur 147, 159, 169
Morris, Graham 228
Mortimer, John 79, 80
Mosey, Don 222, 227
Moss, Alan 101, 104, 188, 189
Muncer, Len 78
Munden, Vic 98

NCA 218
New Zealand 20, 54, 144, 145, 148, 149, 160, 161, 175–7, 209, 230

Nichols, Morris 15
Nicholson, Bill 205
Noble, Alf 200
Northamptonshire CCC 77, 104–7
Nottingham Forest FC 205
Nottinghamshire CCC 48, 69, 107–11
Nutter, Albert 105

Oakes, Charlie 122
Oakes, Jack 122
Oakman, Alan 125
Observer 204
Old, Chris 135
Oldfield, 'Buddy' 105
Olympic Games, Munich 210, 211
O'Reilly, Bill 15
Oxford University 24, 40, 42, 43, 122

Packer, Kerry 230
Padgett, Doug 138
Pakistan 64, 94, 100, 160, 225
Palmer, Charlie 95, 231
Palmer, Les 219
Pamensky, Joe 178
Parfitt, Peter 100, 103
Parker, G. W. 20–2
Parkhouse, Gilbert 168
Parks, Harry 122, 123
Parks snr, Jim 122, 123
Parks jnr, Jim 123, 125
Pataudi jnr, Nawab of 122, 125
Patterson, Bob 60
Pearce, Tom 49–56, 59, 64, 96, 97
Perks, Reg 130, 131
Perrin, Percy 71
Phelan, Paddy 118, 133
Pierre, Lance 70
Place, Winston 92
Pleass, J. E. 79

Pollock, Graeme 224
Preston, Ken 60, 75, 84, 90, 133
Price, John 101
Pritchard, Tom 128
Procter, Mike 79

Quick, Arnold 75

Radley, Clive 100
Ralph, Roy 60, 75, 143
Ramadhin, 'Sonny' 70, 153, 156, 157, 189, 190
Ramsey, Sir Alf 205
Randall, Derek 109
Ray, Ashish 229
Revie, Don 205
Revill, Alan 76
Rice, Clive 108, 136, 224
Richards, Viv 111, 113, 114
Richardson, Peter 132, 154, 180, 181
Ridgway, Fred 89
Ring, Doug 151, 152
Rist, Frank 64, 65
Robertson, Jack 21, 99
Robins, R. W. V. 99, 102, 103
Robinson, Ellis 113, 116
Robinson, Tim 231, 232
Robson, Bobby 205
Roebuck, Peter 111, 112
Rorke, G. F. 173
Rossiter, Donald 202, 203
Rothman Cavaliers 66, 90, 107, 126, 194, 195
Rowan, A. M. B. 158
Rowan, Eric 148
Royal Marines 8, 28–36, 198
Rumsey, Fred 113, 196
Russell, Eric 100

Scarborough Festival 69, 134, 138
Sellers, Brian 135, 141

Shackleton, Derek 82, 85, 86

Sharpe, Phil 136, 138

Shepherd, D. J. 78, 79

Shepherd, J. N. 195

Sheppard, Rev D. S. 122–4, 168

Shirreff, Alan 22

Simmons, Jack 92

Simpson, Bob 153

Simpson, Reg 109, 110, 145, 160, 175, 176

Sivaramakrishnan, Laxman 229

Smith, A. C. 129, 130

Smith, Don 122

Smith, G. J. 130

Smith, M. J. K. 128, 129

Smith, O. G. 153

Smith, Peter 51–3, 59, 60, 90, 100, 103, 141

Smith, Ray 34, 51–3, 59, 60, 70, 106, 116, 132, 141

Snow, John 125, 126

Sobers, Gary 98, 108, 109, 126, 153, 154, 192, 195, 217, 218

Somerset CCC 41, 55, 68, 69, 111–6, 142

South Africa 64, 70, 102, 114, 131, 148–50, 154, 155, 158, 159, 178–84, 224

Southend United FC 43, 197–9, 204

Spooner, Dick 128, 167

Sri Lanka 50

Statham, Brian 92, 149, 151, 160, 169, 171, 180–2, 188, 192

Stewart, Micky 118

Surrey CCC 24, 59, 71, 84, 116–21, 154

Surridge, Stuart 116–8

Sussex CCC 44, 69, 121–6

Sutcliffe, Herbert 180, 181

Swanton, Jim 188, 189, 220, 221

Tallon, Don 159

Tate, Maurice 118

Tattersall, Roy 91, 158, 159

Tayfield, Hugh 181, 182

Taylor, Brian 49, 62, 63, 69, 78, 93, 143

Taylor, Ken 138

Taylor, Reg 51–3

Taylor, Wilf 64

TCCB 63, 64, 216, 217, 231

Test Match Special 138, 208, 212, 220–31

TEST SERIES appearances v
    Australia (1950–51) 163–9; (1953) 145–8, 150–2, 159, 160–2; (1954–55) 169–71; (1956) 152–4; (1958–59) 167, 172–4
    New Zealand (1949) 20, 54, 144, 145, 148, 149, 160, 161; (1950–51) 175; (1954–55) 175; (1958) 158
    Pakistan (1954) 94, 160
    South Africa (1951) 148, 158, 159; (1955) 149, 150, 154, 155; (1956–57) 178–84
    West Indies (1950) 155–7; (1953–54) 167, 185–94, 231; (1957) 153, 154, 157, 158, 161

Thompson, L. B. 34

Thomson, Ian 125

Titmus, Fred 101, 103, 142, 149, 153, 155

Tomlinson, Professor 178, 179

Tompkin, Maurice 97

Tottenham Hotspur FC 205

Townsend, Alan 128

Tremlett, Maurice 114

Tribe, George 107

Trueman, Fred 19, 76, 92, 107, 115, 138, 139, 153, 161, 162, 188, 192, 193, 222, 223

Tuke Hastings, Michael 220, 223

Turner, Mike 96
Tyson, Frank 107, 155, 169, 170, 171, 180

Underwood, Derek 79, 88
Urquhart, J. R. 43

Valentine, Alf 153, 156, 190, 192
van der Bijl, Vintcent 104, 220
van Ryneveld, A. J. 181
Verity, Hedley 140
Vigar, Frank 52, 126
Voce, Bill 108

Wade, Tom 51, 58
Waite, J. H. B. 154, 155
Walcott, Clyde 70, 153, 154, 186, 189
Walcott, J. H. 190
Walker, Peter 143
Walsh, C. A. 82
Walsh, Jack 94, 95
Walthamstow Avenue FC 199, 201, 202
Wardle, Johnny 138, 140, 151, 153, 159, 160, 169, 176, 180, 181, 182, 190, 192
Warner, Sir Pelham 57
Warr, John 76, 98, 102, 165, 168
Warren, Harry 199
Warwickshire CCC 42, 52, 61, 65, 71, 126–30, 216
Washbrook, Cyril 92, 93
Watford FC 203
Watson, Willie 97, 137, 145, 150, 151, 153, 169, 181, 191, 201
Webster, Rudi 130
Weekes, Everton 153, 154, 167, 186, 188, 191, 195
Weeks, Ray 128
Wells, Alan 122
Wells, 'Bomber' 79, 80

Wells, Colin 122
West Indian Board of Control 186
West Indies 70, 101–3, 131, 153–8, 161, 185–96
Westcliff CC 18, 19, 72, 208
Wight, Peter 113, 115
Wilcox, Denys 15, 16, 19, 35, 38, 39, 51, 52
Wilcox, John 39
Willatt, Guy 41, 44
Wilson, Don 136
Wilson, Vic 137, 169, 176
Winslow, P. L. 154, 155
Winterbottom, Sir Walter 205
Wodehouse, P. G. 22
Woodcock, John 183, 221
Wooller, Wilf 77–9
Woolley, Frank 98
Worcestershire CCC 63, 71, 130–4
World Cup (soccer) 209, 210
World Series Cricket 103, 230
Worrell, Frank 153, 161, 186, 195
Wright, Billy 209
Wright, Doug 87, 88, 168, 175
Wrightson, Roger 139
Wrigley Softball Cricket Tournament 217–9
Wyatt, Bob 38

Yardley, Norman 69, 141, 220, 223
Yawar Saeed 113
Yorkshire CCC 34, 49, 58, 63, 69, 84, 105, 115, 134–43, 145, 224
Young, Jack 101

Zaheer Abbas 115